CCM Magazine Presents

CCM TOP 100

GREATEST SONGS IN CHRISTIAN MUSIC

INTEGRITY®
PUBLISHERS
Nashville

Written by Tori Taff and the editorial staff of CCM Magazine,
including Christa Farris, Caroline Mitchell, Stephanie Ottosen,
Jay Swartzendruber, Michael Tenbrink, and Chris Well.

List Crafting by Michael Nolan.

Editorial Assistance by Kelly O'Neil.

Afterword by Steven Curtis Chapman.

Cover Design by Benji Peck.

Interior design by Jay Smith at Juicebox Designs
info@juiceboxdesigns.com

Art Direction by Lee Steffen.

FOREWORD

When I heard that *CCM* had the opportunity to compile this unprecedented volume celebrating contemporary Christian music's greatest songs, the fan inside me started to get excited. Which songs would be highlighted? Would my favorite artists be represented? What would the top 10 look like? And then the growing voice of the professional editor started whispering within: *How will we ensure credibility? How can we best honor Christian music's history? And how broad should the definition of "Christian song" be?*

In some ways the last question would be the toughest of all—with good reason. A majority of the Christian community's most prolific artists emphatically believe that a song honors God when it's an expression of goodness, truth and beauty. That whether it's gospel, praise, an instrumental or has a biblically informed perspective on anything under the sun, God is pleased. These artists might sing about friendship, prayer, sexual purity, money, politics, humility or something as timely and specific as the current HIV/AIDS and poverty crises in Africa.

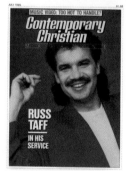

We at *CCM* wholeheartedly agree—this conviction served as the starting place for our approach in creating this book. That said, we did feel it necessary to create two tangible man-made guidelines for the sake of practicality and to specifically honor the history of the Christian music community. To be eligible for nomination, a song had to originate with our songwriters/artists and initially (or simultaneously) be nationally distributed to the Christian market. Hence U2's modern worship classic "Gloria (In Te Domine)," for instance, was not eligible though it eventually impacted the

Christian marketplace thanks to later recordings by Audio Adrenaline and Circadian Rhythm. Secondly, after much debate, we came to the conclusion that it would be most helpful for the purposes of this book if eligibility required that songs be distinctly faith-evident. Thus Phil Keaggy's astounding instrumentals and Sixpence None the Richer's worldwide smash hit "Kiss Me," for example, were not eligible.

Before we began sifting through thousands of potential nominees, we also had to clarify what made for one of Christian music's greatest songs. In this case, did "great" mean excellent, innovative, popular or influential? Actually, all of the above. And that's a significant point. If you asked me to list my 10 favorite Christian songs of all time, for instance, chances are the results would look quite different than a list of what I considered to be the 10 most influential or popular songs of all time. If a song was merely a personal favorite of ours, it didn't come close to making the final cut. But if it was a radio hit, eventually ended up in hymnals, made unprecedented in-roads into culture or was covered by multiple artists, then its chances were significantly better.

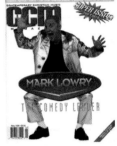

And the actual selection process? First we began by referencing decades of groundbreaking albums, radio airplay charts, Dove Award wins, and downright personal opinions. From these sources we were able to easily list hundreds of landmark songs. We then took this list to a panel of industry pioneers and executives. After asking them to add any songs that were "missing," we invited them to help us dramatically shorten the overall list by constructively debating the merit of each and every song initially nominated. The resulting conversation around *CCM*'s large conference room table was extremely engaging, intense, nostalgic, fun and, without a doubt, productive. And did I mention that it was surreal? One moment I would find myself feeling like a relevant

contributor, and the next an astounded spectator—a fly on the wall of Christian music history. I mean, can you imagine sitting across from legendary producer Michael Omartian as he cheerfully debated with pioneering manager/label founder Michael Blanton about Christian music's most pivotal moments in the 1970s? Me either. I had to see it to believe it. And just what was I thinking during those moments when I actually challenged the opinions of such Christian music giants? It had to be my love for the music. It made me audacious. After all, these were some of the very people who literally helped form my tastes in music.

When this phase was completed, we still had about 250 songs on the list. I'm talking classics—both early and modern. From here on out, it would mean a self-imposed guilt-trip for each and every song that didn't make the final 100. There was only one appropriate way to go from here—it would come down to votes cast by industry leaders and fiercely loyal Christian music fans. In a page borrowed from professional sports leagues that designate their all-stars by differentiating between votes cast by players and votes cast by fans, we decided 50 percent of the final say would be determined by Christian music leaders and the other 50 percent by fans. On the industry side, we contacted dozens of key executives, artists and producers and then randomly selected more than 2,500 *CCM Magazine* subscribers and invited them all to cast their votes. The result? The historic book you now hold in your hands.

For more than 25 years we at *CCM Magazine* have celebrated the increasing influence of Christian music and are honored to serve as our community's primary voice to you, the fan. This book is a substantial expression of what we're all about. We hope that as you read through its pages, you will experience the same joy, wonder and nostalgia that we did in creating it.

Jay Swartzendruber
Editor, CCM Magazine

THE SONGS THEY SUNG:

A SONG-CENTERED TOUR OF CONTEMPORARY CHRISTIAN MUSIC

BY STEVE RABEY

In the beginning was the Word, but music came along pretty soon after. Today virtually every religion in the world uses music in its ceremonies and rituals. Still, when it comes to sacred texts, the Bible that Jews and Christians read and study is the most musical holy book of them all.

While it doesn't contain the lyrics of the love songs Adam and Eve may have sung to one another, the Bible contains hundreds of other songs—some of them composed thousands of years ago by the earliest Jewish musicians, who used harps, trumpets and drums to create the songs they sang as they married and mourned, celebrated victory and endured defeat, and worshiped their Lord.

David, the lowly Jewish shepherd boy who became ancient Israel's greatest king, composed hundreds of songs. Some were solo laments that the ever-moody David would sing to his God. Others were joyous choruses of praise that were designed to be sung by thousands of thankful voices.

Many of David's songs are collected in the Bible's book of Psalms. (There's a rumor going around that the people who first compiled the Bible considered calling the Psalms "The 150 Greatest Songs of Judeo-Christian Music," but these were unavailable for comment.)

In Psalm 145, a song of praise, David catalogs some of the most important reasons for praising God. His greatness is unfathomable. His splendor and majesty are glorious. His works are many and wonderful. He upholds those who fall. And His power is awesome.

A few millennia after David wrote these words, a quirky and creative 20th-century songwriter by the name of Rich Mullins drew inspiration from Psalm 145 when he wrote "Awesome God," the contemporary praise song that leads the list of the 100 Greatest Christian Songs that are described in the book you now hold in your hands.

This, in a nutshell, is one of the main messages of this book. Or to put it another way: A long, long time ago, God created humanity in His image. And part of what it means to be created in God's image is that we have all inherited some of His divine creativity. As a result, people have been creating songs and other things from the beginning of time. And many of the best Christian songs humans have created in the last few decades are described in the pages that follow.

But there's more.

SINGING A NEW SONG

Jews sang Psalms. Later on Christians sang hymns. By 1960, most worship services in the Western world were based around a select list of classic hymns, many of which had been composed a few centuries earlier by reformers like Martin Luther or John and Charles Wesley. Some of the "newer" hymns had been written in the previous few decades by revivalist musicians like Fanny J. Crosby or Ira Sankey, who was evangelist Dwight L. Moody's music man.

By the time the 1960s got rocking and rolling, popular music was undergoing a radical transformation. Pop music, which had once provided little more than background noise for sock hops or beach-blanket barbeques, had been transformed by artists like Bob Dylan and the Beatles into a diverse and lyrically complex art form capable of expressing a generation's loftiest dreams and darkest nightmares.

Spirituality was in the air—along with plenty of idealism, incense and marijuana smoke. A mushrooming youth movement offered a chaotic cornucopia of causes and creeds, including campus sit-ins, anti-war demonstrations, political radicalism, communal living, sexual liberation, recreational (and religious) drug experimentation, a parade of Eastern gurus and home-grown cults, and revolutionary—even revelatory—kinds of music.

After realizing that free love could be costly, trips could be bad, and cults could be expressways to the heart of spiritual darkness, millions of young people turned to Jesus. If these new believers wound up in traditional churches, they were often taught that God wanted them to cut their hair, lengthen their skirts and turn a deaf ear to the "Devil's music."

But those who became part of the Jesus movement, a burgeoning Christian counterculture, argued that God could redeem and use their music just as He had done with them. Or as Larry Norman sang in his signature song, "Why Should the Devil Have All the Good Music?" which ranks at #75 on the list of the 100 Greatest Christian Songs, "They say rock and roll is wrong . . . I say I feel so good I gotta get up and dance."

Norman's history-making debut album, *Upon This Rock*, was released by the mainstream Capitol label in 1969. This record (yes, it was a record, as in a 12-inch disk of black vinyl that rotated on a turntable at 33 1/3 revolutions per minute) combined soft rock, pop, ballads and folk sensibilities, and featured songs like "Sweet Sweet Song of Salvation," "Forget Your Hexagram" and "Moses in the Wilderness." Only later was *Upon This Rock* re-released by gospel label Impact.

Norman and dozens of other unlikely pioneers were the true founders of contemporary Christian music, which was becoming the *lingua franca* of a growing network of coffee houses, communes, street-corner concerts and newfangled fellowships.

"For the masses today, the greatest medium for expressing the gospel is rock 'n' roll," said Randy Matthews, who in 1971 founded Cincinnati's Jesus House and recorded Word's first contemporary album. "It's not even a musical form any more; it's a culture and it's a lifestyle. The pulpit of this generation and the next is the guitar."

SWEET SONGS OF SALVATION

The Jesus movement—along with the often-overlapping charismatic movement that ignited spiritual renewal in thousands of churches in a wide range of denominations— spawned a nationwide awakening, and like earlier religious revivals, it inspired new kinds of music.

Contemporary Christian music borrowed heavily from folk and rock idioms as well as more traditional southern gospel forms. It was also brought to life by a host of important but largely unheralded transitional figures like Jimmy and Carol Owens, Ralph Carmichael, Thurlow Spurr, Kurt Kaiser, Ray Repp and Bill Gaither.

Gaither, who is still filling arenas with his popular "Homecoming" concerts, is on the list of the 100 Greatest Christian Songs at #15 with his classic "Because He Lives" and at #38 with "He Touched Me," a song that was recorded in 1972 by Elvis Presley. Gaither has also served as a mentor to many contemporary Christian artists who appear on the list, including Michael English (#17, #82), Steve Green (#44), Sandi Patty (#56, #65, #73), Russ

Taff (#29), Larnelle Harris (#85) and members of White Heart (#92).

But while many contemporary Christian musicians borrowed from earlier musical forms, others made a clean break with the past or anything that sounded like traditional hymns. "I don't like none of these funeral marches," sang Norman. "I ain't dead yet."

Norman and others like him bore the anger of many older Christians for making the bold assertion that rock music could be used to sing about Christ. It's hard to believe it now, but Christian rock was a controversial subject in many circles, and many major Christian publishers still published virulently anti-rock books well into the '70s and '80s.

Lyrically, the new music expounded on five key elements of Jesus movement theology.

Theme 1) The Son and the Father

Norman's *Only Visiting This Planet*, released in 1972 by the mainstream Verve label and in 1978 by Word, featured "The Outlaw," a folk ballad which presented Jesus as a mystical, magical, countercultural radical who "roamed across the land" with "unschooled ruffians, and a few old fisherman."

The song's final verse was more orthodox, stating that Jesus was "the son of God, a man above all men." Likewise, Norman protégé Randy Stonehill emphasized Christ's role as gracious Savior, describing him as "the King of Hearts."

Over the years, some of the best Christian songs talked more about God the Father than they did Jesus the Son. In addition to Mullins' "Awesome God," songs like Amy Grant's recording of Michael Card's "El Shaddai" (#5) and "God of Wonders" from the City on a Hill collaboration (#11) describe the eternal Creator God in the latest musical styles.

Other songs, such as Mullins' "My Deliverer" (#87) and Keith Green's "There Is a Redeemer" (#54), combine Old and New Testament motifs about God's work of redeeming humanity.

Theme 2) The Holy Spirit

The third member of the Trinity played a renowned role in the lives of many late 20th-century Christians, so it should come as no surprise that the Spirit has also played an emphasized role in contemporary Christian music. Christianity was seen as more than dry, dusty dogma. It was a powerful daily reality.

Annie Herring was the principal songwriter and vocalist for 2nd Chapter of Acts, a group which took its name from the New Testament account of the day of Pentecost. 2nd Chapter's best-known hit is "Easter Song," which appears at #69. But other songs written by Herring combined charismatic enthusiasm with inward mysticism, like "Which Way the Wind Blows" from 1974's *With Footnotes* and in "Something Tells Me" from 1975's *In the Volume of the Book,* in which she beseeches the Holy Spirit to "let it pour on me, let it shine on me."

Half a century ago, an invisible line separated Christians who sang hymns about the Spirit (they were the Pentecostals) from those who sang songs about salvation or the Word of God (they were the Baptists and all the others). But those invisible lines have been

disappearing ever since musicians linked to the Jesus movement and the charismatic movement began writing new songs about the Spirit, some of which will be covered below under "praise."

Theme 3) End Times

Those of you who thought millennial fever began with Y2K or with the mega-best-selling Left Behind series have another thing coming.

Larry Norman's apocalyptic "I Wish We'd All Been Ready" (#13 on the list) was a mournful song that said: "Life was filled with guns and war." The world-weary pessimism of this Jesus movement theme song was a barometer of the anxiety of an age. Back then, you didn't have to be a card-carrying member of the Silent Majority to fear that the world—or perhaps Western Civilization, or at least a certain cherished American way of life—was coming to an end.

Other songs from this period, including Michael Omartian's elaborate jazz-rock opus "White Horse," could have served as a musical soundtrack for *The Late Great Planet Earth,* Hal Lindsey's multi-million-selling book about end times prophecies. The Maranatha! label took its name from Paul's words near the end of 1 Corinthians: "Come, O Lord." Meanwhile, sibling trio 2nd Chapter of Acts expressed the world-weariness of many when they sang that they "would not cry if this was the very last day of my life 'cause I've been waiting for it."

Similar apocalyptic themes appear in songs like Crystal Lewis's "People Get Ready"

(#42) and Andrae Crouch's "Soon and Very Soon" (#64).

Theme 4) Evangelism

It only follows that if Jesus is coming back and Judgment Day is just around the corner, Christians ought to roll up their sleeves and get busy proclaiming the gospel.

Believers have urgent work to do: introducing others to the salvation they've found in Christ. "Why don't you look into Jesus, He's got the answer," sang Norman. Stonehill, 2nd Chapter of Acts and others wrote songs called "Good News." And the title song to Paul Clark's 1974 *Come into His Presence* album (volume three of Clark's Songs from the Savior series) painted an image of Jesus "with his arms stretched out on a tree . . . reaching for you and me."

More recently, artists like dc talk and Newsboys have picked up the torch for songs about evangelism. Newsboys' "Shine" (#9) urges Christians to let their light shine before others, while dc talk's "Jesus Freak" (#2) is a bold declaration of single-hearted faithfulness to Christ in an age when such devotion strikes many as the freakiest kind of fanaticism.

Theme 5) Praise and Worship

People didn't know it at the time, but Jesus movement praise songs like "Seek Ye First," "Father, I Adore You," "I Love You, Lord," "Our God Reigns," "He Has Made Me Glad" and "The Peace That Passes All Understanding" would transform the way people worshiped.

These lively, simple, melodic songs, many of which were based on texts from the Gospels or the Psalms, spread like wildfire from one fellowship to the next before invading mainstream churches and, in many cases, replacing the hymns that Norman and others had found so lifeless. And along with the music came a new, relaxed and informal worship style.

This revolution, which is contemporary Christian music's most important contribution to the church, was described in "Little Country Church," Love Song's 1971 classic, which declared that "People aren't as stuffy as they were before/They just want to praise the Lord." More recently, songs like MercyMe's "I Can Only Imagine" (#4), Delirious?' "I Could Sing of Your Love Forever" (#6) and Darlene Zschech's "Shout to the Lord" (#10) are among the most popular Christian songs of all time, illustrating the perennial power of praise to stir listeners' hearts.

In fact, between one-third and one-half of all the songs on the list of 100 Greatest Christian Songs could be considered praise and worship songs, depending on how broadly you define the category. But this shouldn't be surprising, as Christian music is created and performed not only for human ears but for a heavenly audience that shares with us in the praise and worship we offer up.

CHARTS OR HEARTS?

As the Christian music industry grew in size, popularity and financial clout, a number of artists expressed concern that it was wading into dangerous water by emulating the conventions of the "secular" music industry.

The February 1986 issue of *CCM Magazine* featured an open letter written by Scott Wesley

Brown and Jimmy and Carol Owens and signed by more than 60 artists and executives (including Pat Boone, Michael Card, Steve Green, Darrell Harris, Annie Herring, Phil Keaggy, Michael Omartian, Sandi Patti, Michael W. Smith, John Michael Talbot and Wayne Watson). The letter urged an end to all negative album reviews and airplay and sales charts in the magazine, claiming that such trappings of fame only served to tempt artists and others in the industry away from a pure form of ministry:

"Scripture exhorts us neither to compare ourselves with one another nor to compete with one another. We feel that polls such as these create an unhealthy atmosphere of rivalry between ministries. We can hardly imagine the apostles and prophets being categorized in such a way. . . .

"The whole area of reviewing albums and ripping apart one another's offerings unto the Lord is disgraceful. If you don't like an album, we ask that you simply not review it. . . .

". . . true success is serving God and touching people's lives. Please help us to do this rather than influencing us to follow the world's standards of success."

None of the 100 Greatest Songs deals specifically with the issues of ministry and commerce that were raised in this letter, but a number of artists found their own unique ways to address these issues.

GOD'S ELBOW

With his catchy melodies and earnest lyrics, Keith Green continually crossed the line between pop and praise. But Green's intense spiritual zeal and radical approach to his work left little doubt that he believed God wanted him to minister, not entertain.

"I know that I am a minister of the gospel," said Green, who has two songs on the 100 Greatest Songs list ("Oh Lord, You're Beautiful" at #40 and "There Is a Redeemer" at #54). "I am a musician last—not second, but last. Music is just a tool, and a faulty one at that."

Green was only 23 when Sparrow Records released his debut album, *For Him Who Has Ears to Hear*, in 1977. He was only 28 when he and 11 others were killed in a plane crash on the property of the musician's Last Days Ministries. But during those five years, Green wrote and recorded a surprisingly large and influential body of work.

Capable of creating passionate ballads as well as powerful pop punctuated by his rhythmic honky-tonk piano work, Green filled his songs—some of which he wrote with his wife, Melody—with a potent combination of Jesus movement millennialism and Holy Ghost revivalism, and he preached against "church-ianity," worldliness, sin in the church, Catholicism and a watered-down gospel message of "God loves you and has a wonderful plan for your life." His free-admission concerts frequently contained more preaching than playing, as he lashed out at complacent Christians.

"Some people are hands; some people are elbows," he said. "I'm an elbow. I didn't choose to be that way. I don't want to be that way. I'd much rather be the mercy-shower than the prophetic voice. But I do it in obedience because that's what the Lord called me to do."

Ironically, Green was one of the fledgling Christian music industry's best-selling artists as well as one of its harshest critics.

"The central reason there are record companies is for corporations to make money," he told *Contemporary Christian Music Magazine.* "Anybody who honestly believes that a record company is there as a service is grossly mistaken."

Green put his own money where his mouth was, walking away from a lucrative Sparrow contract, creating his own label—Pretty Good Records—and pledging that any profits would go to support missions and fight world hunger.

His 1980 album *So You Wanna Go Back to Egypt . . .* featured performances by Ralph Carmichael and Bob Dylan, and this bold message on its back cover: "THIS RECORD CANNOT BE SOLD!" Instead, Last Days made it available on a free-will offering basis, and about one-fourth of the nearly 200,000 copies the ministry sent out were given away free, leading some to jokingly call it "the worst-selling gospel album in history."

In a March 1980 cover story entitled, "A non-profit prophet?" Green proclaimed, "I repent of ever having recorded one single song, and ever having played one concert if my music and, more importantly, my life has not provoked you in godly jealousy to sell out completely to Jesus!"

A DIVERSITY OF STYLES AND APPROACHES

It's always been difficult to understand where categories like "gospel" and "contemporary Christian" begin and end. Perhaps gospel, with its Southern roots and twangy, four-part harmonies was easy to grasp. But contemporary Christian music has embraced a staggering diversity of styles, from the crunching hard rock of bands like P.O.D. (their song "Alive" is #76) to beautiful melodies of artists like Twila Paris (whose "How Beautiful," at #20, is just one of four songs on the list).

"I can really see the Lord using all of it," said Don Francisco ("He's Alive," #53) at a 1978 Christian music gathering in Colorado. John Michael Talbot, a secular folk-rocker who became a contemporary Christian music pioneer before converting to Catholicism and creating dozens of albums full of liturgically based worship music, agreed.

"We need to know rock 'n' roll," said Talbot. "We need to know the gentleness of a folk tune. We need to know the majesty of Handel's *Messiah.* We need to know the awesome reverence of the Gregorian chant."

Debates about style eventually took a back seat to arguments about "crossing over," which was one of the hottest issues of the 1980s. During the last two decades, artists like dc talk, Jars of Clay (#7 with "Flood"), Michael W. Smith (with four songs on the list) and Amy Grant have bounced back and forth between the so-called "Christian" and "secular" worlds.

This trend worried artists like Dallas Holm (#52 with "Rise Again"), who had raised questions about lyrical ambiguity back in January 1979. "Quite honestly, there are a lot of Christian songs I can't figure out," he said. "If I, as a Christian, can't figure them out, how in the world is a person out there who isn't even spiritually minded going to figure them out? If I'm failing to communicate the message of Jesus, if anybody sitting out there is wondering what in the world I'm talking about, then I've failed as far as I'm concerned."

Some Christian artists, like guitar virtuoso Phil Keaggy (#62 with "Your Love Broke Thru"), had started out as "secular" performers before recording for Christian labels. Others, like those mentioned above, started in the Christian market before signing with mainstream labels. Rarer still were mainstream artists like U2 and Lifehouse who recorded exclusively with mainstream labels but were still able to attract a sizable audience of Christian listeners.

By far, the most celebrated (and most controversial) crossover artist of all time was Bob Dylan, the American music icon who shocked the world when he released three consecutive Christian albums: 1979's *Slow Train Coming*, 1980's *Saved* and 1981's *Shot of Love.*

The first and most influential Christian artist to cross over to the mainstream was Amy Grant, who has five songs on the list—more than any other artist.

In 1985, Grant boldly went where none had gone before with "Find a Way," contemporary Christian music's first Top 40 hit. The song's bridge presented the clear gospel message of "our God His Son not sparing."

Like any trailblazer, Grant paid the price for her innovations. When she performed on a live television broadcast of the Grammy Awards, some Christians cheered her while others criticized the fact that she performed with BARE FEET and clingy LEOPARD-PRINT PANTS!

Another history-making crossover artist was Bob Carlisle, the hard-working veteran singer whose song "Butterfly Kisses" (#18) was a surprise hit in June 1997 and helped the album of the same name become the first Christian-label release to reach the top spot on the Billboard 200 chart.

The song, a radio-friendly, sob-inducing ode to family values, made an "overnight sensation" out of Carlisle, who had made his debut in the early 1970s with the Maranatha! band, Good News, and later recorded a handful of albums with the Allies before launching his solo career.

About the same time Carlisle was king of the album charts, a song called "Stomp" (#55) rumbled from radios across the land. Kirk Franklin's Nu Nation and singing group God's Property teamed up for a top-notch hip-hop hymn about the transforming love of Jesus—a love that made themselves and audiences "wanna stomp."

But Franklin's spoken introduction to the song hinted at the cultural battle lines that still divided the church: "For those of you that think that gospel music has gone too far, you think we've gotten too radical with our message, well I got news for you: you ain't heard nothing yet!"

On the heels of Franklin's initial success, Sixpence None the Richer released a string of four radio hits that further undermined the marginalization of artistic Christians. After Casey Kasem announced Sixpence's "Kiss Me" as the #1 pop song in America in the summer of 1999, the band spent the next few years invading the radio charts with "There She Goes," "Breathe Your Name" and "Don't Dream It's Over." Then, when P.O.D. overlapped with its explosive assault on alternative radio and MTV with standouts such as "Alive" and "Youth of the Nation," the stage had been set for the Christian music community's biggest surge ever into the world of mainstream music.

During 2003 alone, MercyMe, Stacie Orrico, Switchfoot, Pillar, Smokie Norful, Steven Curtis Chapman and Natalie Grant each landed on major mainstream radio charts. And the faith-based Tooth & Nail Records label saw MTV and MTV2 combine to play seven of their videos that year. As Switchfoot, MercyMe and Pillar continued their charge with new hits in 2004, they were joined on the general market radio charts by Thousand Foot Krutch, Skillet and Jars of Clay. At one point, Christian market-supported artists accounted for an unprecedented six charting hits during the same week.

TO ROCK OR NOT TO ROCK?

Remember the stir over Amy Grant's leopard-print pants? They weren't half as tight as the spandex tights sported by the four members of Stryper, whose classic "To Hell with the Devil" (#70) was a centerpiece of the Los Angeles-based band's so-called yellow and black attack.

Debuting with a six-song EP in 1984, Stryper was a hard-rocking hair band that created a wailing wall of sound full of screaming guitars and pounding drums. Their label, Enigma, had launched heavy metal bands Mötley Crüe and Ratt.

Though their lyrics were explicitly Christian and the band routinely threw New Testaments to members of its audiences, some anti-rock critics felt their hard rock image spoke louder than their music. Attired in spandex and decorated with chains, leather and studs, Stryper initiated a whole new round of anti-Christian rock hysteria.

In the early days of Christian rock, Bob Larson had made a name for himself by writing books with sensationalistic titles like *Rock & Roll: The Devil's Diversion, The Day Music Died* and *Babylon Reborn.* In these books (as well as his popular lectures), Larson argued that rock—whether so-called-Christian or otherwise—was a powerful pied piper propelled by demonic beats which was leading America's youth right into occultism, drugs and perverted sex. (It apparently wasn't too good for houseplants, either.)

By the 1980s Larson and others among Christian rock's most outspoken critics had largely made their peace with much of the new Christian music, and Larson even wrote an occasional article for *Contemporary Christian Music.* But he felt Stryper went too far.

"I very strongly object to the whole heavy metal frame of reference," he said. Meanwhile, Minnesota's Dan and Steve Peters, who gained national notoriety for burning offensive secular albums, embraced Stryper and the band members' bold public witness for Christ. "I don't think Jesus told us how to look," said Steve. "I would dress as a clown to get on *Entertainment Tonight* and share 10 sentences about Jesus Christ."

The noisiest and most persistent critic was televangelist Jimmy Swaggart, whose self-published 1987 creed, *Religious Rock 'n' Roll: A*

Wolf in Sheep's Clothing, caused less of a stir than his own subsequent moral fall.

Even a decade later, rock music could still send some Christians into a frenzy. Just ask Pat Boone, that paragon of American virtue who ran afoul of the music police in 1997. In a move that was an even bigger risk than his decision decades ago to loan a struggling Randy Stonehill enough money to record his first album, Boone released *In a Metal Mood: No More Mr. Nice Guy*, a collection of heavy metal hits arranged for big band. The album was certainly a sin against heavy metal, and maybe even good taste. But was it a sin against God Almighty? The folks at Trinity Broadcasting Network, which aired Boone's TV show, thought so and canceled the program.

Today such battles seem silly, and rock bands like Third Day and Audio Adrenaline blend meaty rock hooks with powerful praise lyrics. Third Day, with two songs in the top 25 on the list (#16 "Agnus Dei" and #24 "Show Me Your Glory") and AA ("Big House" at #25) should be required to stop, kneel and thank God for Petra, a pioneering band founded by guitarist Bob Hartman in 1972.

By 1973, Petra (the name comes from the Greek word for "rock") was the unofficial house band at The Adam's Apple, a Ft. Wayne, Indiana Christian hangout. The band's self-titled Myrrh debut came out in 1974, even though many Christian bookstores refused to sell it. The rest, as they say, is history.

"For me the name Petra has a dual meaning," said Hartman, who temporarily retired from full-time touring in 1995. "It means rock music, but it also means that we stand upon the rock of our belief in Christ."

Over the years, Petra has given millions of fans muscular music that both stirs the heart and stimulates the body. Along the way, they've logged millions of miles and performed thousands of times, bringing new levels of professionalism and showmanship to Christian concerts and using their substantial international platform to promote the work of established ministries like Josh McDowell and Compassion International.

In its day, each new Petra album pushed the envelope for cutting-edge audio production and snazzy graphics. And while their fan base has evolved almost as much as the band's own personnel, it continues to win the affection of young listeners.

In 1988, the Gospel Music Association, which had originated within the southern gospel culture, announced that it would add rock and heavy metal categories for its annual Dove Awards. Soon Petra and other bands were winning these coveted awards, a further symbol of rock's emergence into the Christian cultural mainstream.

Petra's song on the list is "More Power to Ya" at #72. Though the song isn't one of the band's rockers, it provides a window into one of the towering artists in Christian music history.

THE POWER OF POP

During the '90s, a Pennsylvania-based firm was selling something it called "The Christian Rocker's Creed." Printed on faux parchment so that it resembled America's Bill of Rights, on which it was loosely based, the creed read, in part: "We hold these truths to be self-evident, that all music was created equal—that no instrument or style of music is in itself evil—that the diversity of musical expression which flows forth from man is but one evidence of the boundless creativity of our Heavenly Father."

Rock may have recently become the most popular genre in Christian music, but for most of the past three decades, artists like Steven Curtis Chapman have repeatedly demonstrated that it's pop the people wanted. Chapman, who has become one of the best-selling and most acclaimed artists in Christian music history, is represented on the list by four of his dozens of hits: "The Great Adventure" (#8), "Dive" (#78), "I Will Be Here" (#26) and "For the Sake of the Call" (#37).

Meanwhile, artists like girl group Point of Grace combined a shimmering pop sheen with traditional four-part harmonies on hits like "The Great Divide" (#19) and "Jesus Will Still Be There" (#47).

Jars of Clay, which combined pop sensibilities with the jangly guitar sounds of alternative rock, took their name from a passage in the Apostle Paul's 2 Corinthians. The band came on like gangbusters.

One day the four members were sitting in their dorm room at Greenville College singing songs to each other. The next, their 1995 self-titled debut had sold 1.5 million copies to become the best-selling debut in Christian music history; the video for the song "Flood" (#7) was in regular rotation on MTV and VH-1; and their phenomenal success story was being told in the pages of *Rolling Stone* and

Spin. Their 1997 sequel, *Much Afraid*, debuted at number eight on the Billboard 200 chart.

"Flood" was representative of a new brand of crossover Christian pop. The lyrics were clearly based on the Bible (the account of Noah, to be precise). But listeners who weren't familiar with the Bible weren't forced to find their way through piles of obscure Christian lingo.

But some Christian fans weren't sure they wanted the band to take all this "Go ye into all the world" stuff quite so literally. "I have heard a rumor that Jars of Clay has played in venues where alcohol and drugs have been abundant," wrote one anxious fan in a posting on the band's Web site. "Please, someone, confirm/deny this story!!" (The rumor was true.)

On the other hand, some unchurched fans who bought the band's album after seeing "Flood" on MTV were shocked and offended by the explicitly Christian content of much of the band's music. But Jars kept making new music and winning new fans.

The presence of newer artists on the list of the 100 Greatest Songs indicates that the Christian music industry continues to evolve at an even more rapid pace.

Take Jaci Velasquez, for example. She hadn't even been born by the time Amy Grant released her first album. But by the end of 1997, she was the proud owner of the industry's fastest-selling release—the result of skill, hard work, good looks and Myrrh's relentless marketing campaigns. Her moving song "On My Knees" (#14) ranks with some of Christian music's classics.

Other new artists like Avalon ("Testify to

Love" at #23), Nichole Nordeman ("Holy" at #27) and Switchfoot ("Dare You to Move" at #50) prove that the biblical admonition to "sing a new song" continues to be heard by artists who interpret its command in their own unique ways.

One group that has continually reinvented both itself and its music is dc talk, which is represented by two songs on the list ("Jesus Freak" at #2 and "What If I Stumble?" at #31). The tale of how three young men—two white and one black—from Jerry Falwell's Liberty University became one of Christian music's most important acts is one of the most intriguing success stories of the 1990s.

dc talk's self-titled 1989 debut album wasn't anything to stop the presses. The opening cut, Toby McKeehan's "Heavenbound," had a memorable melody and a nice beat. "Time Ta Jam" offered a challenge to critics who might be tempted to declare rap—even this trio's toned down version—off limits to saints. *Nu Thang* (1990) reaffirmed the band's ambition to redeem a genre:

> *God doesn't change, but he knows the time*
> *From harp to piano and song to rap.*

The album also featured "Walls," the multi-racial trio's first comment on race:

> *Gotta live by example, show brotherly love*
> *We're together on earth, we'll be together above.*

By the time 1992's Grammy-winning *Free At Last* came out, Promise Keepers and other groups were trying to convince evangelicals that racism was a profoundly destructive sin. dc talk presented the same message over an infectious musical accompaniment on "Socially Acceptable."

With 1995's Grammy and Dove Award-winning *Jesus Freak*, dc talk upped the musical ante, mixing hard-edged rock and soulful ballads with in-your-face lyrics. But the message of brotherly love was still front-and-center:

> *We're colored people, and we live in a tainted place*
> *We're colored people,*
> *and they call us the human race*
> *We've got a history so full of mistakes*
> *And we are colored people who depend*
> *on a Holy Grace.*

In 1998, the trio picked up another Grammy for 1997's *Welcome to the Freak Show—Live in Concert* and released their latest album, *Supernatural*. Today it's the band members' solo and side projects that are gaining the most attention for Toby McKeehan, Michael Tait and Kevin Max.

SONGS OF LIFE

Songs have been around from nearly the beginning of time. Over the centuries, songs have been used to accompany brides and grooms as they make their way down the aisles at beautiful wedding celebrations. Other songs have been used to provide encouragement to frightened soldiers who were marching off to near-certain death.

The best songs seem to capture a moment, a feeling or an experience, expressing it in both concrete and universal ways. When such songcraft works, it can have a powerful impact, enabling listeners to enjoy a new song, understand it, embrace it, and ultimately incorporate it into their minds and hearts.

That's exactly what has happened with one of the most successful songs in contemporary Christian music's history. That song, "I Can Only Imagine," illustrates how songwriters reflect and meditate on the raw materials of life—in this case, death—and transform them into art. The song's long and winding road to success also illustrates the many complexities of today's Christian music industry, an industry that would have shocked and amazed some of the musicians who first put contemporary music to timeless lyrics nearly four decades ago.

Of course, MercyMe singer/songwriter Bart Millard wasn't consciously thinking about history or art when he scribbled down the first lyrics to "I Can Only Imagine" in 2001. Millard, who was raised by his dad after his parents divorced, nursed his father through years of cancer-related suffering and medical treatments.

It was after the latest in a series of episodes when he thought his father might die that Millard grabbed paper and pen and began pouring his heart out. The words that emerged from that painful time represent a heartfelt, even joyful expression of the hope that lies within us all:

I can only imagine
When all I will do
Is forever worship You.

First released in 1989 on an independent album, the song was re-released in 1991 and soon won a Song of the Year Dove Award. That would have been amazing enough, but word-of-mouth buzz soon propelled it to mainstream pop success, leading members of MercyMe to jokingly refer to themselves as "the longest overnight success ever."

The many ironies revealed in the song's runaway success are a powerful reminder of the internal tensions that have made contemporary Christian music so interesting for so long.

Like Rich Mullins' "Awesome God," "I Can Only Imagine" was born as a worship song. But somehow its explicitly Christian content didn't prevent it from connecting with the widest possible audience of listeners.

And like Bob Carlisle's "Butterfly Kisses," "I Can Only Imagine" was a mega-successful, laid-back, adult contemporary single from an artist much better known for rockier music.

But such ironies aside, songs like "I Can Only Imagine" illustrate that thousands of years after David played his harp and sang his heart out to God, music still has the power to touch us and move us in ways we continue to find surprising.

Music is one of the most influential of the many good gifts God gave us when he created us in His image. And as the 100 songs described in this book attest, Christian songcraft remains alive and well.

Steve Rabey is a freelance writer living in Colorado (www.rabey.us). This introduction is adapted from "Age to Age," his overview of contemporary Christian music's history from the July 1998 issue of CCM Magazine.

For all the fans,
For all the artists,
And for all the music and stories yet to come

CCM Magazine Presents
The Top 100 Greatest Songs in Christian Music . . .

RICH
MULLINS

AWESOME
GOD

WRITTEN BY RICH MULLINS

RECORDED BY RICH MULLINS
ON WINDS OF HEAVEN, STUFF
OF EARTH (REUNION RECORDS,
1989)

PRODUCED BY REED ARVIN

ALSO RECORDED BY:
JOHN TESH ON
WORSHIP COLLECTION

PAT BOONE ON GREATEST
CONTEMPORARY CHRISTIAN
SONGS

CARMAN ON ESSENTIAL
PRAISE & WORSHIP

RAY BOLTZ ON THE CLASSICS

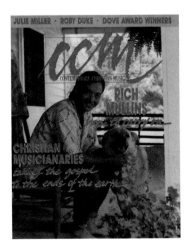

There is an irony in having a Rich Mullins song at the top of this list. Of all the artists and writers represented here, he would probably be the least likely to look upon it as an honor. "Actually," chuckles his brother David Mullins, "it would probably tick him off—I can just hear him, 'It's foolish to try to rate art! Art is not a contest!'"

But for the millions of Rich Mullins fans who still keenly feel his absence since his death in a car accident in 1997, the choice of "Awesome God" as the #1 Christian song is actually no contest at all. Years before praise and worship songs were the mainstay of most artists' repertoires, Rich's simple hymn acknowledging the awesome power of our Creator became one of his signature songs.

"The story about that song, according to what I've been told," says David Mullins, "is that Rich was driving late at night by himself to a youth concert in Colorado and was having trouble staying awake. He said he was thinking about southern preachers, the kind that say short sentences, real strong. So he rolled his window down and started yelling these statements into the night, trying to stay awake: 'There is thunder in His footsteps and lightning in His fists!' He thought it was funny, and then when he got to the concert he taught the kids the song." Almost every Rich Mullins concert after that included a point in which he started singing that song and then stopped, closed his eyes, and let the gentle, a cappella response of the crowd wash over him. "'Awesome God' creates a magic moment," Rich once remarked. "It reminds you that this world is not your home."

Rich Mullins never seemed to feel completely at home anywhere, even in the contemporary Christian music field in which he chose to make his living. Restless, eccentric, enigmatic Rich was not an easy fit in an industry that prefers its artists a little more presentable—and a lot less abrasive. Amy Grant, whose recording of Rich's song "Sing Your Praise to the Lord" brought him to the attention of the industry,

says, "Rich was the uneasy conscience of Christian music. He didn't live like a star. He'd taken a vow of poverty so that what he earned could be used to help others."

Rich's longtime view of Christianity as something you do, not something you talk about, was evident in his writing and his travels. He journeyed to Guatemala, Japan and Korea and spent time in Thailand helping farmers dig septic tanks and plant fruit trees. At the height of his growing career, and much to the chagrin of his record label, Rich left Nashville and moved to Wichita, Kansas to pursue a degree in music education at Friends University. After he graduated from Friends in

1995, he moved to a Navajo reservation in Window Rock, Arizona to teach music to the children there. However, in typical Rich fashion, his brother David says he actually went there to learn more than teach. "Everybody always thinks, 'Oh what a wonderful thing, this Christian music artist moving to a reservation to help those people.' But what I heard Rich say about it was, 'I also went to the Navajo reservation because they are traditionally a shepherding culture, they work with sheep, and so many scriptures were

"Prophets aren't necessarily the best party guests. But if Rich Mullins were better adjusted and better behaved, a lot of art would not exist in this world, and a lot of truth would still be unspoken."

PRODUCER REED ARVIN

3

Patty Masten

"I remember a special night at Cafe Milano in Nashville, where a group of about 10 artists had gathered to celebrate Rich's music. We had all learned one of his songs, and he was sitting in the middle of the room looking like a kid at Christmas, just enjoying hearing the expressions of the artists. He didn't seem overly embarrassed or preoccupied with all of the attention that was on him. He just took it all in with that big, honest smile"

PHIL KEAGGY

written from that perspective. I went there to learn from them what I could about the Lord as our Good Shepherd.'"

Rich always kept one foot in the music business, however, and continued recording, writing and performing concerts. At the time of his death, he was about to begin a new project, which was eventually released posthumously as *The Jesus Record*. The 41-year-old singer's death on September 19, 1997 left the industry reeling, in much the same way that fellow Christian music rebel Keith Green's fatal plane crash had 15 years earlier. Rich's unflinching honesty, startling intellect and wide open heart are what his friends and fellow artists remember most. And his quirky, self-dep-

recating humor is what they will miss the most.

Just days before his death, Rich faxed *Sound and Spirit* magazine his goals and resolutions for 1998 for an upcoming feature. Here is what he wrote:

"My goal is to stop being grumpy. My resolution is my plan of attack:

A. Get up before I have to so I can have a half-hour at least before I have to talk to anyone.

B. Spend an hour each early evening working out—do not hurry.

C. Unplug my phone—use my answering

"When I was around Rich, I was always asking questions and digging into that brain, because he was a great thinker, a real follower of Christ in a really awkward way. Unlike the rest of us, he didn't hide his scars very well; he was more like, 'Hey looky here, I've got scars!' And then he wrote about them."

MARK LOWRY

Patty Masten

machine as a dart board. Throw ice cubes at it when I'm frustrated instead of making cutting remarks to people I love.

D. Stop expecting big successes and start celebrating the little ones.

E. Chart the movements of the Big Dipper and soak in the sun as much as possible. Live in a world that is bigger than my calendar—more permanent than my feelings, more glorious than my accomplishments (that should be easy)."

At a memorial service held in Wichita, Rich's favorite former professor, Dr. Stephen Hooks, concluded his stirring remarks with this: "There's a Ragamuffin loose in heaven. There are bare feet on the streets of gold. And I tell you, heaven will never be the same!"

dc talk

JESUS FREAK

WRITTEN BY MARK HEIMERMANN AND TOBY MCKEEHAN

RECORDED BY DC TALK ON JESUS FREAK (FOREFRONT RECORDS, 1995)

PRODUCED BY TOBY McKEEHAN, MARK HEIMERMANN AND JOHN PAINTER

1996 DOVE AWARDS—SONG OF THE YEAR, ARTIST OF THE YEAR, ROCK RECORDED SONG

1996 GRAMMY—BEST ROCK GOSPEL ALBUM: JESUS FREAK

1997 DOVE AWARD—BEST ROCK ALBUM: WELCOME TO THE FREAK SHOW—DC TALK LIVE IN CONCERT

The superlatives flew when dc talk's "Jesus Freak" first hit the airwaves in 1995. The song and the album marked a decidedly risky metamorphosis by an already unconventional group. Released three years after their successful R & B/pop-tinged *Free At Last* album, *Jesus Freak* was a hybrid of hard-edged, guitar-driven grunge rock and in-your-face Christian lyrics—with the occasional rap break thrown in for good measure. Described by *CCM*'s Thom Granger as "an impressive example of re-imaging and re-inventing an artist's musical identity," the groundbreaking song was also hailed as single-handedly "ushering in Christian music's modern rock era." Even the staid *Chicago Tribune* noted in a 1996 review, "In considering the group's artistic merits, it's time to bury the over-burdened label 'Christian band.'. . . Like Van Morrison or U2—bands with strong Christian themes running through their music—dc talk deserves to be judged by a different standard."

Michael Tait, one-third of the group that also includes Toby McKeehan and Kevin Max, regards *Jesus Freak* as a pivotal, career-making move for dc talk. "It seemed to create a bit of a revolution in our industry," Tait recalls. "Every record we made

had been different from the one before and we had just released *Free At Last*, which was the biggest record to date for us. We knew *Jesus Freak* had to take it to the next level. I think—and I say this as humbly as I can—I really think it raised the bar a little bit, and we are very honored to be a part of it." The message of the song and the style

TALK ABOUT TOWN

5 songs by other artists with guest vocals from members of dc talk

1/ "Throw Yo Hands Up," Kirk Franklin (and Toby)   2/ "There's Just Something About That Name," Sonicflood (and Kevin)

3/ "Say Won't You Say," Jennifer Knapp (and Michael)   4/ "Big Man's Hat," Charlie Peacock (and Kevin)

5/ "Oh Holy Night," Leigh Nash (and Michael)

"I've spent so much of my time over the years, and still do, working with college and high school students at camps and retreats all over the country. One of the most revolutionary songs I have ever come across in the sense of changing people's perspectives on Christian music is 'Jesus Freak.' It's one of those songs that youth ministers play over and over again, just crank it up and watch the kids go nuts. It's so fun to watch the kids' reactions, it's like, 'FINALLY, music for us!' It's not something the 30-year-old sponsors of the trip are necessarily playing for themselves, but it's still something they can get into, bobbing their heads, jumping around, screaming and making fools of themselves—that's what being a Jesus Freak is all about. Everybody always loves it and it means so much to me too."

CHRIS RICE

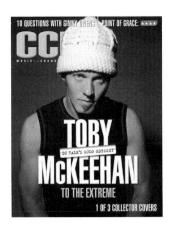

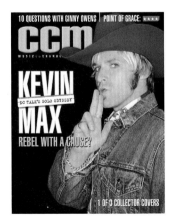

in which it was delivered rang especially true to Michael. "I was totally into rock and roll at that time," he says. "I really wanted to make a rock record, and of all of the albums we've made, I think I just kind of lost myself in that one. I really gave it everything I had, and it's like I became the music and the song in some ways. So there's *Jesus Freak* in all of its true rock glory, just bad and kickin', but with this blatant message about being completely sold out to the Creator of the Universe—who's gonna argue with that?"

Toby McKeehan explained the inspiration behind the song in a 1996 interview for *Music News* this way: "'Jesus Freak' is obviously a throw-back phrase. It was a negative phrase back in the late '60s and early '70s. If you were a 'Jesus Freak,' that meant people were talking down to you. We've chosen to take the opposite approach and say that it's something to be happy about. The word *freak*, I actually looked up in the dictionary as I was writing the song. The third definition in the copy of Webster's I have says the word *freak* is a noun meaning 'an ardent enthusiast.' So, you can definitely label us Jesus Freaks!"

The song that brought a new twist to an old label also helped redefine dc talk as serious artists and innovators. The

album went on to sell over two million copies and spawned numerous "Jesus Freak" books, youth group devotionals, journals and study guides. "We always wanted to be relevant," Tait says. "We wanted to write songs that would hopefully touch a generation. But this one became a phenomenon

way beyond anything we imagined. The song is very, very outspoken about our faith, because it truly takes a freak, a crazy man, a very daring person to live the Christian life and to walk the walk. So, be a freak for Jesus and never be ashamed of it."

"The first time I met Kevin Max, I was producing a Christmas project with various artists on it and he was going to be singing one of the songs. When he got to the studio, he came walking through the door and just tossed these t-shirts at the three of us behind the board—the co-producer, the engineer and me. We were all surprised; we'd never met him before, so I looked down at the shirt and it was this really brightly colored thing that said 'JESUS FREAK' all over the front of it. I thought he was joking with us, so I said, 'Man, this is horrible,' thinking that was the desired response. There's this kind of awkward silence and then Derri the engineer said, 'Uh, Steve, I think that's their new album . . .' Oh, well. Great album, great track."

STEVE HINDALONG, PRODUCER AND FOUNDING MEMBER OF THE CHOIR

MICHAEL W. SMITH

FRIENDS

3

WRITTEN BY MICHAEL W. SMITH AND DEBORAH D. SMITH

RECORDED BY MICHAEL W. SMITH ON THE MICHAEL W. SMITH PROJECT (REUNION RECORDS, 1982)

PRODUCED BY MICHAEL W. SMITH

1998 MICHAEL PERFORMED "FRIENDS" AT THE COLUMBINE HIGH SCHOOL MEMORIAL SERVICE IN LITTLETON, COLORADO

RE-RECORDED BY MICHAEL ON:
THE FIRST DECADE
THE SECOND DECADE

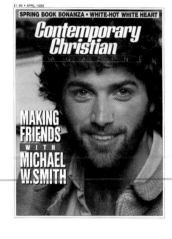

"Friends" is arguably the single most popular song in Christian music history. Even *CCM Magazine* proclaimed it "The #1 Song of All Time" in its 1998 20th Anniversary Issue. The simple chorus with its hopeful, almost child-like lyric has been a part of an entire generation's memory-making moments. It has been responsible for countless lumps in countless throats at weddings, graduations, funerals, birthdays, church camps, anniversaries and youth groups for over 20 years.

Originally appearing in 1983 on Michael's first Reunion record, *The Michael W. Smith Project*, "Friends" included vocals from one of his real friends, Amy Grant. When Smitty was hired to play keyboards on Amy's tour, he joined her on stage every night to close the show with what was becoming his signature song, and it never failed to bring the house down. The song's momentum began to grow, and by the time Michael featured the song again on his 1987 album, *The Live Set*, it was already a classic. "Friends" still graces the set list of every concert Michael performs—he has sung it for the President of the United States at Camp David as well as for the families of the victims of the Columbine tragedy. The power of that simple little song continues to this day.

The sweet story behind the writing of "Friends" has become part of Christian music lore, one of its most well-loved and often-repeated tales. The basic facts are that Michael and his wife, Debbie, wrote the song as a spontaneous farewell gift

for a friend from their church who was moving away . . . But here's the story behind the story, directly from the pen of the recipient of that now-famous gift. Bill Jackson is a missionary in Kijabe, Kenya. In this recent letter, he fondly recalls that long-ago evening and the effect it has had on his life:

Dear Friends,

My story starts when I was doing a youth ministry internship at Belmont Church of Christ in Nashville. My wife, Carol, and I were both interns there. We had a large group of college and young singles that met weekly for Bible study, worship and prayer. We met Debbie first, then Michael, and we gradually got to know each other. Michael also got involved in leading worship and helping with the youth group—he had a real heart for kids (and still does).

After Michael and Debbie Smith got married, we began having the Bible study at their house, and I was fortunate to be able to help lead it. About this time I was preparing to leave Nashville and head to Memphis, where I would be starting an InterVarsity Christian Fellowship Group for college students. The last night that I was to be at the Bible study at the Smith's, Debbie said that she and Michael had a gift for me. That's when

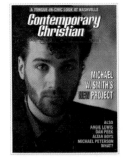

Michael sat down at the piano and sang "Friends." Debbie had written the words, and then Michael wrote the music right before the study was to start. I don't think there was a dry eye in the house after he sang the song. What a gift! To have a song written for me was really something so special.

I knew Michael was working on his first album, but I had no idea that he would include "my song" on his album. He told me later, and gave me a demo of "Friends" which I still have. When the album came out and I actually heard the song, I was really floored. I guess at that time I realized that "Friends" was not going to

MUSIC TO WAVE CANDLES BY

Most artists have at least one song that makes you want to flick your Bic, but we've discovered one guy who really shines in this category.

"We Will Stand"—Russ Taff

"Go Light Your World"—Kathy Troccoli aka "The Candle Song" by Chris Rice

"Keep the Candle Burning"—Point of Grace

"Honestly"—Stryper

"We Are His Hands"—White Heart

"I Will Remember You"—Amy Grant

"Say Once More"—Amy Grant

"It Is You"—Newsboys

"We Are the Reason"—David Meece

"Emily"—Michael W. Smith

"This Is Your Time"—Michael W. Smith

"I Will Be Here for You"—Michael W. Smith

"Place in This World"—Michael W. Smith

used in a setting like that. I couldn't contain myself. I yelled out, "That's my song!" and I started crying. I think most of the folks there thought something was wrong with me!

After Carol and I were married, God really began to speak to us about going into overseas missions. In the summer of 1987 we went to Kenya. We eventually had three sons, and several times when we were back in the States, Michael and Debbie sent us all tickets to his concerts. We always had a great time worshiping the Lord and then getting to see Michael backstage. I committed myself to pray for Michael, Debbie and their children, and I have really tried to be faithful in that.

Presently we are finishing up six and one half years of having lived and ministered in Kijabe, Kenya. My job has been that of a physical therapist for a small hospital called Bethany Crippled Children's Centre of Kenya, which was created for children who were born with terrible disabilities or deformities. We care for them through surgery, counseling to patients and parents, physical and occupational therapy, and spiritually by our trained staff of chaplains. God be praised.

Thanks so much for asking me to tell my story! We don't get a chance to see Debbie and Michael often enough. We miss them and hope to see them soon. But even in the silence in between, I know that we will always be "Friends."

In Him,
Bill Jackson

be just my song anymore, but a song for so many others too.

After I left Nashville for Memphis, Michael and Debbie wrote me a few times to tell me about letters they received from people about what "Friends" meant to them. Once, just before Carol and I were married, we went to a conference, and on the last night before everyone left, someone played "Friends" as the parting song. That was the first time I had heard it

MERCY ME

I CAN ONLY IMAGINE

4

WRITTEN BY BART MILLARD

RECORDED BY MERCYME ON
ALMOST THERE (INO, 2001)

PRODUCED BY PETER KIPLEY

ALSO RECORDED BY:
AMY GRANT ON LEGACY:
HYMNS AND FAITH

A wistful, well-written lyric, a melodic hook, a heartfelt vocal: these are the ingredients of a great song—though not necessarily a hit record. The phenomenon of MercyMe's "I Can Only Imagine" is that it not only turned out to be both, but went on to become one of the most successful crossover records in Christian music history.

The story behind "I Can Only Imagine" begins in 1991 when Bart Millard was a 19-year-old freshman in college. He lost his father after a long, hard-fought battle with cancer. Well-intentioned friends and family assured the grieving son that his father was happy now and would much rather be in heaven with Jesus than living in this troubled world. "I believed that," Bart says slowly, "but it was hard to swallow. I just kept thinking, *What's so great about heaven that my dad would rather be there than here with me?*" He tried to comfort himself by picturing the place his father was now and wondering what it would be like when they were reunited there. A phrase

formed in his mind and repeated itself with such intensity that he found himself writing it on anything he could get his hands on, jotting "I can only imagine" down on napkins or absent-mindedly doodling it while on the phone. But that's as far as it went. The loss was still too raw and the wounds were too fresh —so the words remained unspoken and the song unwritten.

Shortly after his father's death, the youth pastor in Millard's home church in Greeneville, Texas moved to Lakeland, Florida and invited Bart to come work with the youth praise band at the new church. At the end of his freshman year of college he did just that and had his first taste of perform-ing with a band. "It was just a local youth group that played for the

Wednesday night service," Bart says. "But I fell in love with it immediately." He hooked up with keyboardist Jim Bryson, and in the summer of 1994 they traveled to Europe as part of a praise team. The trip opened Bart Millard's eyes to the possibility of full-time music ministry. He and Bryson were soon joined by guitarist Mike Scheuchzer, and the three of them, now living in Oklahoma City, formed MercyMe. The group began to attract the attention of local promoters and eventually made the move to Nashville before finally settling back in Texas. Around that time bassist Nathan Cochran and percussionist Robby Schaefer came on board, turning MercyMe into the five-piece band.

Now based out of Dallas, MercyMe continued to travel and sing, with their schedule growing to over 200 dates a year. They released

"IT JUST FELT LIKE THE RIGHT TIME TO TRY TO PUT IT TO MUSIC," BART RECALLS.

several independent projects over the years and steadily built a solid, if not nationally recognized, ministry. In 1999 while working on their sixth recording, the band discovered that they were one song short. "We already had 10," Bart explains, "but for some weird reason we had this thing about always having more than just 10 songs on our albums; so we were trying to come up with number 11." As Bart leafed back through some of his old journals looking for inspiration, he came upon that phrase "I can only imagine" again and again. "It just felt like the right time to try to put it to music," Bart recalls. "And it only took about 10 minutes from start to finish—which always amazes people, but you have to remember that it had been on my heart for 10 years."

"So 'Imagine' became the eleventh song and we just stuck it on there, kind of like a 'B'

HARD TO IMAGINE . . .

RIAA Gold Certified in under one year. Released on album *Almost There* (INO, 2001)

Almost There* debuted #5 on Top Christian Album charts according to SoundScan. Album sold more than two million copies

Released as a single with "Word of God Speak"

Song was on the charts for 80 weeks (or 289 days) and appeared in six total charts, peaking at #12 in World (US, Canada, Germany, France, UK, Australia) Adult Top 20 Singles and #14 in USA Singles Top 40 compiled by top40-charts.com

Went into rotation on national mainstream AC and Hot AC formats. Song was #1 on Christian radio and was the most played song for 2001

Hit radio countdown shows *American Top 20* with Casey Kasem and *Hollywood Confidential* with Leeza Gibbons

2002 Dove Award Song of the Year

2004 Dove Awards for Artist and Group of the Year

The first contemporary worship song to crack top 40 radio since Sister Janet Mead's double-platinum-selling version of "The Lord's Prayer" in 1974

side," Bart continues. "It was real simple stuff, your basic verse—chorus—verse, but we felt like it had special meaning for us." The song wasn't on their set list, but one night while performing at a church camp, the pastor asked if they would sing "Imagine" during the invitation. "I remember saying, yeah, I guess we can, but we're going to have to learn it because we haven't really played it since we were in the studio. So we worked on it all day, and that night we played it. When we finished, there was just dead silence. I thought, *Oh crud, that's the worst song we've ever sung; we're never playing it again!* But when the lights came up, the band saw to their amazement that the kids weren't applauding because they were all weeping. "We couldn't believe it," Bart says, shaking his head at the memory. "We had no idea the kind of impact the song was going to have on people."

That was just the beginning. "I Can Only Imagine," the simple song with the simple message, became an award-winning, chart-topping, genre-jumping phenomenon. Released in 2001 on MercyMe's *Almost There* album, it racked up a laundry list of accolades and hovered near the top of sales and radio charts for over a year. MercyMe was also propelled into the heady stratosphere of mainstream success as "Imagine" became the pop radio surprise of the year. "It just made no sense," Bart laughs. "This is a straight-up worship song about heaven, for crying out loud! There's no way anyone could have predicted this."

As MercyMe moves into the next phase of their career and releases their next project, the legacy of "the little song that could" has left its mark. The tour production is fancier and the record budgets are larger, but the heart and the message of MercyMe remains the same—and it all began with "I Can Only Imagine."

AMY GRANT

EL SHADDAI

WRITTEN BY MICHAEL CARD AND JOHN THOMPSON

RECORDED BY AMY GRANT ON AGE TO AGE (MYRRH, 1982)

PRODUCED BY BROWN BANNISTER

ALSO RECORDED BY:
MICHAEL CARD ON LEGACY

BRYAN DUNCAN ON MY UTMOST FOR HIS HIGHEST

WINANS PHASE 2 ON SONGS FROM THE BOOK

5

Twenty-one-year-old Amy Grant was thrilled to be sitting behind the console board in the control room of the famed Caribou Ranch recording studio. So many of her musical heroes had recorded at this exclusive Colorado ranch—Dan Fogelberg, Elton John, Chicago—and bright and early the next morning she was slated to begin her own project there. "It was so exciting, I felt like I was looking behind the magic curtain in *The Wizard of Oz*," Amy recalls with a smile.

This was to be Amy's first studio recording since *Never Alone* in 1980, which had been followed by two back-to-back live concert releases. There was a lot of advance preparation for this album; the material had been chosen and the direction was clear. But that night in the studio, Mike Blanton—Amy's manager who was also the A & R director for the record—suddenly remembered a cassette that had come in at the eleventh hour. He had hurriedly stuck it in his suitcase on his way out of town and decided to pull it out now

> " 'El Shaddai' is still one of the most powerful worship songs today and will remain so. Amy is just an awesome force to me."
> CECE WINANS

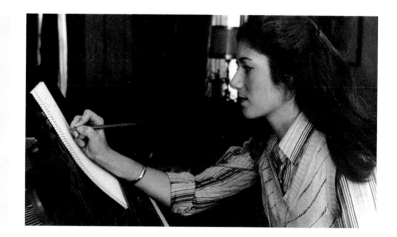

and give it a listen. "So we're all sitting in the control room poised and ready, when out of the speakers comes 'El Shaddai,'" Amy says. "And there went all of our carefully laid plans for the record! It was probably the most concise Bible history I'd ever heard in one song. It's all there—the human plight and God's mercy, from creation to crucifixion to resurrection. It was just unbelievable, and that one last-minute cassette tape changed everything for us."

In the days before worship songs regularly dominated the charts, "El Shaddai" seemed an unlikely choice

to release as a radio single. But the combination of Michael Card's powerful lyric performed by Amy's

achingly young voice layered over a lushly orchestrated soundtrack proved a winner. The song won numerous awards, including a 1983 Dove Award for Song of the Year, and *Age to Age* earned Amy her very first Grammy, for Best Contemporary Gospel Album.

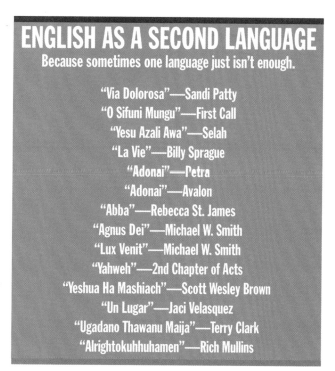

ENGLISH AS A SECOND LANGUAGE
Because sometimes one language just isn't enough.

"Via Dolorosa"—Sandi Patty
"O Sifuni Mungu"—First Call
"Yesu Azali Awa"—Selah
"La Vie"—Billy Sprague
"Adonai"—Petra
"Adonai"—Avalon
"Abba"—Rebecca St. James
"Agnus Dei"—Michael W. Smith
"Lux Venit"—Michael W. Smith
"Yahweh"—2nd Chapter of Acts
"Yeshua Ha Mashiach"—Scott Wesley Brown
"Un Lugar"—Jaci Velasquez
"Ugadano Thawanu Maija"—Terry Clark
"Alrightokuhhuhamen"—Rich Mullins

"I remember Amy Grant coming to England and playing Greenbelt Festival when I was about 17. Of course we were all huge fans, and of course we were all in love with her——Amy, the sweetheart from America, singing 'El Shaddai' and the whole place just going nuts, you know."

MARTIN SMITH OF DELIRIOUS?

"EL SHADDAI" AWARDS

1982 Grammy——Best Gospel
Performance, Contemporary:
AGE TO AGE

1983 Dove Award——Song of the Year

1983 Dove Award——Songwriter of
the Year for Michael Card

1983 Dove Award——
Artist of the Year

1983 Dove Award——
Pop/Contemporary Album:
AGE TO AGE

MICHAEL CARD, co-writer of "EL SHADDAI"

I went to college at Western Kentucky University and in the first half of my second year, I got linked up with this world-class Bible scholar named Dr. William Lane. He had his PhD from Harvard; he spoke 16 languages and was the author of two major commentaries on the Bible. I signed up for every single class he taught. He also had a real heart for discipleship, and he basically poured his life into me for the next six years while I was in college—in fact, he discipled me for 21 more years after that. I always tell people he created me the way Dr. Frankenstein created his monster! I can't even tell you all of the things he meant to my life. I named my son after him, and I was holding his hand when he died. That's one of my favorite stories about Bill, actually. He was in Seattle, this was years later of course, and he found out that he had multiple myeloma. He called me at my home in Franklin, Tennessee and asked if he could come there. He said, "I've got six months to live. Can I come to Franklin and show you how a Christian man dies?" I'm telling you this because a lot of my songs came from his sermons, but this song in particular, "El Shaddai," is a direct result of what William Lane taught me.

When I wrote "El Shaddai" I had just graduated with a master's degree in biblical studies and I had spent six years studying really hard. The good news is that a lot of the themes I had been studying and most of the Hebrew was still fresh in my head. My friend John Thompson played some music for me that he had been working on, and he asked, "What does that sound like to you?" I said, "Well, there's a strength to it; it's got kind of an 'almighty' feel to it." John said, "'God Almighty'?" And I said, "You know, that's 'El Shaddai' in Hebrew." So John told me to just take it and see what I could do with it. Since I was right out of college, I was still living at my parents' house and I went straight down to the basement and wrote it that night. I've probably written over 300 songs by now, and that's the only song that came out almost verbatim. When I played it for some people, they thought it held together well, so we went ahead and did a demo on it. Amy was planning on recording another song I had written called "I Have Decided" for her new album, and they called me and asked if I had anything else. So I said, "Well, I've just finished this song; let me run it over to you." And that's how it happened.

But the reason I could write it was because of the six years I had just spent under the discipleship of that amazing man. So when people compliment me on "El Shaddai," when they say there is such depth to it, I just always smile and tell them, "Well, that's Bill Lane!"

6

**RECORDED BY DELIRIOUS?
ON CUTTING EDGE
(FURIOUS RECORDS /
SPARROW RECORDS, 1997)**

**PRODUCED BY ANDY PIERCY
AND DELIRIOUS?**

**ALSO RECORDED BY:
SONICFLOOD ON SONIC
FLOOD**

SALVADOR ON WORSHIP LIVE

**JOHN TESH ON A DEEPER
FAITH**

Martin Smith, lead guitarist and vocalist for the British band Delirious?, cheerfully admits that "I Could Sing of Your Love Forever" is: a) not his personal favorite of all the songs he's written, and b) not the result of exhaustive creative effort. "I'd like to say that I spent three or four days solidly on my face before God sweating and crying over it," Martin says. "But the truth is, it just sort of fell out in half an hour—this simple little ditty."

The year was 1994, and Martin and his new wife were on holiday on the western coast of England with some other members of his family. "The house we were staying in overlooked this beautiful countryside with mountains, trees and a kind of a hill with this little river just jingling around below it," he recalls. "I always had my guitar with me, and I had been sitting around tinkering about with it, as you do. That's how the song came, and I thought nothing of it at the time."

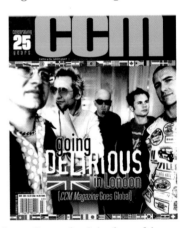

A couple of weeks later Martin was back home at the Arun Community Church in Littlehampton, England, a humble fellowship that held a small youth group meeting once a month. Martin and the four other members of the newly formed Delirious? regularly performed original worship music at these gatherings, which were locally referred to rather grandly as the "Cutting Edge" services. Eventually the band performed "I Could Sing of Your Love Forever" for the first time

there, receiving, to Martin's surprise, "a fantastic response."

Young Christians in Europe were experiencing a massive renewal movement during this time, and the Cutting Edge meetings soon began attracting up to 1,000 kids a month. Delirious?

went through all of the obligatory garage-band experiences—local gigs, home-recorded projects and selling albums out of the trunk of the drummer's car after their concerts. But as the movement grew, so did the popularity of the band, and it soon became apparent that they were in the middle of a full-time career instead of a part-time hobby. A climactic, near-fatal car accident in the summer of 1995 almost spelled the end of the group, but Martin Smith and bassist Jon Hatcher left the hospital after a lengthy recovery with a new resolve. They had escaped death and were determined to get on with the business of living. Within months, the rest of the band had all quit their day jobs and the first full-length studio album was in the works—Delirious? was off and running.

Ever the entrepreneurs, the band decided to start their own record label, Furious? Records, where each member of the band took on duties: Stew the drummer handled the graphic design, Jon the bass player worked the stockroom, Stu G the guitar player booked the overseas concerts, Tim the keyboard player managed the business, and Martin produced and engineered the tracks. Their first release on Furious? Records was *King of Fools*, which debuted at #13 on the British pop charts. Its success caught the attention of music companies across the pond, and soon EMI execs came courting. In 1998 Delirious? released *The Cutting Edge*, a double-disc compilation of their early worship recordings including "I Could Sing of Your Love Forever." Sparrow/ Chordant signed the band for American distribution, and soon Martin's initially underrated song was climbing the charts and helping to firmly establish

QUIET LITTLE SONGS THAT PACK A PUNCH

Just as Elijah heard God as a still, small voice, sometimes it's the quiet little songs that come through loud and clear.

"Just Come In"—Margaret Becker
"Come to Jesus"—Chris Rice
"I Wish We'd All Been Ready"—Larry Norman
"Boundless Love"—Farrell and Farrell
"No One Knows My Heart"—Susan Ashton
"Beyond Justice to Mercy"—Susan Ashton
"Simple Song"—Honeytree
"A Little More Like Jesus"—Brent Bourgeois
"The Hammer Holds"—Bebo Norman
"Sometimes Alleluia"—Chuck Girard
"Tremble"—Nichole Nordeman
"Small Enough"—Nichole Nordeman
"All I Ever Have to Be"—Amy Grant
"All I Must Do"—Kathy Troccoli
"If You Want Me To"—Ginny Owens
"Make My Life a Prayer"—Keith Green
"When You Cry"—The Winans
"Strength of My Life"—Leslie Phillips
"Hymn"—Randy Stonehill
"Let Me Sing"—Andrew Peterson
"Create in Me"—Brown Bannister
"Hold On to Jesus"—Steven Curtis Chapman
"By His Wounds"—Wes King
"When I Stand with You"—Charlie Peacock
"Tomorrow"—The Winans

Delirious? as a one band born-again British invasion. "I Could Sing of Your Love Forever" became a praise and worship standard. "Many, many people covered the song, especially in America," Martin says. "I think Sonicflood had the most radio success with it, so that's great." (Sonicflood's remake went #1 at Christian pop radio.)

Martin sums up his feelings about the little song that "just sort of fell out in half an hour" this way: "When you're writing, you're just thinking, *I want to create something that actually makes God smile.* That's all you're really interested in at that moment in time. Then later on you start to think, *Oh, I wonder if I could do this one in church, or if we will want to record it, or if it will work on the radio* . . . Those kinds of thoughts may kick in later, but right at the moment you're just pleased because you've created something. And that's enough. Because I guess if we could see the future, it would freak us out a bit, wouldn't it?"

Andy Hutch

25

JARS
OF CLAY

FLOOD

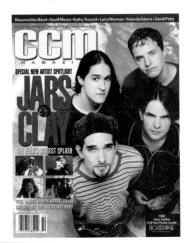

7

WRITTEN BY DAN HASELTINE, MATT ODMARK, STEPHEN MASON AND CHARLIE LOWELL

RECORDED BY RICH MULLINS ON WINDS OF HEAVEN, STUFF OF EARTH (REUNION RECORDS, 1989)

PRODUCED BY REED ARVIN

#37 ON BILLBOARD CHART

#2 ON THE TRIPLE A COLLEGE RADIO CHART

GRAMMY NOMINATION— BEST ROCK SONG

FEATURED IN THE MOVIE HARD RAIN AND IN COCA-COLA COMMERCIALS

If you are wearing a Toad the Wet Sprocket t-shirt on the campus of a Christian college, chances are someone is going to notice. At Greenville College in the early '90s, the t-shirt wearer was Dan Haseltine, and Charlie Lowell was the one who noticed. Having established their mutual admiration for the alternative pop/rock band, the two college freshmen struck up a friendship. A year later, wearing the same t-shirt, Dan met another Toad fan named Steve Mason. The three contemporary Christian music majors eventually moved into the same dorm, and a band was born.

In 1994, the new group decided to enter the Spotlight

Talent Competition run by the Gospel Music Association. On the strength of their demo tape alone, Jars of Clay traveled to Nashville, performed for industry executives (complete with choreographed moves and baby pacifiers in their mouths) and won the contest. They headed back to Greenville College and put together a self-released demo CD called *Frail*. When record company executives started calling the pay phone at their

> " 'Flood' absolutely floored me the first time I heard it. I'm someone who loves melody, that always catches me first in a song, and that one is so strong. The blend of their voices and the dynamics of the music—it was just totally unique. I'm pig-headed enough that I don't say this very often, but that's one song I wish I'd written!"
>
> PETER FURLER OF NEWSBOYS

dorm hoping to sign them, the guys decided that maybe Nashville was where they needed to be. Charlie Lowell's childhood friend Matt Odmark joined the band when the original second guitarist, Matt Bronleewe, decided to stay in college.

Jars of Clay signed with Essential Records and began recording a self-titled debut album. But their demo CD *Frail* had somehow come to the attention of progressive rock guitarist and recent Christian convert Adrian Belew. Belew, who had toured with David Bowie, King Crimson and the Talking Heads, was so impressed by *Frail* that he called and offered to produce a couple of tracks for the new record. "When we heard that he was interested in working with us, at first we didn't really believe it," laughs Dan Haseltine. "But he had picked out two of our songs he wanted to produce." One of those songs was "Flood."

"'Flood' was the last song written for that first album," Dan says. "I remember the day that we wrote it, because it was this really bright sunny day in Greenville, Illinois. We sat down under a tree, looking up at that beauti- ful blue sky, and wrote this song about torrential downpours and mud."

Jars of Clay was not too happy when the label decided that "Flood" would be the first single. "We thought it wasn't representative of the whole album," Dan says. "But it was released in the Christian market for a year, and all of a sudden mainstream radio picked up the song, back in the days when radio could still champion a song, and it started to grow. We were just amazed, watching all this, and felt very sure it was a case of God opening doors for us that we could never have done on our own. It just seemed like it was the right timing —the, you know, post-grunge. People were looking for something that was still aggressive but had slightly less of a pessimistic take on the world. And that song had this small spark of hope in it, and I think people gravitated towards that."

The "Flood"-gates were opened and the boys from the little Christian college were soon riding the wave of a double platinum record. They burned up the charts and won MTV Awards. They opened for Sting, worked for

"I remember we were in Chicago the first time we heard 'Flood' on the radio. We had been having this discussion within the band about some of our songs and how we needed to incorporate harmony, which was a new concept for us. 'Flood' came on, and our bass player started yelling, 'Listen to that! That's good harmony right there!' I do have one beef with them, though. Every time we do a festival with them and they do 'Flood,' it starts raining instantly. That's almost not a lie. Seriously, it's like it's a Native American rain dance or something. What is great about Jars, though, is that they never tried to do a 'Flood, Part Two.' They just put out this great song that turned out to be this huge hit and almost spawned its own radio format, and then they went on to make other great music. To this day, they're my favorite band in Christian music."

MARK LEE AND MAC POWELL OF THIRD DAY

African AIDS relief with Bono and received intense scrutiny from both sides of the music business. "That

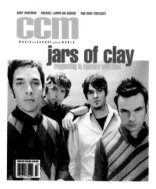

was a season in our lives that we began to ask some really good questions, you know, what does it look like to be a Christian in the world? Lifestyle evangelism took on a whole new level for us. It was in some ways a difficult time, but we survived and now, 10 years later we're more inspired as a band and more connected to

each other than we've ever been."

STEVEN CURTIS CHAPMAN

THE GREAT ADVENTURE

WRITTEN BY STEVEN CURTIS CHAPMAN AND GEOFF MOORE

RECORDED BY STEVEN CURTIS CHAPMAN ON THE GREAT ADVENTURE (SPARROW, 1992)

PRODUCED BY PHIL NAISH

1993 DOVE AWARD—SHORT FORM MUSIC VIDEO OF THE YEAR

SONG PARODY BY MARK LOWRY, "THE DATE ADVENTURE," ON MOUTH IN MOTION

"**O**K, I don't really even care for horses all that much." This smiling admission comes from Steven Curtis Chapman, who is musing aloud about the writing of one of his most recognizable and well-loved songs, "The Great Adventure." He continues, "So I don't know why I wrote this song about saddling one up and heading out! Although I guess in my heart I probably always wanted to be a cowboy. . . . I mean, what's the most freeing, exciting thing that I can imagine? Jumping on the back of a wild horse and just tearing out to see where it takes me! That's the picture I had in my head when I wrote it."

But cowboy fantasies aside, it was a much more serious kind of introspection that led to "The Great Adventure." "It's interesting how some songs are birthed," Steven begins. "I had been sitting with a group of pastors who were serving as my advisory board at that season in my ministry. I was meeting with these guys to kind of check in and talk about the new album I was supposed to be writing songs for. But it was one of those times

in my life that I just felt like a complete failure as a dad and as a husband. I was bummed, and I was weary. When we sat down they asked me, 'So, how are you doing?' I made an offhanded comment; I said something like, 'Well, I really feel like I need to just sit down and cry for a while—but I'm great!'" Though no one said anything right away, the statement did not go unnoticed by the pastors. Steven continues, "Then I kind of put on my happy face and we started talking about the new album and other

www.lamoine.com

business stuff. But after a while one of them said, 'I want to return to something you said earlier, that comment you made about feeling like you need to sit and cry for a while.' I reluctantly began to talk about it. I told them that I felt like I was just blowing it. Here I was, supposedly the one with all of the great, profound things to say, and I didn't really feel like I knew how to be a dad or a husband, or even a Christian half the time." The pastors on Steven's advisory board heard his frustration and pain, and rallied to encourage him. "They began to talk to me about the grace of God," Steven remembers. "And one pastor friend of mine said this— 'Here's the great news about grace: there's absolutely nothing you can do that will cause God to love you any more, and there's nothing you can do that will cause Him to love you any less. That's what grace is.'" Steven pauses, then says, "As they began to minister to me in that time of discouragement, it's like these little walls I had put up around myself in my futile attempts to try to do it all on my own just came down. Those guys just blew those walls down by reminding me of what it's really all about. I began to see myself, as I later wrote in the song, standing out in 'the wild blue yonder of God's amazing grace.'"

Steven walked out of that meeting with a renewed appreciation for godly counsel, an insight into grace, and the idea for a new song buzzing around in his head. He collaborated with his longtime friend and songwriting partner Geoff Moore, and eventually emerged with what was to become the title cut of his next album. The song begins with a buoyant invitation to "Saddle up your horses," and challenges the listener to jump headlong into "the great adventure" of life with the assurance that God will always be right there with them. Musically, it fit easily into the contemporary pop niche, but Chapman's country roots were definitely showing. The song was a hugely popular radio hit, occupying the charts for over 11 weeks. The accompanying video enjoyed some play on CMT, briefly sparking rumors of a country music crossover for Chapman. "The Great Adventure" also earned a bevy of industry acknowledgments, including four Dove Awards and a 1993 Grammy.

A REWARDING ADVENTURE

1993 DOVES:
SONGWRITER OF THE YEAR
ARTIST OF THE YEAR
SONG OF THE YEAR
POP/CONTEMPORARY ALBUM
SHORT FORM MUSIC VIDEO

1992 GRAMMY:
BEST POP GOSPEL ALBUM

1993 GRAMMY:
BEST POP/CONTEMPORARY GOSPEL ALBUM: *The Great Adventure*

Nashville Songwriter's Association International Award

OTHER "GREAT" SONGS

"Great, Great Joy"—Chris Christian
"Great Is the Lord"—Michael W. Smith
"The Great Divide"—Point of Grace
"The Great Exchange"—Bruce Carroll
"Great Big Stupid World"—Randy Stonehill

NEWSBOYS
SHINE

WRITTEN BY STEVE TAYLOR AND PETER FURLER

9

RECORDED BY NEWSBOYS ON GOING PUBLIC (STARSONG RECORDS, 1994)

PRODUCED BY STEVE TAYLOR AND PETER FURLER

1995 DOVE AWARD FOR GOING PUBLIC; RECORDED ROCK SONG OF THE YEAR FOR "SHINE"

THE BAND HAS HAD 16 #1 HITS ON CHRISTIAN RADIO CHARTS

1996 THE VIDEO FOR "SHINE" WAS FEATURED IN THE STEVE TAYLOR PRODUCED NEWSBOYS' MOVIE DOWN UNDER THE BIG TOP

1997 THE NEWSBOYS PERFORMED FOR POPE JOHN PAUL II'S WORLD YOUTH DAY

Only Steve Taylor could lyrically conjure images of former dictators teaching origami to the poor and vegetarians barbequing hamsters. And only the Newsboys could turn that bouncy and slightly bizarre paean to God's life-changing power into a song that jumped to #1 on the charts and then stayed there for six weeks.

"Shine" is instantly recognizable and ridiculously catchy, due in no small part to its unique musical intro. Peter Furler recalls the happy accident that produced the sound:

"We were recording the CD *Going Public* in a down-town studio in Nashville. We had just about finished nine songs, but the record companies always really like you to have more than that. Contractually we had to come up with one more, and we just didn't have it. So while the rest of the crew was in another section of the studio recording their parts, it was deemed my job to go and find that tenth song. I felt a little bit of pressure, because Steve Taylor and I both felt like we were still missing the cornerstone piece of the album. You know, on every project it seems that we always find that one song that you build the rest of the record around. And we just didn't have that yet."

As Peter tried to figure out where the last song was going to come from, he wandered into an empty vocal booth in another part of the recording studio. "So I'm sitting there, locked in this little glass room trying to write a song, trying to come up with the main theme," he says. "I was definitely feeling the pressure, but at the same time I thought, *Well, worrying isn't going to make the song come any faster!"*

Peter started noodling around with a new keyboard he had purchased specifically for the record project. "I usually write songs on the guitar," he says, "but for some reason I had bought this new thing called a Korg Wavestation module. I thought it might help with the making of the record; maybe I could find some of the latest sounds and that sort of stuff." While he was scrolling through sounds, he came upon something called "Frippertronic," named after famed British guitarist Peter Fripper. Furler continues, "I found this weird sound and it sort of intrigued me. It was like, 'Mah, mah mah mah!' I just started pressing the keys and rolling this little beat, and all of a sudden I started to come up with this melody. To get the intro sound, I had to record one track with my little tape recorder there, and then play over the top of it. When we play it now in concerts, Jeff our keyboard guy is so great he can just do the whole thing at once, but not me. So after a while I came walking out with the song, and when I played it for them, Steve Taylor and all the crew thought I was absolutely such a genius, you know. They didn't realize it was obviously the hand of the Lord being merciful on me. Steve finished off the lyrics to it and we were done. I think we recorded the song that day, maybe tidied it up in the next few days and then finished the vocals. And even though it was for our *Going Public* project, to this day people think the album's title is *Shine!* From a marketing standpoint, that probably would have

been a better choice, but the cover was already done; everything was already done. We were lucky it made the record at all."

Steve Taylor has played an important role in the career of the Newsboys, and in Peter Furler's life as well. "He's been my confirmation," Peter explains. "Steve is one of the few people in my life—my wife and my manager are the other two—that I always depend on for creative input. When I take a new song to show him, if he likes it he'll say, 'Yeah, I think we're on to something here; go run it by our other ears.' He means my wife and manager, because when the four of us agree that we've got a good song, we haven't missed yet."

That kind of confidence can come in handy when the audience doesn't immediately latch on to a new song. The first few times the Newsboys played "Shine" in concert, it didn't exactly bring the house down. Peter smiles, "It's a good thing we don't completely let the crowd's opinion tell us if a new song is going to work or not, because probably the first 10 times we did

Kristen Barlowe

'Shine' in concert, it bombed. We were all kind of going, 'Whoa!' But when it went out to radio, it just flew up the charts and became #1. So our instincts were right about it."

Apparently so. *Going Public* won the 1995 Dove Award Album of the Year and was nominated for a Grammy. "Shine" won the Dove Award for Recorded Rock Song of the Year and was also nominated in two other categories.

The funky little Korg keyboard that started it all, unfortunately, didn't fare as well. A couple of years later, it was stolen along with the rest of the Newsboys' entire keyboard rig. When the Newsboys tried to replace it, they made the interesting discovery that not only did the company not manufacture that model anymore, it was also the only keyboard module in existence that had that particular Frippertronic sound sample on it. Peter laughs at the memory. "We had to search the entire continent to find one," he says. "Just think—that famous weird 'Shine' sound was almost gone forever!"

"My kids have grown up listening to the Newsboys, which I am so grateful for. In fact, when I think of my song 'Mirror' I can't help but think of 'Shine,' because 'Mirror' talks about letting your face reflect Jesus Christ and His love and 'Shine' tells us that if we do that, it will make the world wonder what we've got! Even though the songs are 20 years apart, it's the same message, just different styles. The Word doesn't change."

EVIE

DARLENE ZSCHECH

SHOUT TO THE LORD

WRITTEN BY DARLENE ZSCHECH

RECORDED BY DARLENE ZSCHECH ON SHOUT TO THE LORD (HOSANNA/INTEGRITY 1996)

PRODUCED BY DARLENE ZSCHECH AND RUSSELL FRAGAR

DARLENE ZSCHECH WAS THE FIRST FEMALE WORSHIP LEADER EVER IN THE LONG-RUNNING, CRITICALLY ACCLAIMED HILLSONG MUSIC SERIES FROM INTEGRITY

ALSO RECORDED BY:
CARMAN ON PASSION FOR PRAISE

The "praise and worship movement" is a genuine phenomenon in contemporary Christian music and has changed the face of the industry. If that sounds like a bit of an overstatement, just try "Google-ing" that phrase on your laptop and see what comes up: you'll find praise and worship leader workshops, alternative praise and worship manuals, praise and worship dancewear, praise and worship seminars, praise and worship coffee mugs . . . and the name "Darlene Zschech." A native of Queensland, Australia, Darlene's self-penned "Shout to the Lord" is practically the theme song for the entire movement. It is sung by an estimated 25–30 million churchgoers every week, has been covered by at least 20 other artists and has been performed for the President of the United States and the Pope at the Vatican.

Darlene Zschech is not entirely comfortable with all of the attention "Shout to the Lord" has caused. A pretty, soft-spoken mother of three with a self-deprecating sense of humor, Darlene has reconciled herself to the fact that her days of anonymity as a member of the worship team at Hillsong Church in Sydney are long over.

A child star on a weekly children's television show, a precocious 10-year-old Darlene sang, danced and hosted interview segments for *Happy Go 'Round*. With eight years of vocal training and nine years of dance training behind her, she then toured internationally as a background vocalist, worked as a session singer and sang jingles for companies including

McDonalds, KFC and Diet Coke. But she also endured her parents' shattering divorce and subsequent custody battle at the tender age of 13, and struggled for several years with bulimia. When her father rededicated his life to Christ and began attending church,

Lee Steffen

Hillsong Church, a well-known and respected 10,000-member church with its own praise and worship recording label. It was there in 1993, while serving on the staff of the church, that Darlene wrote the now-famous anthem. It was released on the church's Hillsong Music Australia label, and then in 1996 "Shout to the Lord" was released in the United States as the title cut for a Hosanna! Music project that went on to become gold-certified and topped the Praise and Worship charts for over 30 weeks. But the bold lyrics and soaring melody were born out of a particularly hard time in Darlene's life, a time when a less gentle soul might have been tempted to shout *at* the Lord.

"We had totally come to the end of ourselves, and we were losing our way," says Darlene, recalling those anxious days when she and her husband, Mark, were struggling to make ends meet with two young children and a failing motorcycle-parts business. "There were all

he brought his hurting daughter with him, and Darlene began her own relationship with the God that she grew to write about so passionately. She also met her future husband at that church, and after dating for a year and a half, married Mark just one week after her nineteenth birthday. The newlyweds moved to Sydney and eventually found their way to

these dreams, all these things we wanted to do, but nothing was happening." The frustration wasn't only for financial reasons, but spiritual ones as well. "All I really wanted to do was serve God," Darlene says. "But it was like, 'How are we ever going to get there; how are we ever going to serve You in a greater capacity?' It felt like we kept hitting our heads against a brick wall, and I

"Sing to the LORD a new song; sing to the LORD, all the earth. Let the heavens rejoice, let the earth be glad; let the sea resound and all that is in it; let the fields be jubilant and everything in them. Then all the trees of the forest will sing for joy."

was just sort of over it." One particularly trying day, Darlene wandered into her daughter's toy room and sat down at the rickety old piano there. "That poor thing was already ancient when I got it at five years old," Darlene laughs. "It was out of tune and mouse-infested—you know, really glam! But I had some words I'd been thinking about from Psalm 96 and Psalm 100, and I just started singing them. I've always been a worshiper, that's where I naturally go, so I sat there and sang and that song simply flowed out of me."

Initially Darlene was too shy to even sing it for her worship pastor, but she finally gathered

"'Shout to the Lord' moves me because I love a song that encourages people to praise God, to exalt and lift Him up. I get real excited about worship!"

CECE WINANS

1997—Received Dove Award Nomination for Album of the Year

1998—Received Dove Award Nomination for Song of the Year ("Shout to the Lord")

1999—Received the Gospel Music Association's International Impact of the Year Award

1999—The album *Shout to the Lord* received gold certification status from the Recording Industry Association of America

2000—Received Dove Award Nominations for Songwriter of the Year and Praise and Worship Album of the Year (Album: *Shout to the Lord*)

2000—Chosen as Executive Director for Mercy Ministries Australia

2001—Received Dove Award Nomination for Praise and Worship Album of the Year

her courage and oh-so-casually mentioned that she thought she might have written a song. When he asked to hear it, she obliged, but with the condition that he and the music director stand with their backs to her while she sang it. "I was so embarrassed," Darlene says, "I just fumbled my way through it!" Several weeks later she performed it for the first time in church, and before the end of the first chorus, people were standing to their feet. "I started looking around because I thought maybe something else was going on," Darlene smiles. "Then I realized that it was the song, and I said, 'What is happening here?' It had taken on a life of its own, as if the breath of God had just jumped into it."

That worship service was only the beginning. "Shout to the Lord" has gone on to become the standard by which all other worship songs are judged, and it launched an international, award-winning career for Darlene Zschech. "I am honored and overwhelmed and humbled to be part of something that causes such a response in the hearts of believers," Darlene says. "Ultimately it's just a song from an ordinary woman who is loved by a magnificent God."

"The first time I heard Darlene Zschech sing that song, I just went straight to the throne room. 'Shout to the Lord' brought the church and the body of Christ together through the power of music."

HEATHER PAYNE OF POINT OF GRACE

CITY ON A HILL

GOD OF WONDERS

WRITTEN BY MARC BYRD
AND STEVE HINDALONG

RECORDED BY CITY ON A HILL/VARIOUS ARTISTS: LEIGH NASH, MAC POWELL, CLIFF YOUNG, DANIELLE YOUNG ON CITY ON A HILL: SONGS OF WORSHIP AND PRAISE (ESSENTIAL RECORDS, 2000)

PRODUCED BY STEVE HINDALONG

ALSO RECORDED BY:
THIRD DAY ON OFFERINGS II

REBECCA ST. JAMES ON HERE I AM TO WORSHIP

STEVE GREEN ON WOVEN IN TIME

CAEDMON'S CALL ON IN THE COMPANY OF ANGELS: A CALL TO WORSHIP

11

ompilation albums are not a radical new concept. They usually consist of gathering a collection of already-recorded songs by different artists under one heading and releasing it as an album. Or sometimes there will be a concept record with original music—*My Utmost for His Highest* or *Traveling Light*, for example—and the artists will come in separately and record their tracks, usually never crossing paths with anyone else on the project. *City on a Hill*, however, broke new ground with an artists-in-community approach that had never been attempted.

Producer Steve Hindalong brought the idea for *City on a Hill*, which was originally conceived with the title *Holy Communion*, to Essential Records President Robert Beeson, who gave it a green light. Hindalong explains, "Our concept of 'community' was one that takes the emphasis off of the particular artist who may have his or her name on the song and places it where it belongs—in worship and exaltation of God." The idea may have sounded a bit esoteric, but the actual process was, as Cliff Young of Caedmon's Call describes it, "really amazing, just a blast!"

The songs from the album all focused on the grace and goodness of God, with the artists teaming up in various combinations to record and worship together. The roster included Jars of Clay, Sixpence None the Richer, Third Day, FFH, Peter Furler, Gene Eugene, The Choir,

Kristin Barlowe

Sonicflood and Caedmon's Call. There were no spotlight-grabbing star turns, and the method for pairing artists with songs, and artists with each other, was kept rather, well, loose. Cliff Young recalls, "Everybody was really cooperative, and you never knew what you were going to be singing on. It was like, 'Hey, would you sing on this song with so and so?' 'Yeah, great!' 'How about you and you, together?' 'Sure, no problem!' It was

pretty cool; I'd never experienced that kind of atmosphere before. And I remember Leigh Nash was in the middle of the whole crazy 'Kiss Me' thing, selling millions of records, and she was absolutely right in there with *City on a Hill*—I mean, she was into it."

"God of Wonders," which became the biggest hit from the album, features no less than 12 different artists and musicians. As reviewer Anthony

City on a Hill artists pose at the unveiling of the album's cover art with painter Kim Thomas.

43

DeBarros describes it, "'God of Wonders' is a simple declaration of the holiness and majesty of God. From the outset, when Leigh Nash of Sixpence sings the gentle intro 'Lord of heaven and earth,' the focus is toward God. Nash then passes the vocal to Third Day's Mac Powell, who takes a verse and chorus before handing off to Caedmon's Call singer Cliff Young. By the time it wraps, Caedmon's singer Danielle Young is weaving in a line from the old hymn 'Holy, Holy, Holy! Lord God

Kristin Barlowe

Kristin Barlowe

MEGA-MULTI-ARTIST COLLABORATIONS

We'll spare you the roll call of the 100+ artists who contributed to "Fight the Fight" back in the mid-1980s. But here are a few songs brimming with talent.

"Lean on Me"—Kirk Franklin, R. Kelly, Crystal Lewis, Mary J. Blige and Bono

"Friends 2003"—Michael W. Smith, Amy Grant, Steven Curtis Chapman, Michael Tait, Point of Grace, Mac Powell, Anointed, Joy Williams and Avalon

"Do Something Now"—Amy Grant, Larry Norman, Kathy Troccoli, Russ Taff, Evie, Phil Keaggy, Scott Wesley Brown, Michele Pillar, Steve Camp, Sandi Patty, Dana Key, Mylon LeFevre, Jessy Dixon, Steve Taylor, Matthew Ward, 2nd Chapter of Acts, Sheila Walsh, Chris Christian, Gary Chapman, Rob Frazier, Bobby Jones and Newlife, Tami Gunden, Larry Bryant, Angie Lewis, Kim Perry, Geoff Moore, Lanny Wolfe, Candy Hemphill, DMB Band, Sue Dodge, Pete Carlson, Billy Crockett, Karen Kelly, Cam Floria, Flo Price, Glad, Owen Brock, Jim Murray, Shirley Caesar, David Meece, Sherman Andrus, Lisa Whelchel, Robin Crow, Pam Mark Hall, Brown Bannister, Billy Sprague, Doug Oldham, Amy Fletcher, Michael Card, Steve Green, Silverwind, Connie Scott, Rick Cua, Glen Kaiser, Dennis Agajanian, Bob Farrell, Morgan Cryar, Bill and Gloria Gaither, Found Free, Rusty Goodman and Gary McSpadde

Almighty!'" The song immediately became one of the most popular songs on Christian radio and eventually appeared on both Third Day and Caedmon's Call albums.

According to Mark Lee of Third Day, the group originally passed on the song. "We heard the demo and loved the song, but we didn't think it would work for us. So we recorded this other song for the project, but I guess Steve still had Mac's voice in mind for 'Wonders,' so one day he pulls Mac into the studio and has him sing on it. It's been one of our most popular songs, and we almost turned it down. Yeah, that would have been a really good career move for us!"

Cliff Young gave the song a test run at his church in Houston months before it was actually recorded for the project. "We had the demo of it, and one Sunday morning I was leading worship and taught it to the congregation," Cliff says. "It was just incredible; we had to sing it every Sunday. I finally called Steve and said, 'Man, you've got to hear this; we've got 5,000 people singing your song and they are just loving it!'"

The simple beauty and collaborative

Lee Steffen

vision of that song defined the *City on a Hill* project. "You can't walk into that kind of thing and ever really know how it's going to turn out," Steve Hindalong says. "I was just writing with my good friend Marc Byrd, who's like a brother to me. He had this melody and just a few words going, and it made the hair stand up on my arms as soon as he started strumming the guitar. There was just so much emotion in it. Typically, we both tend to write in a more lyrically introspective direction, but I said, 'Marc, this just has to be BIG, with the biggest language I can possibly think of.' That's why I wrote, 'God of wonders, beyond our galaxy . . .' Galaxies are big!" Steve laughs and then says, "But the second verse to me is where the song really has its power. It says, 'When I stumble in the darkness, I will call Your name by night.' I wanted to say that the God we worship is that big and vast, beyond even our world, but yet He listens to us when we're in trouble and He cares for us like a loving, tender Father. That's a powerful truth, that song, and it's a privilege to offer something like that."

"Before I'd ever heard the recording, I heard 'God of Wonders' at church on a Sunday morning. I was immediately drawn into a more appreciative worship—a place of responding to the majesty of God. Any song that accomplishes this in the human heart is made of greatness and goodness. Plus, I wish I'd written it!"

CHARLIE PEACOCK

NICOLE C. MULLEN

REDEEMER

WRITTEN BY NICOLE C. MULLEN

RECORDED BY NICOLE C. MULLEN ON NICOLE C. MULLEN (WORD ENTERTAINMENT, 2000)

PRODUCED BY DAVID MULLEN AND JASON NIEBANK

2001 DOVE AWARD— POP/CONTEMPORARY RECORDED SONG OF THE YEAR; SONGWRITER OF THE YEAR

NICOLE ONCE CHOREO- GRAPHED TOURS FOR AMY GRANT, THE NEWSBOYS AND MICHAEL W. SMITH

NICOLE RECORDED THE VEGGIE TALES CLASSIC "LARRY BOY"

12

The audience members at the 2001 Dove Awards got more than they bargained for. In addition to the usual glitz and glamour of the performance-packed show, they also got to witness a little history being made. When the winner was announced for Song of the Year and then Songwriter of the Year, it wasn't Steven Curtis Chapman who mounted the stage. Instead, all eyes were on a beauti- ful, elegantly dressed African-American woman with a face-splitting smile and a humble, articulate acceptance speech. Nicole C. Mullen, who won a total of four Dove Awards that night, was the first woman in 14 years to win Songwriter of the Year and the first African-American ever to take home Song of the Year honors. A paradigm shift was in the air.

Nicole's self-penned "Redeemer" was a single from her

first Word album, *Nicole C. Mullen*. It was not only an immediate hit, rap- idly rising to #1, but it seemed to reach beyond airplay and chart action straight into the hearts of the listeners. "Redeemer" brought well- deserved attention to her prodigious songwriting skills, which had first been recognized by the industry in 1998 when Jaci Velasquez's version of her song "On My Knees" won the Dove Award for Song of the Year.

But it is Nicole's amazing vocal prowess and patented style—a combination of pop, funk, black gospel, hillbilly and urban sounds she refers to as "funkabilly"—that sets her apart from her peers. She also brings her unique talents as a

"One girl that I think is the absolute bomb is Nicole C. Mullen. Her testimony, her lyrics ... She's such a marvelous woman of God and an exceptional poet. If I am driving when her song 'Redeemer' comes on, I want to stop and get out and just yell, 'YEAH!' She is magnificent."

DARLENE ZSCHECH

storyteller, actress, choreographer and dancer to everything she does. This ability to successfully blend different elements is reflected in Nicole's private life as well.

Nicole has chosen to take the bold and unusual step of tackling the subject of race head-on in her music and ministry. "I feel called to be a bridge builder, and to help others celebrate our differences and our sameness," she says. She also speaks openly about God's divine diversity, a concept she well understands. Nicole is one happy half of an interracial couple, married for over a decade to producer David Mullen. They have two biological bi-racial children, Jasmine and Josiah, and an adopted African-American son, Maxwell. "We tell our kids that the color of skin is meant to be a description, not a definition," she says. "It tells you nothing about whether a person is rich, poor, smart, whatever. Character tells you that."

When Nicole tells the story of how she came to write "Redeemer," she remembers that she was sitting on the couch in her music room with her Bible, flipping through the story of Job. "You know, Job is one of those books that can really mess with your theology!" Nicole laughs. "I had gotten to the part of the story where God is having this conversation with the devil and brings up the fact that His

"I think lyrically one of the best songs that has ever been written is 'Redeemer' by Nicole C. Mullen. As a songwriter, the first time I heard it I was literally jealous—I was like, 'How in the world did you think to say it that way?' As Christian artists, we're all trying to put a new spin on an old story that's obviously still relevant. And the way she wrote that song, the way she expressed it, was like a breath of fresh air. When I finally met her I was able to tell her how many times I had worshiped listening to that song. I'm just real appreciative of great songwriters and great songs, and Nicole is unbelievable. Another great song that I wish I had written."

BART MILLARD OF MERCYME

servant Job was blameless in all his ways, perfect and upright. And the devil came back saying, 'Well, he only worships and serves You because You've given him all this stuff and made his life good. If I lift my hand and strike him, he'll curse You to Your face.' God says, 'OK, do whatever you want; take your best shot. But you can't kill him.'"

Nicole continues, "And so sure enough, the devil goes and wreaks havoc. He kills all 10 of Job's kids; he steals all his animals in one day; his finances are gone, everything's gone. But instead of cursing God like the devil said he would, Job said, 'Naked I came into the world and naked I'm going to leave. The Lord giveth and the Lord taketh away. Blessed be the name of the Lord.' Then his friends came and kept telling him he must have done something really bad to deserve all this, and poor Job's lying there saying, 'What's my crime? Have I been sinful? Somebody tell me what it was!'" Nicole pauses and then says, "But right in the middle of all Job's loss and confusion, he still finds hope. He began to prophesy; he said, 'I know that my Redeemer lives.' And I remember seeing that and thinking, *If Job can go through all this and still reach out to God, how much more can I?*"

As Nicole picked up her guitar and started strumming, the entire chorus of "Redeemer" came to her. Then the first verse poured out, but when she tried to write the second verse and the bridge, nothing came. So she tried again. Nothing. Nicole laughs and says, "Finally I put it on my 'to be completed' list in my stack of songs and it just sat there. Actually, I was going to pitch it to Point of Grace, but I didn't finish it in time for their deadlines. Eventually, I think probably about a year later, I went back to it. That's when the second verse and the bridge finally came. But even in the interim before I had the other verses, that song was kind of a comfort to me. There were nights that I would just sit there on my bed with my guitar and start singing, 'I know my Redeemer lives . . .' I didn't think of it as a song that everybody was going to love. I just knew that it was going to be special to me."

POWER LIST OF POWER BALLADS

You know how these work: they quietly build through the verse until everything hits you full-force on the chorus, often with a key change prior to that last reprise.

"We Are the Reason"—David Meece

"Holding Out Hope"—Michael English

"I Surrender All"—Clay Crosse

"Stubborn Love"—Kathy Troccoli

"Blessed Are the Tears"—Bryan Duncan

"Amazed"—Steve Archer

"Praise the Lord"—Imperials

"God So Loved"—Jaci Velasquez

"No Greater Love"—Rachael Lampa

"The Robe"—Wes King

"We All Need"—Bryan Duncan

"I Will Be Free"—Cindy Morgan

LARRY NORMAN

I WISH WE'D ALL BEEN READY

WRITTEN BY LARRY NORMAN

RECORDED BY LARRY NORMAN ON UPON THIS ROCK (CAPITOL, 1969)

PRODUCED BY HAL YOERGLER

COVERED BY RANDY MATTHEWS, CLIFF RICHARD AND DC TALK, PLUS A REMIX (USING ORIGINAL TAPES) BY BRIAN HARDIN

13

Credited by many as the first songwriter to combine faith-based lyrics with rock 'n' roll, Larry Norman has a career steeped in legend. He started songwriting and performing in 1956. Then, 10 years later, long before anything like the Christian music business existed, he and his band People signed to Capitol Records, the same label as the Beach Boys and the Beatles. The band, which had a Top 20 hit with "I Love You" in 1968, opened for such secular groups as The Doors, The Byrds and many others.

Norman signed a solo deal with Capitol in 1969. His first solo record, *Upon This Rock*, furthered Norman's unlikely mix of gospel messages, love songs, sarcasm and political outrage. Produced by Hal Yoergler (who also produced The Bugaloos), the album was a glimpse of what was to come for the revolutionary songwriter.

"*Upon This Rock* was written to stand outside the Christian culture," Norman told *CCM* in 1998. "I tried to create songs for which there was no anticipated acceptance. I wanted to display the flexibility of the gospel and that there was no limitation to how God could be presented. . . . No, it was not a Christian album for those believers who wanted everything spelled out. It was more like a street fight. I was saying [to Christians], 'I'm going to present the gospel, and I'm not going to say it like you want. This album is not for you.'"

One highlight of the album was the enduring "I Wish We'd All Been Ready," a mournful, bittersweet ballad about the return of Christ. (Norman must have

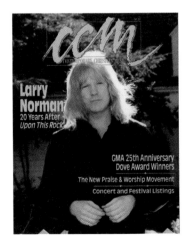

liked the song a lot, because he recorded it again for the very next album). One of the earliest examples of eschatological pop, it became the cornerstone of the 1972 end-times film *A Thief in the Night* and an anthem for a generation reading Hal Lindsey's *The Late Great Planet Earth* and looking to the skies for the Second Coming.

Petra founder Bob Hartman considers it one of the best Christian songs ever written. "It brought some urgency to understand the imminency of the return of Christ, put in a way that people grasped it and were almost shocked by it. I think it's a very powerful song, and it's one that represented the needs of believers in a very big way. The Jesus movement and that song are kind of linked."

"When you think of 'I Wish We'd All Been Ready,' you think of nylon-stringed guitar, youth group, headbands," remarks Steve Hindalong, who remembers learning to play guitar in youth group in the early 1970s. "It's a song for an era."

It's also one of the first Christian songs that Chris Rice can remember from when he was a kid in the '70s. "I remember my brothers and I

singing through that song, not really understanding what we were singing. 'Two men walking up a hill, one disappears, and one's left standing still'— kind of a scary thought for an 11- or 12-year-old. But it was a big song for me, my introduction to Christian music. Growing up through those early teenage years, going to a lot of festivals and seeing Larry Norman actually perform the songs. It began something in me. So many of my songs talk about heaven, talk about looking forward to a time and place where there will be no more sin or suffering or pain or sorrow. I'm sure that began because of the influence of Larry Norman."

"And there's that line that says something about 'the demons dined,'" adds Third Day guitarist Mark Lee,

"and I remember when dc talk did it at their concerts, all the kids would think they were saying, 'the demons died,' and everybody'd be like, 'YEAH!' But, no, wait a minute; I don't think that's the line. I don't think they should be clapping there."

The roots of dc talk's popular remake of that song go back to when dc talk alum Michael Tait was a kid. "Back in the '70s so many preachers preached fire, hell, brimstone—the whole nine yards—and it was so impactful to have a song that went along with those messages. Larry was before his time, man. I think he was way underappreciated, but that's all right, because I think he affected the people he needed to."

Norman followed up on the "end-times" riff on subsequent albums with such songs as "U.F.O.," "Six Sixty Six" (later covered by The Pixies' Frank Black) and "Here Comes the King." But none matched the sweet accessibility of "I Wish We'd All Been Ready," a campfire-ready song that swept up a generation.

"Larry Norman! What a legend; 'I Wish We'd All Been Ready' was one of the first songs I learned on the guitar. It's great."
MARTIN SMITH OF DELIRIOUS?

SONGS ABOUT THE END

"When He Comes Back"—DeGarmo & Key
"Here He Comes, Second Time"—Terry Scott Taylor
"Is This a Dream?"—Sup the Chemist (with Project 86)
"Here He Comes"—Michael Omartian
"It Might Be Today"—Seven Places
"You Don't Belong Here"—Tonio K.
"The Judge"—Dynamic Twins
"Six Sixty Six"—Larry Norman
"Waiting for the Aliens"—Barnabus
"Sorry"—Phil Keaggy Band
"Thief in the Night"—Cliff Richard
"This Is What Time It Is"—ETW
"Six, Six, Six"—DeGarmo & Key
"Coming Back"—P.O.D.
"Ground Zero"—Kerry Livgren
"Mothership"—Glisten
"Here Comes the King"—Larry Norman
"Fallout"—Bride
"Midnight Oil"—Petra
"Alleluia, Christ Is Coming"—DeGarmo & Key
"Ready or Not"—Tourniquet
"Time"—Phil Keaggy
"A Thief in the Night"—T-Bone
"White Horse"—Michael Omartian
"Soon and Very Soon"—Andrae Crouch & The Disciples
"People Get Ready ... Jesus Is Comin' "—Crystal Lewis
"Ready or Not"—DeGarmo & Key

JACI
VELASQUEZ

ON MY KNEES

WRITTEN BY DAVID MULLEN, NICOLE C. MULLEN AND MICHAEL OCHS

RECORDED BY JACI VELASQUEZ ON HEAVENLY PLACE (WORD RECORDS, 1996)

PRODUCED BY MARK HEIMERMANN AND PHIL NAISH

ALSO RECORDED BY:
NICOLE MULLEN ON GREAT GOSPEL MOMENTS: WOMEN OF GOSPEL

BOB CARLISLE ON SHADES OF GRACE

14

In 1969, the Gospel Music Association's Dove Awards were only two years old. The list of winners from that year included names like the Blackwood Brothers, the Oak Ridge Boys and the Speer Family. A promising young writer named Bill Gaither got the nod for Songwriter of the Year. And farther on down the list, a young group called The Four Galileans, featuring lead singer David Velasquez, won the Most Promising New Gospel Talent Award.

Fast forward to the Dove Awards, 1997. David Velasquez's baby girl, Jaci, on the strength of her stunningly successful debut album *Heavenly Place*, tearfully accepts her very own New Artist of the Year Award at the ripe old age of 17. But it wasn't just about "passing the torch"—it was more like watching a precociously talented young woman light her own.

Jaci Velasquez was a baby-faced teenager when she recorded her first major label release in 1996. She was discovered two

> "We took Jaci out on tour to open for us when she was just 14—she and her mom went on the road with us. And we just couldn't get over The Voice! We knew she was something special. When she was recording her first record, she played some of the rough mixes for us and I especially remember 'On My Knees.' We listened to it and then just said, 'Well, all right—get ready, girl.' Because you could tell that it was all just about to explode."
>
> **ANDY CHRISMAN OF 4HIM**

years earlier in Houston, Texas by one of Christian music's top managers, Mike Atkins, who has helped launch the careers of 4HIM and Point of Grace. Jaci is the youngest of six siblings in a Brady Bunch-type blended family —she is the "ours" among the "his" and "hers" from previous marriages. Her father is a former pastor who began a traveling ministry with his wife and daughter in 1989, and Jaci's first performances were the solos she sang before her father's sermons. Atkins, intrigued by the big voice coming from the little girl, quickly signed her to an exclusive management deal and brought her to the attention of Word Records.

Jaci immediately began working on her debut album and remembers hearing "On My Knees" for the first time during pre-production. "Nicole Mullen, David Mullen and Michael Ochs—the guys that wrote the song—walked in one day and said, 'Hey, you ought to cut this song on your new release,'" Jaci explains. "So I put my voice on the demo, and then I took off to Michigan for a concert. I was still singing with my parents at that time. And in the middle of the night my mom woke up singing 'On My Knees.' It was the weirdest thing! It was like we knew from that first time we heard it that it was going to change our lives." But right before Jaci's record was going to be released, Nicole C. Mullen was also entering the studio to work on her first project. When her creative team realized she had "given away" "On My Knees" to another new artist, they told Nicole she needed to get her song back for her own album. Jaci laughs, "I was like, 'But it's already on my record—no fair!' Anyway, it all worked out; and she had 'Redeemer' on hers, so she didn't miss out on a thing!"

Heavenly Place resulted in some impressive accolades for a first-timer. In addition to the New Artist of the Year Dove Award, she was also voted Best New Artist in both *CRR* and *CCM*'s Reporters polls. She had three other 1997 Dove nominations, including Album of the Year and Inspirational Song of the Year for "On My Knees," which actually won the prestigious Song of the Year category the following year. All four of the singles released from her album became #1 songs, and by the end of the year, *Heavenly Place* was officially certified platinum.

Jaci also released several top-selling albums in the Latin pop market, and

PRAYER TIME

Bow your head . . . and sing along.

"Pray, Pray, Pray"—James Ward

"Pray for Me"—Michael W. Smith

"Pray for Me"—Scott Wesley Brown

"Pray for Me"—B. J. Thomas

"Somebody's Prayin'"—Ricky Skaggs

"Pray in the USA"—Morgan Cryar

"When God's People Pray"—Wayne Watson

"Make My Life a Prayer to You"—Keith Green

"Let Us Pray"—Steven Curtis Chapman

"Prayer"—Petra

"This Town"—Rob Frazier

"Pray"—Rebecca St. James

"Why Pray"—Angie Lewis

"Say a Prayer"—Lenny LeBlanc

"I'm Praying for You"—Dick & Mel Tunney

"Down on My Knees"—Susan Ashton

"Have a Talk with God"—Jon Gibson

"I have to tell the truth, when Michael Ochs first came up with the idea of a song with the words 'on my knees' in it, David and I just kind of looked at each other and said, 'Corny.' But as soon as he started playing the piano and the music got to the place where he sang those words—that's the only part of the lyric he had—we started thinking, *OK, this could work!* We were all probably thinking that I might sing it, but I didn't have a record deal at the time. And when Jaci and her mom heard it, it went right to their hearts; they just knew that this was her song. And I have never regretted it. I do think it was definitely written for her to sing first; she does such an incredible job on it."

NICOLE C. MULLEN

her career has continued to grow with unprecedented success at radio, retail and on the road. However, the last few years have changed the exuberant, high-spirited teenager into a stronger, perhaps wiser, young woman. She has been through some difficult life experiences with the divorce of her parents when she was 19 and her own history of rocky personal relationships. She is on the other side of that now, being a newlywed and having a renewed energy for her career. Asked to describe her life now, Jaci just smiles and says, "It's all good."

GAITHERS

BECAUSE HE LIVES

WRITTEN BY BILL AND GLORIA GAITHER

RECORDED BY THE BILL GAITHER TRIO ON BECAUSE HE LIVES (HEARTWARMING RECORDS, 1972)

PRODUCED BY BOB MACKENZIE

ALSO RECORDED BY: KRISTEN CHENOWETH ON HYMNS FOR WORSHIP: AMAZING GRACE

LARNELLE HARRIS ON A STORY TO TELL: HYMNS & PRAISES

"BECAUSE HE LIVES" APPEARS IN MANY HYMNALS AND CHURCH SONGBOOKS

15

Bill and Gloria Gaither have an interesting effect on people. Journalists can't write about them without using words like "history-making" and "living legends." Artists and songwriters get all reverential and awe-struck, shaking their hands too enthusiastically and rambling on about what an inspiration the two of them have been. And the fans just want to hug their necks and take them home for Sunday dinner.

While the Gaithers' achievements in Christian music are unrivaled, it is their ability to wear that mantle loosely that has endeared them to the industry and audiences alike. They are remarkably accessible and approachable, especially in their small Indiana hometown where Gaither sightings occur so regularly they have ceased to cause a stir. Bill and Gloria live in the same house, go to the same church and have many of the same friends that they did before the world knew their names. And that's just the way they like it.

Bill was a schoolteacher with a passion for quartet music and Indiana basketball when he met and married fellow teacher Gloria Sickal. His love of gospel music and her gifted ability to express herself with words were a perfect fit, and they soon began collaborating on writing and eventually singing songs together. For several years they juggled teaching, writing, recording and publishing before the music demanded their full-time attention in 1967. Bill's brother, Danny, joined them, and they traveled and performed as the Bill Gaither Trio with ever-increasing success. It was during those hectic years, as their family and career were both growing by leaps and

> "'Because He Lives' is a song that will never die. It still rings true today, and people still weep when they sing it. We talk a lot about all of the talented contemporary writers, but there's only one Bill Gaither—and he can still pen a song from time to time . . ."
>
> MICHAEL W. SMITH

bounds, that some of their most famous songs were written. "Because He Lives" was one of them.

Gloria remembers that time, the late '60s, as a period of great turmoil and change in America, and in the Gaither household as well. Their first child, Suzanne, was four and her baby sister, Amy, just three months old when an exhausted Gloria found out that she was expecting again. Bill had contracted mononucleosis, which left him depleted and depressed, and he had recently learned that his beloved only sister, Mary Ann, was in the throes of a devastating divorce. Their black-and-white television set brought the world into their living room every night, with pictures of the raging war in Vietnam, mounting racial tensions and widespread drug abuse. It suddenly felt like a very scary time to bring another child into the world.

"Bill and I would sit and talk about all the circumstances of the world and the discouragement he was going through," says Gloria. "We would wind up looking at each other and saying, 'If the world is like this now, what will it be in 15 or 20 years? What will this child have to face?'" After the prayerful intervention of a Christian friend, Bill gradually began to get better. As Gloria described it, "Physically and spiritually he saw a growing ray of light in the darkness." Though the world situation hadn't changed much, Bill and Gloria's view of it had.

In the spring of that year, Bill's father, George, came into their office one morning and beckoned Bill and Gloria to come outside with him. They followed him to the middle of the new parking lot, which had been leveled, graded, layered and blacktopped the previous fall. He pointed down to the pavement and said, "Look there." Pushing up through all of the layers of stone, sand and blacktop was a tiny blade of green grass. Gloria describes it this way, "George just grinned and walked back into the office, leaving us there to marvel at this amazing story of Easter from a tiny blade of grass. It was confirming a truth that had been pushing its way to the surface of our souls: Life wins!"

Gloria with her inspiration—young son Benjy

> "You know, to tell the truth, I'm not sure that I've ever even actually heard the Gaithers sing 'Because He Lives.' I've just always grown up singing it in church; it was one of the staples. It's such a great lyric. And when you're a 10-year-old kid singing that, the old ladies just lose it."
>
> **MAC POWELL OF THIRD DAY**

Out of that experience and the subsequent birth of their son, Benjy, "Because He Lives" was written. Bill explains what he was feeling at the time. "For whatever reason, in a lot of my writing I have always asked the question, 'Why is this song going to make a difference?' And in this song, I wanted to say that because of the theological absolute around which I have built my life—which is the truth of the Resurrection—I can face tomorrow, no matter what it brings. I wanted to make that statement so strong that the guy in the

GLORIA GAITHER'S FAVORITE (GAITHER) SONGS:

"Because He Lives"
"He Touched Me"
"The King Is Coming"
"It Is Finished"
"The Church Triumphant"
"Something Beautiful"
"I've Just Seen Jesus"
"Let Freedom Ring"
"I Am a Promise"
"I Believe in a Hill Called Mount Calvary"
"Let's Just Praise the Lord"
"The Old Rugged Cross Made a Difference"

> "ASCAP gave Bill and Gloria Gaither the Songwriters of the Century Award—think about that! Bill writes music that we can't stop singing, and Gloria is the greatest lyricist in the history of Christian music. And I'd say that even if I didn't love them both so much. 'Because He Lives' will live on and on."
>
> **RUSS TAFF**

street could take that with him through whatever difficult circumstances he was walking through. 'Because He lives I can face tomorrow. Because He lives all fear is gone . . . ' I believe that! Christ is freedom."

"Because He Lives" is sung in thousands of churches every Sunday and in Gaither Homecoming concerts around the world.

The whole family, from left to right:
Benjy, Gloria, Bill, Suzanne and Amy

THIRD DAY

AGNUS DEI

WRITTEN BY MICHAEL W. SMITH

RECORDED BY THIRD DAY ON EXODUS (ROCKETOWN RECORDS, 1998)

PRODUCED BY MICHAEL W. SMITH

ALSO RECORDED BY: MICHAEL W. SMITH ON WORSHIP

"AGNUS DEI" IS LATIN FOR LAMB OF GOD

16

"**W**e have a really wild idea . . ."

The year was 1998, and Mac Powell of Third Day was tentatively approaching Michael W. Smith with a request. Smitty was in the initial stages of matching artists with material for an upcoming praise and worship project on his fledgling Rocketown Records label. "We want to cut 'Agnus Dei' for the *Exodus* album," Mac said.

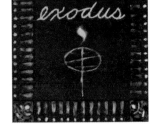

Michael freely admits that his initial thought was *How in the wide world of sports is that gonna work?* "Agnus Dei" was a classically based worship song, and a rock and roll band like Third Day didn't exactly seem like a natural fit to cover it.

Smitty was also especially fond, and maybe just a little protective, of that particular song. "It was one of those songs that I wrote in five minutes, because it all just came flooding out," he says. "I actually cried on that one; I had a meltdown. There's nothing necessarily profound about it musically. But it's kind of haunting and reverent—holy, really. I can't explain it; it just works."

> "The true test of a great song is if it still stands up and is relevant years on down the line. 'Agnus Dei' is one of those songs. In Michael's original style, or with Third Day rocking it hard, 'Agnus Dei' delivers."
>
> RUSS TAFF

63

"I've got to talk about 'Agnus Dei,' because I'm one of the few people that isn't afraid to pronounce it. In my estimation, it is such a great blend of Smitty's classical training and the beautiful simplicity that he always writes with. And it also has some of those weird rhythm things that he tenaciously holds on to, even though good sense should tell him he needs to write it in a way that people can tap their foot and still sing that lead line! It's mysterious and timeless and just a beautiful song."

AMY GRANT

Kristen Barlowe

But unbeknownst to Smitty, Third Day had a special connection to his song as well. "In 1994 we were working at a YMCA summer camp, and we were like the house band for the whole camp," Mac remembers. "The very first Christian music I ever listened to was Michael W. Smith. I heard his *I 2 Eye* record and thought it was just incredible. So I went right out and bought *Go West Young Man,* and that's where I found 'Agnus Dei.' When I heard it, I just loved it and told the guys, 'We've gotta do this for the camp!' And we did, and of course all the kids dug it and it was awesome. We played it all the time after that." So the idea of

finally recording it for a praise and worship project made perfect sense to Third Day—if not, at least at first, to Smitty. "I could tell they wanted to do some kind of rock version of 'Agnus Dei,' which was making me real nervous," laughs Michael. "But finally I just said, 'You know what—let's give it a try!'"

What happened next was one of those rare, everything-just-fell-into-place recording experiences. "Michael W. Smith himself actually produced us doing that song," Mac marvels. "We went from leading a few kids in worship at this little camp in the north Georgia mountains to being able to go into the studio and

record it with the writer and artist that had inspired us in the first place. It was just the coolest thing." Mark Lee chimes in, "'Agnus Dei' ended up being one of our biggest rock radio hits ever. We even re-cut it in 2000 for the *Offerings* album. And last year we did the 'Come Together and Worship' Tour with Michael, so we got to be up there on stage playing the song with him every night."

Smitty agrees that the odd coupling was indeed inspired. "It all came together and turned out to be a big song for them," he says. "I think I hear their version on the radio more than I ever did mine! So it was definitely the right move—good instincts by Mac and the guys!"

" 'Agnus Dei' was a song that was written on the core of my heart at a young age. It inspired me to worship. The song embraces and includes; it gathers your emotions and brings you to your knees. I sing it everywhere I go."

DARLENE ZSCHECH

MICHAEL ENGLISH

MARY, DID YOU KNOW?

WRITTEN BY MARK LOWRY AND BUDDY GREENE

RECORDED BY MICHAEL ENGLISH ON MICHAEL ENGLISH (WARNER ALLIANCE, 1991)

PRODUCED BY BROWN BANNISTER

ALSO RECORDED BY:

MARK LOWRY ON REMOTELY CONTROLLED

MICHAEL CRAWFORD ON A CHRISTMAS ALBUM

NATALIE COLE ON THE MAGIC OF CHRISTMAS

DONNY OSMOND ON CHRISTMAS AT HOME

REBA MCENTYRE ON THE SECRET OF GIVING

KATHY MATTEA ON GOOD NEWS

P oignant, profound, tender and reverent—frankly, these are not the first words that come to mind when you think of comedian Mark Lowry. But the lyric he wrote for the much-loved Christmas song, "Mary, Did You Know?" is all of those things.

In 1984, Mark was asked to write a Christmas musical for his church. "I'd never written a musical," Mark admits. "But I knew how to put on a production, because I had done that for four years. So I just got all of these great Christmas songs together and then wrote monologues to connect them." One idea that he wanted to explore was based on something he had heard his mother say a few years before. "She said that if anybody knew Jesus was virgin-born, Mary knew. That stuck in my head, and I thought about it through the years, and it came up again when I was trying to write this musical." Mark says, "I started waxing eloquent on this monologue that I planned on reciting between the scenes in the musical. I wrote about wondering if

Photos courtesy of Gospel Music Association
Photo taken by Harry Butler

"Michael English is one of the greatest singers I have ever been privileged to work with. When he would sing 'Mary, Did You Know?' it would make you weep and put chill bumps on top of chill bumps. I don't think anyone's ever sung it the same way."

BONNIE KEEN OF FIRST CALL

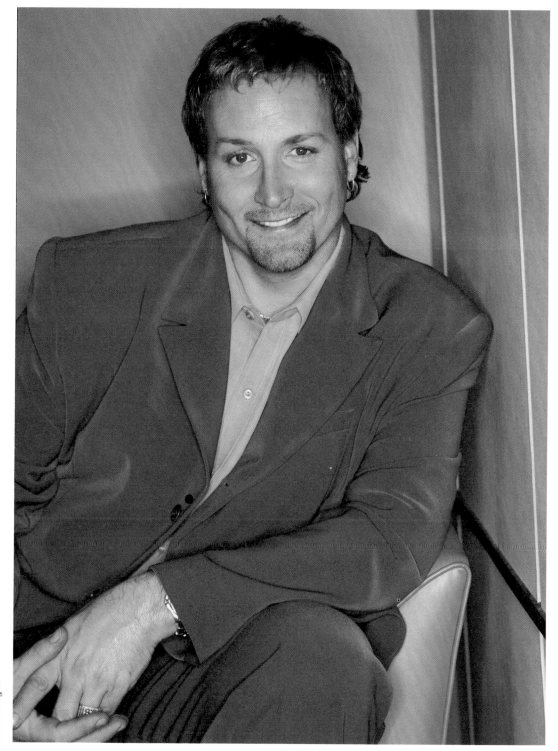

MUSICAL QUESTIONS

Because inquiring minds want to know.

"Who"——Newsboys

"Who Am I"——Margaret Becker

"Who Am I"——Casting Crowns

"Who Will Be Jesus"——Bruce Carroll

"Who Will Call Him King of Kings"——Sandi Patty

"Who Will Save the Children"——Randy Stonehill and Phil Keaggy

"Who Do You Think You're Fooling"——Don Francisco

"Who Do You Say That I Am"——Pam Mark Hall

"What Kind of Love Is This"——Steven Curtis Chapman

"What Am I Without You"——Twila Paris

"What Did He Die For"——Twila Paris

"What I Can Do For You"——Imperials

"What Have We Become"——dc talk

"What Are the Words"——Steve Green

"What Sin"——Morgan Cryar

"Whatcha Gonna Do When Your Number's Up"——Steve Taylor

"Where Do You Hide Your Heart"——Amy Grant

"Where Are the Other Nine"——Geoff Moore

"Why"——Michael Card

"Why Should the Devil Have All the Good Music"——Larry Norman

"Why Should the Father Bother"——Petra

"How Could I Ask for More"——Cindy Morgan

"How Can You Say No"——Billy Sprague

"How Can They Live Without Jesus"——Keith Green

"How Can It Be"——Michael Card

"How Long"——Michael Card

"Can You Reach My Friend"——Debby Boone

"Was It a Morning Like This"——Sandi Patty

"Whatever Happened to Sin"——Steve Taylor

"Will There Be Hippies in Heaven"——Gary S. Paxton

Mary knew the authority that was compressed in that eight-pound bundle lying in her lap. I wonder if she really understood that those little lips now uttering unintelligible baby noises were the same lips that had spoken worlds into existence. And that those hands were the hands that had scooped out the oceans and formed the rivers." As he warmed to the idea, Mark started thinking of questions he'd love to ask Mary if he could sit down and have a cup of coffee with her. "Like, did you know that one day He would walk on water? Did you know that He'd save our sons and daughters? And then there were the questions I didn't put in the monologue, like, did you ever walk into His room and say, 'Goodness gracious, clean

"There is a mystical, spiritual quality about that song, and it explains the Incarnation in a more tangible way than any song I've heard in the last 50 years. It hits me every Christmas when I hear it sung. All of a sudden you realize the importance of the mother of God. It connects you with her humanity, but it's a humanity that is tied to the eternal. And it is one of the best examples I've seen of a lyric married to a melody. In fact, it's hard to think that it was written by two different people. That's one of those divine God things."

BILL GAITHER

up this mess! What, do You think You were raised in a barn? I couldn't figure out how to work that in."

It was another six years before the monologue became a song. Mark held on to the poem and sometimes recited it to friends, including his fellow Gaither Vocal Band member Michael English. Michael was about to cut his first solo album and was looking for material. "Mark had quoted this amazing poem to some of us," Michael says, "and then he decided to put it on his Christmas card. So he hands one to me and I told him that I honestly wouldn't send this out on a card, that I thought he'd be crazy not to make a song out of it." Mark took Michael's advice and turned his poem over to musician, writer

and harmonica virtuoso Buddy Greene, who, legend has it, wrote the music in about 15 minutes. Michael remembers hearing the demo of the completed song for the first time. "It was just Buddy Greene and his guitar, and it was unbelievable. I know that the lyric is beautiful and timeless, but I think the music is just as important. And that music is perfect."

The Christmas card verse has now become a modern classic, recorded by over 30 artists including Wynonna, Kenny Rogers, Kathy Mattea, Kathleen Battle, Reba McEntyre and Natalie Cole. "I can't take credit for anything other than singing it," Michael English smiles. "But I bet this song is going to be around for the next 300 years, if the Lord tarries."

Mark Lowry

69

BOB CARLISLE

BUTTERFLY KISSES

18

**WRITTEN BY BOB CARLISLE
AND RANDY THOMAS**

RECORDED BY BOB CARLISLE
ON BUTTERFLY KISSES
(SHADES OF GRACE)
(DIADEM RECORDS, 1997)

PRODUCED BY BOB CARLISLE

ALSO RECORDED BY:
JEFF CARSON ON BUTTERFLY
KISSES

RANDY THOMAS ON
FOREVER YOURS

**#1 ON BILLBOARD 200
ALBUM SALES CHART**

"Butterfly Kisses" is not cool. And it's not hip, cutting edge or avant-garde. What it is, is a totally unexpected Grammy- and Dove Award-winning, three million-selling, crossover smash hit—and a father's tender love song to a daughter poised on the brink of womanhood.

Bob Carlisle was not exactly the new kid on the block when "Butterfly Kisses" exploded onto the Christian, pop and country music charts in 1997. A veteran of the Southern California music scene, Bob was the lead singer and guitarist of the Christian pop/rock band Allies in the '80s and early '90s. After the group disbanded, Bob scored a songwriting coup when his song, "Why'd You Come in Here Looking Like That?" became a #1 single for Dolly Parton. On the strength of that success, Bob moved his family to Nashville, Tennessee to continue writing. In 1993 he began his solo Christian music career with the release of a self-titled album on Sparrow Records, followed by *The Hope of a Man* in 1994.

Russ Harrington

70

Both were moderately successful, but Bob moved over to Diadem Records for his next album.

"Butterfly Kisses" was never intended for mass consumption. Bob's only daughter, Brooke, was nearing her sixteenth birthday and his wife, Jacque, planned to make a collage of family photos to mark the day. She had left the pictures laid out in order across the table when Bob wandered by and was struck by the photographic record of his daughter's metamorphosis into a beautiful young woman. As Bob describes it, "The reality was in front of me that my baby girl had grown up and she would not be under my roof for too much longer. The joy of so many happy memories and the burden of missed opportunities collided in my heart, and the song just poured out."

Brooke, now a young married woman living in Nevada, takes up the story. "I didn't even see it until about six months later," she recalls. "I think he wanted to have it all done before I knew anything about it. But I was in his office one night and saw the lyrics on his computer. I just stood there reading it, and all of a sudden I said out loud, 'This is about me!' I had no idea he was writing it; I was just overwhelmed that I had inspired such an incredible song. Later he

"My dad took his guitar and learned to play and sing 'Butterfly Kisses' for me. At my wedding, that was the song we danced to, and he sang it in my ear. It's a precious moment between us that I will never forget."

MELISSA GREENE OF AVALON

played me a rough mix of the music, and I was so excited I took it to school and kept saying, 'Listen to my song!' Dad's track record is to take the really strong feelings in his life and write about them, turning them into these little works of art. What a talent to be able to portray what you are feeling so beautifully with words. That's where all of his love and emotion and passion come spilling out. And he is passionate about his children."

The song remained a tape in Brooke's cassette player until one night when several record company executives were having a preproduction meeting at Bob's house. At Jacque's insistence, a reluctant Bob agreed to play his daughter's song for them, but excused himself from the room while they were listening to it because the song just felt too personal. When he walked back in the room, he faced a sofa full of teary executives, determined to put that song on the new album.

The album, *Shades of Grace*, had been out a year before the song hit. "Butterfly Kisses" crossed over from Christian radio and got played on just one pop station in Louisiana and took off. It jumped from the 195th position to the #1 spot on the Billboard Pop chart in one week. The Bob Carlisle family was in for the ride of their lives.

The next year brought the kind of whirlwind publicity junkets, television appearances and command performances that few artists ever get to experience. Brooke and her little brother Evan had a ball. "We took advantage of every opportunity!" Brooke says with a smile. "We were honestly such a humble little family that we didn't expect anything special. So every experience was enjoyed to the fullest. We got to be on VH1 and *Good Morning America*, we got to meet

KIDSTUFF

A little list celebrating children of all ages.

"Butterfly"—Nicole C. Mullen

"Bullfrogs and Butterflies"—Barry McGuire

"Fingerprints of God"—Steven Curtis Chapman

"Watercolour Ponies"—Wayne Watson

"Kumquat May"—Billy Sprague

"FATHER'S LOVE"—BOB CARLISLE

"We've Been Waiting for You"—Carolyn Arends

"Even the Wallflowers"—Carolyn Arends

"Emily"—Michael W. Smith

"I Know"—Michael W. Smith

"The Coloring Song"—Petra

"Somewhere in the World"—Wayne Watson

Russ Harrington

Oprah. . . . But the best thing was Disney World; we spent two days there being treated like royalty and running all over the park. People would recognize my dad, and he would have to smile and just keep walking because they would start coming from everywhere. I was like, 'Wow, Dad's a big star! Who knew?'"

"Butterfly Kisses"—Brooke's gift from her doting daddy—broke records, touched hearts and became a pop standard. "My family is the strongest and best thing in my life," Brooke says today. "I can't think of a single negative thing to say about my dad. You know that saying, 'It couldn't happen to a nicer guy?' Well, it's the truth!"

POINT OF GRACE

THE GREAT DIVIDE

WRITTEN BY GRANT
CUNNINGHAM AND MATT
HUESMANN

RECORDED BY POINT OF
GRACE ON THE WHOLE TRUTH
(WORD RECORDS, 1995)

PRODUCED BY JOHN MAYS,
ROBERT STERLING

1996 DOVE AWARD—
ALBUM: THE WHOLE
TRUTH

1996 DOVE AWARD—
GROUP OF THE YEAR

19

The Point of Grace girls—and that is inevitably what they are called, though they are all married with children—have never suffered from an identity crisis. There may be the stray critic or two who would love to see the group push the boundaries and come out with a brooding, angst-ridden album, but POG serenely declines. They know exactly who they are, what they are called to do and who they are singing to.

Point of Grace, originally known as Say So, was formed in 1991 on the campus of Ouachita Baptist College in Arkadelphia, Arkansas. Heather Payne and Denise Jones had been friends since fifth grade, and they met Terry Jones in middle school. When the three hooked up with the fourth original member, Shelley Breen, at the Baptist college where they were all studying music education, they decided to see what they sounded like together. The young women knew immediately that their four voices created an extraordinary sound. "It felt magical the first time we sang together," Denise recalls. "It was amazing." The foursome started singing on campus, then branched out to churches, banquets and women's

Russ Harrington

74

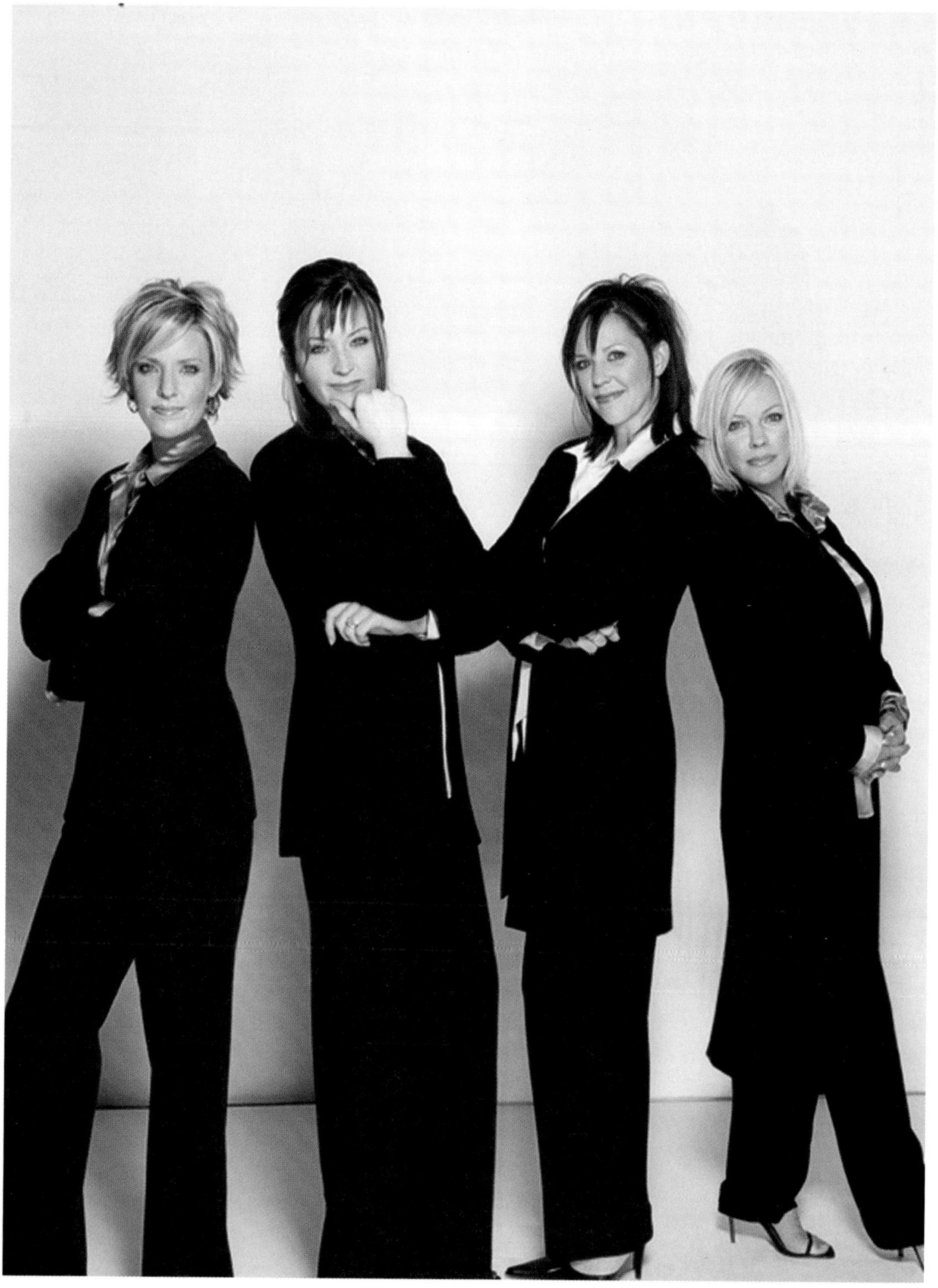

Russ Harrington

conferences. After a couple years of local performances, they went to the annual Christian Artists Seminar in Estes Park, Colorado. There they caught the eyes of talent scouts from Word Records. A few demo tapes and trips to Nashville later, POG signed a record and management deal with Mike Atkins.

In 1993, the girls released their self-titled debut album, which earned six #1 singles, an achievement still unmatched by any artist in any genre of music. By the time their second project, *The Whole Truth*, was released, Point of Grace had honed its sound and perfected the trademark harmonies. "The Great Divide" turned out to be yet another #1 single and ended up winning the 1996 Dove Award for Pop/Contemporary Song of the Year. The four women have a long-standing tradition that they must all agree on a song before the group can record it, and there were no disagreements on this one.

"'The Great Divide' is my favorite Point of Grace song," says Heather. "I think it has made the biggest impact of anything we have ever recorded. It has the straight-up message of the gospel in it, and there is always something powerful about a song that does that. If someone didn't understand salvation or didn't really know the gospel, this is the kind of song you could take to them and say, 'Here, listen to this and you will get a picture of what it's all about.'"

"The Great Divide" was co-written by the late Grant Cunningham, who was the vice president of A&R at EMI and a dear friend of Point

Photo Courtesy of Gospel Music Association
Photo Taken by Harry Butler

of Grace. Cunningham, only 37 years old, died suddenly and unexpectedly in 2002 as the result of a head injury sustained while playing soccer with friends. Denise says, "When we sing it now, it makes me realize that Grant sees the whole picture of 'the great divide.' He's crossed over to the other side and sees Jesus face to face. I can't sing the song without thinking about that and about what Jesus did for us."

As the years passed and their career continued to flourish, the women of Point of Grace began to find opportunities to use their platform to call attention to issues that the girls felt were important. They became increasingly involved with an organization they were introduced to in 1993, Nashville-based Mercy Ministries, headed by Nancy Alcorn. Mercy Ministries is a groundbreaking residential program that helps girls struggling with eating disorders, unwed pregnancies, addictions and abuse, and challenges them to have a personal relationship with Jesus Christ. Point of Grace serves as national spokespersons for the organization, and they have taken that role to heart. They have performed at countless benefits and dedicate a brief portion of their own concert every night

to endorse Mercy Ministries. The women have also personally volunteered at the residence and can speak with first-hand knowledge of the power of the program. Point of Grace recently paired with Nancy Alcorn and launched a series of nationwide "Girls of Grace" conferences for teenage girls. They feature concerts by POG and special guests, as well as speakers and workshops designed to openly discuss issues about relationships, sex, self-esteem and developing a more personal walk with God. "This is something we have dreamed about doing for 10 years," Shelley explains. "And it is finally coming true in a big way."

Point of Grace now has plenty of laurels to rest on, if they were so inclined. But that doesn't seem likely. With a fresh face, Leigh Cappillino, who replaced Terry Jones, and a tour bus filled with diapers, strollers and babies—five, at last count   there are no plans to slow down. Denise says, "We've had so many people that have come up to us and said, 'I've started listening to your music and I came to understand the gospel message through it. Thank you for helping me see it clearer.' Who wants to walk away from that?"

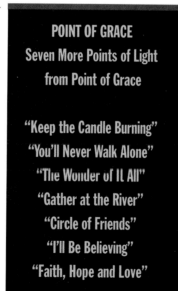

POINT OF GRACE
Seven More Points of Light from Point of Grace

"Keep the Candle Burning"
"You'll Never Walk Alone"
"The Wonder of It All"
"Gather at the River"
"Circle of Friends"
"I'll Be Believing"
"Faith, Hope and Love"

TWILA PARIS

HOW BEAUTIFUL

WRITTEN BY TWILA PARIS

RECORDED BY TWILA PARIS
ON CRY FOR THE DESERT
(STAR SONG, 1991)

PRODUCED BY BROWN
BANNISTER

TWILA PARIS HAS BEEN
CALLED THE "MODERN-DAY
HYMN WRITER"

20

"Writing songs is my very favorite part of what I do," Twila Paris says. You know, I love getting to sing for people, I love getting to work in the studio; all of that is wonderful. But only in songwriting do you get those rare moments when it all comes together and you just get up and run around the room!"

Fortunately for Christian music lovers, Twila has had a lot of those run-around-the-room moments over the years, and we have all benefited from them. Her career highlights include an astonishing 32 #1 songs, five Dove Awards, three American Songwriter Awards and more than two million albums sold. As Twila reflects on one of her most beloved songs, "How Beautiful," she marvels at the mysterious way God continues to supply the music.

"Without being overly mystical, I have always had to give a lot of credit to the inspiration of the Holy Spirit," says Twila. "Because, you know how there are those people who hear a nice phrase and remember to write it down, and then they go write a hit song later when they have time? Well, I'm not one of those people!" Twila bursts out laughing and

then says, "There have certainly been those times when I've tried to operate in the flesh and depend on my human skills, even though I've learned over and over again that I'm not very good at it. But the best songs are the ones that I can't explain. I think, *How did I think of that chord progression? What in the world made me stumble onto*

78

feels like a direct result of having the privilege of my dad also being my pastor my whole life. One thing Dad's always emphasized that has always found its way into my music, is the importance of loving one another. 'How Beautiful' was just one of those moments where all of a sudden, after those years of hearing that teaching, it just became crystal clear and real to me." Twila continues, "I mean, we all know that we're supposed to love each other; God commanded us to. But let's face it—sometimes it's easier to love the perfect Christian in China that we never met more than the guy sitting in the next pew that irritates us every Sunday by taking our parking place! But about the time I

that? I look back now at some of the songs that I've written and I really do know that I'm not that smart!"

According to Twila, "How Beautiful" falls into that category. "Musically, it feels like it's a little beyond me," she says. "And lyrically, it

was writing that song, God was doing this wonderful thing in my heart. He began giving me this family kind of love for the body of Christ. You know, the kind of feelings that you have for your family where no matter how irritated you get at them, you still always love

"I love songs that connect with ordinances in worship. This song is so often used with communion, but in our church, we still believe in washing feet, and this is the consummate song for the washing of one another's feet. She is writing about 'How Beautiful' is the body of Christ, and that means all the way down to that most humbling part of it."

GLORIA GAITHER

79

them. That love is an unbreakable bond, and He just began to give me a revelation of that."

Twila's gently compelling songs have been her trademark for over 20 years. She was definitely "praise and worship when praise and worship wasn't cool." Her demeanor and way of expressing herself clearly mark her for the preacher's kid she is. But she's not just parroting beliefs she learned at her daddy's knee. Twila's strong sense of who God is comes as the result of surviving a series of unforeseen difficulties, with her faith and humor intact.

Jack Wright is Twila's husband of over 20 years and the father of their son, J. P. He has also fought a courageous, behind-the-scenes battle with a mysterious debilitating illness that was misdiagnosed and mistreated for 10 years. Originally thought to be chronic fatigue syndrome, Jack's body was intermittently racked with pain and low-grade fevers that would disappear as quickly as they came. He was often unable to leave the house at all. Finally he was re-tested and the real culprit was found— Hepatitis C. As frightening as it was to receive that news, there was a measure of relief that the enemy finally had the correct name. Jack and his medical team, which includes a nutritionist, have aggressively fought back and are seeing the results. Twila thanks God every day for a husband who can now participate in their life, and for the child they never thought they could have.

"That's the reason I write songs," Twila concludes. "To try to put into words who God is, who I am in relation to Him, and what He has done and continues to do in me and through me. That's eternal; that's the central message of our faith."

TWILA PARIS
Paris Praise

"We Bow Down"
"He Is Exalted"
"Lamb of God"
"How Beautiful"
"We Will Glorify"
"Joy of the Lord"

"As a woman, she carved the way for a lot of us. She wrote about things that no one had really touched on before; she expressed thoughts and feelings that had never been communicated quite the way she communicated them. Twila seems to capture the essence of the true worshiper. 'How Beautiful' is just a stunning, stunning piece of music that I believe has caused all the heavens to smile."

DARLENE ZSCHECH

RICH MULLINS

STEP BY STEP

WRITTEN BY RICH MULLINS AND BEAKER

RECORDED BY RICH MULLINS ON THE WORLD AS BEST I REMEMBER IT, VOL. 1 (REUNION RECORDS, 1992)

PRODUCED BY REED ARVIN

ALSO RECORDED BY: MICHAEL W. SMITH ON WORSHIP

21

I n late 1992, Reunion Records held a private party for Rich Mullins to celebrate his seventh #1 single, "Sometimes by Step," and his first #1-selling album, *The World As Best I Remember It, Vol. 2.* He was photographed holding an inscribed plaque listing his career accomplishments, and then Reunion CEO Terry Hemmings surprised him with a special gift—a beautiful new custom-made hammered dulcimer. Rich's old dulcimer had gotten damaged on the road, and he was flabbergasted and thrilled. "My first hammered dulcimer was a gift from a church," he said. "I appreciate this one so much because I hate spending money on musical instruments, but I love having them!" He gratefully took his new dulcimer home—and left the plaque at the party.

"The first time I met Rich, I was in high school. He did a concert at my church and I was the youth group guy in charge of taking him around. He and Beaker wanted some Mexican food, so while we were sitting there, I started telling them what a great concert it had been. I mean, these were the guys that wrote 'Step by Step' and 'Awesome God,' and I was like this little worship chorus snob. I remember saying something like, 'Man, these new choruses are so great; I couldn't really worship to those old-style hymns.' And then he and Beaker proceeded to do a tag-team rebuke for the next 45 minutes, rebuking me for trying to define and limit worship... I never did that again."

CLIFF YOUNG OF CAEDMON'S CALL

The chorus of "Sometimes by Step" first appeared on *The World As Best I Remember It, Vol. 1* as a simple chorus written by Beaker called "Step by Step." It was sung by a young child, and opened and closed the album. By the following project, *Vol. 2*, Rich had reworked it and written new lyrics to form verses around the now-familiar chorus. *CCM Magazine* reviewed it by saying, "It's a quantum leap from the simplicity of the *Vol. 1* version, where it was sung at first by a child, then by a child-like Mullins. Now the writer is older, pre-sumably wiser, but with seemingly more questions than answers; yet the trusting innocence of the chorus becomes a spiritual compass for this artist's complex journey through the Kingdom of God." In an interview in 1993, Rich described it this way: "If I had to make an overall statement about 'Sometimes by Step,' it would be that faith simply means 'walking with God.' The biggest problem with life is that it's just so . . . daily! But every day we have the chance to make the right choices, one at a time, step by step."

MICHAEL W. SMITH

PLACE IN THIS WORLD

WRITTEN BY WAYNE KIRKPATRICK, AMY GRANT AND MICHAEL W. SMITH

RECORDED BY MICHAEL W. SMITH ON GO WEST YOUNG MAN (REUNION RECORDS, 1990)

PRODUCED BY MICHAEL W. SMITH

1991 FAVORITE ADULT CONTEMPORARY AMERICAN MUSIC AWARD RECIPIENT

1991 #1 IN CHRISTIAN RADIO

1991 #6 ON TOP 40 CHART

22

During the same time that songs like Extreme's "More Than Words," Paula Abdul's "Rush, Rush" and R.E.M's "Losing My Religion" were dominating the pop charts in July of 1991, a face known primarily within the walls of the church was now being embraced by the masses.

Like his longtime friend Amy Grant with her pop radio smashes "Baby Baby" and "Every Heartbeat," Michael W. Smith also found wider, general market acceptance later that year with "Place in This World," an anthem birthed out of a songwriting experience that Smith says he'll never forget.

"I was in my basement in my house, and when I wrote it, I just thought, *This sounds like a pop hit,*" Michael recalls. "I got chills and the whole deal; and it was just one of those things where it was like, 'Wow, I think I'm really onto something.' Actually it was an idea that was inspired by a letter I got from a girl who was suicidal and very, very depressed. To some degree, she said, 'I'm just trying to find my place in this world.' I called on Wayne [Kirkpatrick] and Amy [Grant] to help, and I think they wrote the lyric of a lifetime."

"Place in This World" had a universal theme that everyone from corporate ladder climbers, to youth group kids, to those falling somewhere in between could relate to. The accompanying video was shot with Michael playing the piano on a scenic beach and officially introduced him to the VH1 set as the clip was featured in regular rotation. Later on, Smith also served as a guest host of VH1's *Top 21 Countdown.*

Fellow artist and crossover act in the Latin market Jaci Velasquez says she was "about 10" when she first caught the video on VH1. "That song changed so many people's lives—even in the secular, general market world," she comments. "I mean, how many times have young people really felt so out of place,

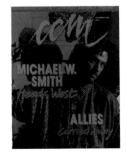

Lee Steffen

although we're all connected? And 'Place in This World' reminds you, 'Hey look, we're all in the same predicament, but we can have a place in this world through Jesus Christ. We're all His babies, whether we believe in Him or not.'"

But in some instances, Smith's newfound crossover success didn't always sit well with the audience that helped launch his career, as Grant also discovered when "Baby Baby" climbed the pop charts. The question "Is Michael W. Smith selling out?" was consistently a popular topic that generated many heated discussions that still continue in the church today with the success of artists such as Kirk Franklin, Stacie Orrico and Switchfoot.

Patty Masten

But despite the controversy, Smith remained outspoken about his faith and resolve to reach a broader audience with a message they weren't typically hearing.

One of Smith's peers in Christian music, Nathan Walters (one-third of the pop/rock band Plus One), remembers the profound impact the song had on him as a teenager. "When I first heard it, I was 14 years old and in a youth group when someone threw out his CD into a crowd, and I caught it. And I'm listening to these songs and going 'Who is this? I've seen this guy before,'" Walters says. "And so I would start listening to these songs and 'Place in This World' really stuck out. I heard it on VH1, and that's when I fell in love with Michael W. Smith's music and wanted to write songs. His writing actually influences me a lot today."

"Isn't Michael W. Smith like the President of Christian Music in America? Actually, I've just had the pleasure of writing with him recently, and I was like a kid in a toyshop. I'm embarrassed to say it, but I didn't really know a lot of his music at first. He was talking about some of his songs, like 'Place in This World,' and I didn't have any of those records. So now I have the whole collection, and I'm trucking through about 15 CDs—what a writer!"

MARTIN SMITH OF DELIRIOUS?

AVALON

TESTIFY TO LOVE

WRITTEN BY PAUL FIELD, HENK POOL, RALPH VAN MANEN AND ROBERT RIEKERK

RECORDED BY AVALON ON A MAZE OF GRACE (SPARROW RECORDS, 1997)

PRODUCED BY CHARLIE PEACOCK AND CHRIS HARRIS

ALSO RECORDED BY: WYNONNA ON TOUCHED BY AN ANGEL (THE SOUNDTRACK)

#1 FOR SIX WEEKS ON ADULT CONTEMPORARY CHART

1998 DOVE AWARD— NEW ARTIST OF THE YEAR

1999 DOVE AWARD—POP/ CONTEMPORARY SONG OF THE YEAR

Every successful group has that one song, the one that die-hard fans expect to hear every performance no matter what. For Avalon, that song is, without question, "Testify to Love." "If we don't sing it, people riot and rush the stage and start throwing stuff," Jody McBrayer deadpans. "So it's a concert staple, for sure."

"Testify to Love" first appeared on Avalon's second album, *A Maze of Grace.* The pop newcomers had enjoyed remarkable success right out of the starting gate with their 1996 self-titled debut producing four straight #1 radio hits. Their crystalline harmonies and polished stage presence had created quite a buzz, but widespread audience acceptance didn't automatically translate into artistic respect. Some critics and industry insiders harrumphed that the group was simply a carefully manufactured marketing machine, created with more calculation than inspiration. So the stage was set for this all-important sophomore release, and there was a lot riding on it. With expectations to live up to and skeptics to silence, the right material was crucial.

"Testify to Love" was originally found, oddly enough, on a

custom record from Denmark. One of the four writers was also an artist, and his self-produced version of the song was the track that was pitched to Avalon. "Actually when we first heard the demo, it didn't really thrill us all that much," Jody says. "I mean, we thought it was a great song with a great message, but we had no idea that it would take off the way it did. We decided to just put it on there, and then it ended up starting out the whole record. When we finally heard the finished product, we thought, *Well gosh, that is pretty cool after all!*"

Apparently the public agreed. "Testify to Love" turned out to be a career-making song for Avalon and broke all the records when it remained #1 for six consecutive weeks on the Christian adult contemporary charts. The album silenced the critics and took Avalon to the next level, due in no small part to the power of "Testify to Love." And when the group takes the stage, they are more than happy to give the fans what they came to hear. "We have all kinds of folks at our concerts," Jody smiles. "We have crazy people jumping pews and quiet people who never move from their pews. But as soon as 'Testify' starts, every one of them are on their feet singing every word. What a rush, to see people worshiping Christ right along with us every night because of that song."

THIRD DAY

SHOW ME YOUR GLORY

24

WRITTEN BY MARK LEE,
MARC BYRD AND THIRD DAY

RECORDED BY THIRD DAY
ON COME TOGETHER
(ESSENTIAL RECORDS, 2001)

PRODUCED BY MONROE
JONES

2001 PEAKS AT #1 ON ROCK
AND POP CHARTS, CHRISTIAN
HIT RADIO AND ADULT
CONTEMPORARY

Third Day guitarist Mark Lee describes "Show Me Your Glory" this way: "The songs that I try to write by thinking commercially or try to write 'for our audience' are usually the ones that end up on the Third Day scrap heap. But the ones that I write just for myself, out of that personal place, are the ones that, for whatever reason, people end up latching onto." "Show Me Your Glory" was definitely one of those.

In 2001, Third Day was in the studio working on their *Come Together* album. As frontman Mac Powell remembers it, "We had pretty much finished the record, but after listening to it a few times, we thought that we maybe needed to go back into the studio for one week and try to come up with a couple more rock songs—we really wanted more rock stuff on it. So Mark, being the great guy that he is, went right home and wrote a worship song!"

Mark laughs, "Well, I did wonder if writing a worship song was the best use of my time right then, but for whatever reason I had this idea going. I just really felt like that was the

REFLECTIONS ON COMMUNION

"This cup is the new covenant in my blood; do this, whenever you drink it, in remembrance of me."
(1 Cor. 11:25b)

"Communion Song"—John Michael Talbot
"Remember Me"—Barry McGuire
"Peace"—Rich Mullins
"Here's to the Day"—Billy Crockett
"Say Once More"—Amy Grant
"Come to the Table"—Michael Card

thing I was supposed to do. When I finished it and played it for my wife, I told her, 'You know what, we're not going to end up doing anything with this song.' But I really liked it and felt like I had spent my time wisely."

When the rest of the band heard the song, they decided that, rock song or not, "Show Me Your Glory" belonged on the record. "It wasn't really what we were looking for," Mac says, "but we all thought it was great." Because of the last-minute timing, the turnaround was unusually quick. Mark says, "What was really wild is that I wrote it, and then two days later we recorded it. Then they decided to make it the single, and it was playing on the radio like, literally, two weeks later. You just never see it happen like that; it was really funny."

"Well, not ha-ha funny," interjects Mac.

"More like ironic funny."

At any rate, the last-minute addition of "Show Me Your Glory" was a key ingredient in the enormous success of the *Come Together* album. One reviewer singled out the song as a "praise-styled gentle jam, showing Powell's gritty vocal patterns stripped down to a soothing tone, while the rest of the band shows their versatility. Guitarists Brad Avery and Mark Lee trade off between acoustic and electric riffs with an incredible amount of continuity and transitional ease."

"Show Me Your Glory" continued Third Day's legacy of well-crafted songs of praise.

AUDIO
ADRENALINE

BIG
HOUSE

WRITTEN BY MARK STUART, BARRY BLAIR, WILL McGINNESS AND BOB HERDMAN

RECORDED BY AUDIO ADRENALINE ON DON'T CENSOR ME (FOREFRONT RECORDS, 1993)

PRODUCED BY GOTEE BROTHERS

AUDIO ADRENALINE ESTABLISHED "BIG HOUSE" BASS, AN EBAY CHARITY AUCTION TO AID MISSIONS

Mark Stuart's dad is a missionary to Haiti, but he might want to consider a second career in the music business. According to Tyler Burkum, Mr. Stuart takes full credit for the fact that Audio Adrenaline's most famous

25

song, "Big House," ever saw the light of day. "I think he was a pastor in Kentucky at the time," Tyler says. "And from the very first time he heard the song, he kept saying, 'That song's going to go somewhere; if you don't put it on the CD, you're going to regret it forever.' The weird thing is, he had a pretty good track record, because almost every time he said something like that about a song, it turned out to be a hit! So when he said that 'Big House' was a special song and the kids were really gonna love it, we were like, 'Really? You think so?'"

But not even Mark's dad could have foreseen the impact the "fun little song" would have on AA's career. "Big House" is easily the group's most recognizable and best-loved song, the one they can't possibly leave off the set list for the rest of their careers. Tyler laughs, "When we do 'Big House' in concert, I can literally play the first guitar riff and it's like starting a car.

Kerri Stuart

ting all caught up in our lives and are taking things so seriously, that simple, child-like faith in God is so powerful. And it also made me realize what a miracle it is that God took a bunch of weirdo Midwestern guys and has done some really cool things with us and through us."

"Big House" became an unexpected #1 hit for Audio Adrenaline and was even named the *CCM* #1 Song of the Decade for the 1990s, to the surprise of many industry pundits. But not Mark Stuart's dad. "He's so much fun; he's like the band mascot and cheerleader," Tyler says. "And he'll never let us forget his claim to fame. Even now he says, 'I told you to put that on the record! What would you guys do without me?'"

We come out onstage and get it going, and then we can walk away because the crowd is going to finish it; they'll just drive that baby on home!"

Audio Adrenaline would be the first to admit that "Big House" is not exactly the height

of lyrical profundity. But it was never intended to be. Tyler says, "The poetic justice of it all is that it's not this amazingly deep song that makes us all look like philosophical geniuses. It's just a simple way to rejoice about the place that God's preparing for us, and the promise that we would someday be in heaven with Him."

One of Tyler's favorite "Big House" memories happened when the band was in Guatemala and taught the song to the village children. "Listening to those voices sing it back to us was such a reminder to me that when we start get-

OTHER BIG SONGS

"Big Enough"—Prism

"Big God"—Imperials

"Big Boy"—Sheila Walsh

"Big Fish"—FFH

"Big Blue Sky"—Bebo Norman

"Big Rubber Bumper"—Billy Crockett

"Big Time"—Michael and Stormie Omartian

"Big Town"—Ashley Cleveland

"Big Bad Wolf"—Disciple

"Big Fat Happy Day"—Hoi Polloi

"How to Grow Up Big and Strong"—Mark Heard

"NEVER GONNA BE AS BIG AS JESUS"—AUDIO ADRENALINE

"Murder in the Big House"—Chagall Guevara

STEVEN CURTIS CHAPMAN

I WILL BE HERE

26

WRITTEN BY STEVEN CURTIS CHAPMAN

RECORDED BY STEVEN CURTIS CHAPMAN ON MORE TO THIS LIFE (SPARROW, 1989)

PRODUCED BY PHIL NAISH

STEVEN CURTIS CHAPMAN MET MARY BETH IN COLLEGE; THEY MARRIED AT 21 AND 19 AND HONEYMOONED AT THE CINCINNATI ZOO BEFORE MOVING TO NASHVILLE

The tender lyrics to Steven Curtis Chapman's "I Will Be Here" paint such a beautiful picture of love and commitment that when producer Phil Naish heard them for the first time, he predicted, "This is going to be a HUGE wedding song!" He turned out to be exactly right, much to the surprise of SCC himself. "I thought, *Are you serious? Who wants to hear 'Tomorrow morning, if you wake up and the sun does not appear . . .' at their wedding?*" laughed Steven. "Actually, in essence it's really a love song to my wife—which also makes it a worship song, because when we love well the people God has put in our lives, that's a great act of worship."

Although "I Will Be Here"

has become synonymous with some of life's happiest moments, it was actually born out of some of life's most difficult ones: the unexpected divorce of Chapman's parents after almost 30 years of marriage. "It completely stunned my brother and me and everybody that knew them," he said. "I think it especially pulled the rug out from under Mary Beth and me, because we were only three years into our own marriage and had always thought that my parents had it so together. We were sort of patterning ourselves after them; our relationship with each other, with God, with everything." The

"I was in college when that record came out, and I bought it at the college bookstore and took it back to my room. I went to a Baptist college, and this was a guy's dorm, full of soccer players and manly men. So I'm playing 'I Will Be Here,' and one by one all these guys' heads start poking in the doorway saying, 'What song is that?' Before you know it, all of these big soccer jocks are sitting around my room crying. Like, sniff, sniff, 'I'll be here too, I promise, Father; I'll be here!' It's such a great song. And they were all just bawling. . . . Cheesy, but true."

JODY MCBRAYER OF AVALON

"'I Will Be Here' has been sung at every wedding since the early 1800s, I think. I got asked to sing that song all the time—I finally had to stop doing weddings because I think I've sung that song more than I've sung 'Imagine!' But yeah, it's definitely one of my favorites. I remember when I first heard it, I was like, 'One day—no one else has ever had this idea—but one day I will have that played when I get married! But don't tell anybody, because I don't want the secret to get out.' Well, apparently somebody told."

BART MILLARD OF MERCYME

sobering realization that even seemingly successful, solid Christian marriages can fall apart caused Steven and Mary Beth to take a hard look at their own. And out of the hurt and disillusionment of his shattered family came a new resolve. Steven said, "This song definitely marked a time of pain and heartache in our lives. But it was also the beginning of this kind of steely determination in us. We were saying to each other, 'We will not give up, no matter what we feel like when we wake up tomorrow. I'm going to be there for you. I am committed to the vows I've made, by the grace of God.'"

It is that underlying sense of purpose that distinguishes "I Will Be Here" from other perennial nuptial favorites. The gentle, acoustic ballad makes a strong statement about the power of a promise. It is simply, as Steven Curtis Chapman says, "a very special song."

NICHOLE NORDEMAN

HOLY

 **27**

WRITTEN BY NICHOLE NORDEMAN AND MARK HAMMOND

RECORDED BY NICHOLE NORDEMAN ON WOVEN & SPUN (SPARROW RECORDS, 2002)

PRODUCED BY MARK HAMMOND

2003 DOVE AWARDS— SONG OF THE YEAR; POP/CONTEMPORARY RECORDED SONG OF THE YEAR

Nichole Nordeman has been dubbed "the wrestling poet" because of her thought-provoking, intensely introspective lyrical style on songs like "Every Season," "This Mystery" and "Why." So she had some pretty high expectations to live up to when beginning work on her third album, *Woven & Spun*.

Those kinds of expectations were something she tried not to worry about too much. "I'm tired of trying to be the artist," she told *CCM Magazine* before the album's release, "—tired of trying to be 'The Nichole Nordeman.' I'm just exhausted with the whole thing.

"Why is it so much easier to write about my own struggle than to write about how good God is?" she asks. "This concerns me." Deliberating, she offers, "Have I spent so much time in the self-absorbed land of questioning and reasoning that I am unable to just worship?"

Like many writers at one point or another in their literary pursuits, Nordeman was also wrestling with something different altogether: a horrible case of writer's block. "I knew I'd reached a breakthrough with 'Holy' because it came from such an honest place," she explains. "It's about my journey away from God and then prodigal-type return to Him."

Having grown up in a Christian home where she attended Christian grade and prep schools, the transition to a liberal southern California college was a journey full of investigation—namely one of claiming her Christian faith as her own. As many often do in this process, Nordeman strayed from the faith during these formative years— a period when she felt "enlightened" by various philosophies.

"Soon the absolutes of my faith became compromised," she says. Although she wandered from God, eventually she found herself exactly where she began. "Many people take the long way around, but then they reach the conclusion that God is holy, and that's all that matters."

And it's this simple, unabashed declaration of faith from the self-described "introvert" that really resonated with Christian radio listeners, the Christian music industry (as she proved to be the "Norah Jones" of the Dove Awards in 2003 with a slew of trophies just like Jones, who cleaned house at the Grammy Awards earlier that year) and even her fellow artists.

"I love Nichole Nordeman. She's a dear friend of mine, and I think she's probably one of the most prolific songwriters in Christian music," says labelmate Jody McBrayer, a member of Avalon and a solo artist. "However, 'Holy' stayed #1 long enough to keep me at #2, and I never made it to #1 with my song. So we're still friends, but I'm bitter," he jokes.

"It's really a great song, though. I still hear it, and I love it. It's an amazing track, but then again, that whole record, *Woven & Spun,* is fantastic."

Also singing Nordeman's praises, Plus One's Nathan Walters likens her to another one of his favorite artists. "When I heard Nichole Nordeman, I really liked her a lot because she kind of reminds me of a female Michael W. Smith. I really liked her hooks, her song, her voice, and the fact she played the piano," he comments. "To this day I have this album in my CD player actually, and it's been out forever. I listen to it a lot because it's catchy, it's very worshipful, and it takes me to a place that's very intimate with God."

NEWSBOYS

HE REIGNS

WRITTEN BY PETER FURLER
AND STEVE TAYLOR

RECORDED BY NEWSBOYS
ON ADORATION: THE
WORSHIP ALBUM
(SPARROW RECORDS, 2003)

PRODUCED BY STEVE TAYLOR

NEWSBOYS VERSION OF "HE
REIGNS" IS ALSO FEATURED
ON DOVE HITS 2004 (WORD
RECORDS)

ADORATION DEBUTED AT #1
ON THE CHRISTIAN ALBUM
SALES CHARTS AND #33 ON
THE BILLBOARD 200 CHART

2004 ASCAP CHRISTIAN
MUSIC AWARD—SONG OF
THE YEAR

The Newsboys and longtime songwriting partner/producer Steve Taylor (Sixpence None the Richer, Waterdeep) might have sported sweaty palms as they entered the studio to record 2003's *Adoration: The Worship Album.* True, the Newsboys had been king of the Christian pop band hill for almost a decade, and Taylor had years of gold and platinum album notches in his production belt, but this was new territory. Sacred territory—literally. For the first time in each of their prestigious careers, the band and producer were preparing to record a worship album.

28

Months later they would watch in amazement as *Adoration* became 2003's best-selling artist-worship album on its way to landing both Grammy and Dove Award nominations. The song "He Reigns" anchored the album and fueled the public's strong response as it claimed the #1

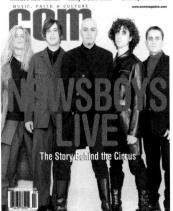

spot on Christian pop radio for five consecutive weeks en route to becoming the most-played single of the year.

"The band always had a kind of a joke with me when I presented a new song to them," recalls Newsboys frontman Peter Furler. "They would always say to me, 'Well, what three chords is it this time?' And I actually do know four chords; I just keep the other one to myself. But it was funny—them joking and messing with me, and I sort of took it to heart at one point and I thought, *Alright, I'm gonna teach you dogs a lesson. I'm gonna write a song with three chords in it.* And so I sat down and I just started singing that chorus, 'He reigns,' and singing, 'Glory, glory, hallelujah, He reigns.'

96

And I was sort of having my own time with my guitar with the Lord and then the phrase, 'All God's children' came. And I put it away—I put it away for about four years.

"When we started working on *Adoration*, I just went back and looked through my old demo CDs. I usually document everything I'm sort of working on and just keep it. And I went back and listened to the song and I thought, *Man, there's something in this.* So I put together the verses and the chorus and the sections, and then I showed it to Steve Taylor."

Taylor gave insight into his response to the song in a statement highlighted in The GMA 35th Music Awards program book:

"When Peter first played me the chorus for 'He Reigns,' I had two immediate impressions: 1. This is a chorus that could be sung Sunday mornings in church, therefore . . . 2. I'm not the guy to finish it. Then I recalled extraordinary images from travels to the corners of the earth. A thousand Masai children singing praises to God on a Tanzanian plain. A town square in Krakow packed with fellow Christians singing hymns in defiance of Soviet-era authorities. A Japanese house church. A ballroom in Chile. A van in Nepal. I couldn't speak the language in any of these places. Yet when I heard my brothers and sisters raise their voices to heaven, I understood perfectly. May 'He Reigns' fill you with the same joy and gratitude that Peter and I experienced writing it."

"He Reigns" drew nominations for GMA (Dove) Awards in two categories—Song of the Year and Worship Song of the Year.

David Dobson

The Newsboys were also Group of the Year and Praise and Worship Album of the Year nominees.

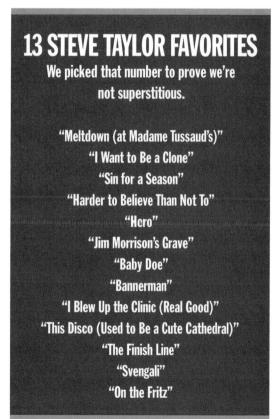

13 STEVE TAYLOR FAVORITES
We picked that number to prove we're not superstitious.

"Meltdown (at Madame Tussaud's)"
"I Want to Be a Clone"
"Sin for a Season"
"Harder to Believe Than Not To"
"Hero"
"Jim Morrison's Grave"
"Baby Doe"
"Bannerman"
"I Blew Up the Clinic (Real Good)"
"This Disco (Used to Be a Cute Cathedral)"
"The Finish Line"
"Svengali"
"On the Fritz"

RUSS TAFF

WE WILL STAND

RECORDED BY RUSS TAFF
ON WALLS OF GLASS
(WORD RECORDS, 1983)

PRODUCED BY BILL SCHNEE

1983 GRAMMY AWARD—
BEST MALE GOSPEL
PERFORMANCE:
WALLS OF GLASS

1984 DOVE AWARD—BEST
MALE VOCALIST

29

R uss Taff was born the fourth of five sons to a fire-breathing Pentecostal preacher father and a gospel music-loving mother. He grew up in tiny Farmersville, California, in the heart of the verdant San Joaquin Valley, surrounded by fruit orchards and itinerant migrant workers. "We were old-time Pentecostal," Russ explains with a smile. "Growing up in that church, I always felt kind of on the fringes of the rest of the body of Christ, because we were just so out there! I also saw how all the Hispanic workers in our town were treated by the locals. It gave me an understanding early on of what it was like to be an outsider, of how it felt to stand alone."

Russ Taff left his hometown at 17 and eventually made his way to Nashville, where the new kid in town quickly found success as the lead singer of the legendary Imperials. By 1982, he had struck out on his own and was getting ready to record his first solo album for Word Records.

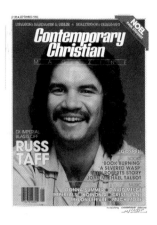

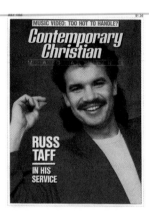

"I was blown away the first time I heard 'We Will Stand.' I love the theme of that song; it makes me glad I'm part of the family of God. I wish Gloria and I had been paying closer attention the day that one was floating around in the air . . . but I'm glad Russ and Tori were!"

BILL GAITHER

"I saw Russ Taff play this big outdoor festival, in '92 or '93. He did the guitar thing, just sat there singing those words, and I was completely overcome with emotion. The message, the passion and just the whole aura of who he is as an artist and a writer... I saw him and thought, *I want to do that—I want to write songs and move people toward God."*

MICHAEL TAIT OF dc talk

Late one night, Russ sat on the living room floor of the apartment he shared with his wife, Tori, strumming his guitar and trying to come up with something for the new record. "I was thinking about this story I had heard from a guy named Archie Dennis," Russ remembers. "He was a singer that traveled with the evangelist Kathryn Kulhman. He was a black man, and he had this huge voice like an opera singer. When he sang, you

couldn't tell what color he was; I guess on the radio most people thought he was white. He told about being invited to Alabama in the early '60s to sing at this big church. It was Sunday morning, and when he got there early to set up his little sound system, the pastor walked in and asked who he was. When Archie told him he was the guest singer, the pastor said, 'This is not going to work. This is Alabama, and there's just no way this can happen. You are not going to be able to sing this morning.' So Archie started packing up his equipment, tears running down his face. He walked out

to the steps of the church on the way to his car and almost collapsed crying, saying, 'God, You know we're all brothers and sisters in Christ—why won't they let me in?' And he said he felt a voice say back to him, 'They won't let Me in either.'"

As Russ recalled the story that he had carried with him for years, a theme of looking beyond our differences and finding unity in Christ began to form in his mind. "By about 4:00 in the morning, I had the chorus," Russ says. "I went upstairs and woke up Tori to sing it to her, and the next day we finished the verses." "We Will Stand" became one of Taff's signature songs, and has been performed at Presidential rallies, Billy Graham crusades, on

Gaither Homecoming videos and in churches of every color and kind across the country. "We just don't have room in the body of Christ for prejudice towards anyone," Taff concludes. "No matter what denomination, race or culture—like the song says, 'If you believe in Jesus, you belong with me, and the bond we share is all I care to see.'"

AMY GRANT

THY WORD

WRITTEN BY AMY GRANT AND MICHAEL W. SMITH

RECORDED BY AMY GRANT
ON STRAIGHT AHEAD
(MYRRH/WORD, 1984)
PRODUCED BY
BROWN BANNISTER

**ALSO RECORDED BY:
MICHAEL W. SMITH ON
FREEDOM**

**STEVE HALL ON IN THIS VERY
ROOM**

**DAVID OSBORNE ON JUST AS
I AM**

In the mid-'80s, Amy Grant was poised on the brink of becoming the first contemporary Christian music artist to truly cross over into the big leagues of pop stardom. Although a bona-fide mainstream hit song was still a few years and a couple of albums away, *Straight Ahead*

30

set her firmly on that path. The album also showcased Amy's new-found vocal aggressiveness: a gutsy, growly edge to her voice that had not been heard before and that left many of her faithful fans a little confused—this was not the sweet, girlish warbler they knew and loved. When the Grammy Awards rolled around that year, there was even more to talk about as a barefoot Amy gleefully danced all over the stage with her band members during a televised performance of "Angels."

"Thy Word," a worshipful, melodic hymn based on Psalm 119:105, did a lot to allay the growing concerns in the Christian community over the musical direction "our" Amy was heading. Co-written with Michael W. Smith, the song was as close to sacred music as anything she had ever done, and was a comforting, soothing island in the middle of a decid-

edly pop/rock project. *Straight Ahead* marked a return to the Caribou Ranch recording studio setup that "Team Amy" had found so effective for her 1982 chartbuster *Age to Age*. High in

the crisp Rocky Mountain air of Nederland, Colorado, the famed studio had played host to artists such as Elton John, Dan Fogelberg and Chicago, and was one of Amy's favorite places in the world. She recalls, "Recording at Caribou was amazing because it was rustic and elegant and the musical experience was just so rich. We'd go for two weeks at a time; first week we'd invite all the musicians and their families up, and the second week I'd invite my whole family up. I was usually working, but we'd find time to ride horses during the day, and we'd go hiking . . . It's just unbelievably beautiful." Michael W. Smith was part of the Caribou Ranch gang for *Straight Ahead*, and he has a favorite story about the writing of "Thy Word."

"I had come up with this melody," Smitty begins. "I actually had some words too, straight from David's Psalms. Amy fell in love with it, but I had no idea what the verses were supposed to say, so I just gave it to her and told her she could write it. I think she struggled a few days with it. Now, at Caribou the nights get very, very dark, and one night Amy left the studio to go back to her cabin and got totally lost—and you don't want to get lost up there; there are bears and mountain lions around. So finally, she saw a lantern in a window and she just kept stumbling towards that light until she walked right up to it and saw that it was her cabin. She went inside and just said, 'Wow,' and sat down right there and wrote the verses (including the line 'Thy Word is a lamp unto my feet, and a light unto my path'), wrote the whole song. And the next day she was in the studio singing it."

dc talk

WHAT IF I STUMBLE?

WRITTEN BY TOBY McKEEHAN AND DANIEL JOSEPH

RECORDED BY DC TALK ON JESUS FREAK (FOREFRONT RECORDS, 1995)

PRODUCED BY TOBY McKEEHAN, MARK HEIMERMANN AND JOHN PAINTER

1997 #1 FOR 6 WEEKS ON CHRISTIAN RADIO

1996 GRAMMY AWARD— BEST GOSPEL ALBUM: JESUS FREAK

1996 DOVE AWARD—BEST ROCK GOSPEL ALBUM: JESUS FREAK

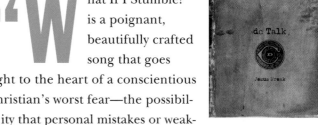

31

"What If I Stumble?" is a poignant, beautifully crafted song that goes right to the heart of a conscientious Christian's worst fear—the possibility that personal mistakes or weaknesses will bring shame to the cause of Christ. dc talk's song is especially meaningful in the context of what was happening to the group's career in 1995.

After three solidly successful records aimed primarily at Christian music audiences, general market mega-label Virgin Records came calling and offered dc talk an avenue to the mainstream. "It was such an exciting time, but it was kind of scary for us too," says Michael Tait, one-third of the group that also includes Toby McKeehan and Kevin Max. "Everybody always says that Hollywood will eat you up and spit you out, and we feared that. We knew that if God was calling us

there, then He would guard us and we would have His armor—but you know, the thing about armor is that it only covers the front; the back is open!"

This golden opportunity also came at a time when the group was inundated at every performance by, as Michael describes it, ". . . youth pastors that said, 'My kids love you guys!' and moms that said, 'Please don't mess up.'" It was a crushing sense of responsibility that made Toby, Kevin and Michael feel vaguely uneasy. At one point, Michael even remembers confronting a fan directly about her expectations for the group by saying, "Ma'am, with all due respect, I can't be Jesus for your kid."

Looking back on that time, he continues, "It's not that I was shirking my responsibility. I know 'to whom much is given, much is required,' and we were all doing our best. But what kept going through my head was, *What if I stumble? What happens to your faith then?*"

Toby McKeehan and Daniel Joseph

expanded on that thought, and the resulting song was a sobering reality check not only for the verging-on-stardom group, but their fans as well. "We've always been the kind of band that tries to not just write a bunch of Hallmark lyrics," Michael says. "I feel like kids are living in extreme days, extreme times, and you really have to touch their hearts and reach them where they are. So we tried to address them honestly with issues we were all going through."

Years after the song was written, "What If I Stumble?" continues to be personally relevant to dc talk, and one of their most requested songs in concert. "I think it hits a nerve with all of us," Michael concludes, "because the truth is, hey everybody, you know what? We will let you down. And your parents are going to let you down; your best friend is gonna let you down. . . . And it's OK; we're all human, we're all fallible. But God is perfect and all-knowing, and at the end of the day, His heart still beckons us."

David Dobson

THIRD DAY

CONSUMING FIRE

32

WRITTEN BY MAC POWELL
AND THIRD DAY

RECORDED BY THIRD DAY
ON THIRD DAY (REUNION
RECORDS, 1996)

PRODUCED BY DAVID MARDIS

1996 SELF-TITLED ALBUM
DEBUTS AT #18 ON CHRISTIAN
RETAIL, PEAKING AT #6

BILLBOARD VIDEO MUSIC
AWARD—BEST
CONTEMPORARY CHRISTIAN
NEW ARTIST VIDEO

1997 DOVE AWARD
NOMINATION—NEW ARTIST
OF THE YEAR

Many times in music circles, the fans' favorite songs—which usually turn out to be the first single an artist releases and end up becoming huge success stories—aren't always the artists' favorite songs, especially in terms of playing them live. It's not that these artists aren't grateful for the mass approval. It's just that sometimes there is a small annoyance factor of having to continue to play the same song night after night when the artist may be more excited about much newer material.

But for the Atlanta-based rockers Third Day, the artists and fans seem to be on the same page with "Consuming Fire." According to its gravelly voiced frontman Mac Powell, "People ask us all the time 'What is your favorite Third Day song?' And we always go back to 'Consuming Fire.' That was one of the very first ones, and I want to say it's the quintessential Third Day song because it combines a worship lyric with a rock sound."

When Third Day debuted in 1996, they offered a diverse southern rock element that was a real departure from what was currently happening in Christian music. Their signature sound was the result of an eclectic mix of personalities and

David Dobson

Photos by Kristin Barlowe

playing styles that was honed from years of playing together. "Consuming Fire" perfectly represents that fusion.

"There's a really cool thing that happened with that song and how it all came together," Mac explains. "Mark [Lee] and I have been together since high school, playing music in garage bands and all kinds of things, and we started Third Day right after we graduated. We spent about a year playing acoustic stuff together, then a year later we added David [Carr], our drummer, and Tai [Anderson], our bass player. They went to school and grew up together, so we had this one set of two friends and then this other set of two friends. It's like the peanut butter and the chocolate combined . . ."

Kristin Barlowe

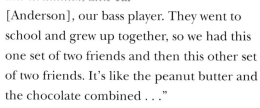

That recipe did indeed turn into something special. But unfortunately there still was one crucial ingredient missing—a louder guitar punch. "It was mostly an acoustic band, but we were missing this rock element we wanted to bring into it," Powell recalls. "So we auditioned Brad Avery. The first song that he auditioned on was 'Consuming Fire,' and from the very first harmonic note that he played, we just knew right away, this is it; this is the band!"

"In case y'all don't know that already, he got the job," Lee chimes in with a laugh.

That easy camaraderie is one of the key elements that has made Third Day a fan favorite for many years. They also share a firm commitment to connecting with their audience and have created a special online community for their fans, known affectionately as "Gomers." The popularity of "Consuming Fire" may have set the tone for Third Day's emergence as one of contemporary Christian music's premier bands, but it is the spirit of its members that keeps them there.

CLAY CROSSE

I SURRENDER ALL

33

WRITTEN BY DAVID E. MOFFIT AND REGIE HAMM

RECORDED BY CLAY CROSSE ON MY PLACE IS WITH YOU (REUNION RECORDS, 1992)

PRODUCED BY REGIE HAMM

1995 DOVE AWARD— NEW ARTIST OF THE YEAR

NOMINATED FOR GMA SONG OF THE YEAR

With the kind of soulful, memorable vocal range that listeners don't easily forget, you'd assume Clay Crosse had been singing all his life. But the truth is, the Memphis native with the given name Walter Clayton Crossnoe didn't sing for the first time in public until he was 14. That performance of "Pillar of Ages" was in front of a very supportive church congregation.

It turns out that despite having an incredible voice, Crosse battled an extreme case of stage fright until a performance at a local theme park made him feel more comfortable with the stage limelight. With this new-found confidence, the singer recorded a demo that eventually landed in the hands of Reunion Records president Terry Hemmings, who wasted no time signing him.

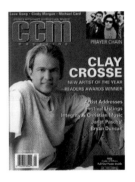

But even with a budding career, this Fed Ex employee didn't quit his day job for quite a while, until a memorable ballad called "I Surrender All" changed everything for the singer. With its confessional declaration of submission to God and goose-bump-inducing crescendo, it became "the song" in Christian music in the early '90s, something that fellow artist Jaci Velasquez remembers well.

"When I heard Clay Crosse for the first time, I knew that

he was going to change Christian music. There was a hole in the market for an amazing male vocalist who could sing a song and tell a story like nobody could with drama and with conviction," Velasquez says. "And Clay Crosse was one of those. The song 'I Surrender All' was probably his biggest

hit. One night I was on tour with him, and when he was doing that song, it was easy to see that it was one of the most powerful songs he's ever recorded. The song presented that feeling of, 'Look, forget about me—forget about all the things that I can't live without and that are holding me down. I want to surrender everything to You and give it up. Because if it's not about You, then I don't want it.' Clay Crosse had the voice to do that, and it definitely changed Christian music."

Another artist known for her tremendous vocal range, CeCe Winans, can't help but agree. "'I Surrender All' is probably one of the greatest songs ever written in life, and definitely the greatest message. Because if we would just learn how to surrender and move out of God's way, we would allow Him to do those things that only He can do. And who else better to deliver that song than Clay

Crosse? He's a wonderful young man and an awesome, awesome talent. I surrender all—that is my prayer, that I can just continue to surrender to the Lord for the rest of my life."

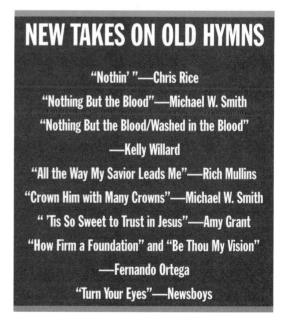

NEW TAKES ON OLD HYMNS

"Nothin' "—Chris Rice

"Nothing But the Blood"—Michael W. Smith

"Nothing But the Blood/Washed in the Blood"
—Kelly Willard

"All the Way My Savior Leads Me"—Rich Mullins

"Crown Him with Many Crowns"—Michael W. Smith

" 'Tis So Sweet to Trust in Jesus"—Amy Grant

"How Firm a Foundation" and "Be Thou My Vision"
—Fernando Ortega

"Turn Your Eyes"—Newsboys

AMY GRANT

SING YOUR PRAISE TO THE LORD

34

WRITTEN BY RICH MULLINS

RECORDED BY AMY GRANT ON
AGE TO AGE (MYRRH, 1982)

PRODUCED BY
BROWN BANNISTER

ALSO RECORDED BY:
RICH MULLINS ON SONGS

A lot changed in Amy Grant's life in 1982. The 21-year-old married singer/songwriter Gary Chapman, for one. She also released an album that would not only change her life forever—its success finally convinced her that maybe she could make a career of music after all—but would literally change the entire course of contemporary Christian music.

Age to Age, Grant's fourth studio album, exploded out of the starting gate at #1 and never looked back. The album spent 22 months in the #1 position (knocked out only by Grant's follow-up release, *Straight Ahead*) and over five years in the Top 50 of the Christian albums chart. To put that into perspective in today's musical climate, the longest-running Top 50 Christian titles are often on the chart less than two years. In 1984, *Age to Age* became the first album ever by a Christian artist to be certified gold (for sales of 500,000 copies), and in 1985 it broke another barrier when it was certified platinum (sales of one million). The album also resulted in Grant winning her first of four Dove Awards from the Gospel Music Association for Artist of the Year. Oddly enough, Grant has never won the lesser title of Female Vocalist of the Year.

Age to Age is full of songs that are now classics, including our #5 song, "El Shaddai." But "Sing Your Praise to the Lord" is significant for another reason: it introduced the world to the music of Rich Mullins, who penned the song. Mullins went on to write several other songs for Grant, including "Doubly Good to You" and "Love of Another Kind."

Grant herself gently pokes fun at all the hoopla, recalling a humorous story about the incredible song with a climactic

> "I love Amy's spirit, and I love her. Her songs have always been so powerful, and this is just a beautiful song."
>
> CECE WINANS

minute-plus intro taken from Bach's Fugue No. 2. "I remember turning on the TV one time, years later, on a beach trip with my family. They were doing some big show at the Radio City Music Hall (in New York City), and the Rockettes were doing can-cans across the stage to a re-written 'Sing Your Praise to the Stars.' It just goes to show there are no sacred cows!"

"I was on Amy Grant's first tour ever with a band. I had never been to a Christian concert, and here I was singing background vocals for Amy! I cried the whole time because I couldn't believe how incredible it was that somebody could sing about their faith. I remember her being just so real . . . so incredibly honest and real about her faith. And it literally changed my life."

BONNIE KEEN OF FIRST CALL

RICH
MULLINS

HOLD
ME
JESUS

35

WRITTEN BY RICH MULLINS

RECORDED BY RICH MULLINS
ON A LITURGY, A LEGACY
AND A RAGAMUFFIN BAND
(REUNION RECORDS, 1993)

PRODUCED BY REED ARVIN

ALSO RECORDED BY:
REBECCA ST. JAMES ON
PRAY

AMY GRANT ON AWESOME
GOD: A TRIBUTE TO
RICH MULLINS

A ccording to his brother, Rich Mullins was the kind of kid who cried when he watched westerns on TV because he couldn't stand watching the Indians get a raw deal. "But it's their land!" he'd wail to the living room at large. No surprise, then, that the boy grew into a man whose anger at injustice and compassion for the underdog colored everything he did.

The kind of music Rich chose to make came with strings attached. He wrote with a level of unflinching honesty that left no religious illusions to hide behind, for the writer or the listener. He was unafraid to admit that he was confused, or scared, or that his faith was wavering, which gave his audience permission to say, "Me too." Songs like "Hold Me Jesus" eloquently illustrate that confessional aspect of Rich's

writing. In a *CCM Magazine* interview around the time of the release of his seventh album, *A Liturgy, a Legacy and a Ragamuffin Band,* Rich addressed the issue. "I generally live on the idea that everyone is pretty much the same," he said, "and that whatever is true for me is probably true of 90 percent of everybody else in the world."

The project was conceived as a concept album of sorts, with the first half in the form of a tool used for collective worship, a "liturgy." The remainder of the album salutes the "legacy" of our heritage, with the issues and traditions that have shaped our country and our selves. The Ragamuffin

> "Rich was so compelling and offensive in such a fabulous way. He followed the depths of his own humanity to the edge, and then pulled back and really had something to say."
>
> AMY GRANT

110

Band was named after a book on grace that Rich was particularly moved by—author Brennan Manning's *The Ragamuffin Gospel*. The stellar lineup, which brilliantly executes the material, is made up of Rick Elias, Jimmy Abegg, Danny O'Lannerty, Chris McHugh, Lee Lundgren, Eric Darken, Billy Crockett and longtime Mullins collaborator Beaker. "Hold Me Jesus" went to #1 and was nominated for two 1994 Dove Awards: Song of the Year and Contemporary Recorded Song of the Year.

With songs like "Hold Me Jesus," and particularly in his live performances, Rich said he wanted his music to ask the audience, "Don't you ever want to say this; don't you ever want to look up to heaven and say, 'Hold me, Christ; I'm shaking like a leaf'? Aren't you tired of being Mr. Together and aren't you tired of healing everybody and aren't you tired of being Mr.

Holy Joe? Don't you ever feel like this? And if you can join me and sing here, that will be good for all of us."

SO HONEST THEY'RE SCARY

We may root for heroes but we're drawn to people who struggle as we do. These songs may make you squirm —but you'll know you're not alone.

"Blister Soul"—Vigilantes of Love
"Beautiful"—Bethany Dillon
"The Turning"—Leslie Phillips
"Expectation"—Leslie Phillips
"Bottom Line"—The Seventy-Sevens
"Answers Don't Come Easy"—Leslie Phillips
"Frail"—Jars of Clay
"Restore My Soul"—The Choir
"Faithless Heart"—Amy Grant
"I Could Laugh"—The Seventy-Sevens
"Hang My Head and Cry"—David Mullen
"Man After Your Own Heart"—Gary Chapman
"Personal Revolution"—Charlie Peacock
"Almost Threw It All Away"—Charlie Peacock
"All I Must Do"—Kathy Troccoli
"What If I Stumble?"—dc talk
"Nod Over Coffee"—Mark Heard
"All I Ever Have to Be"—Amy Grant
"Thought You'd Be Here"—Wes King
"I Remember"—Patsy Moore
"I'll Lead You Home"—Michael W. Smith
"Roll to the Middle"—Sara Groves
"Too Many Times"—Michael W. Smith
"Innocence Lost"—Susan Ashton

Patty Masten

111

RAY BOLTZ

THANK YOU

WRITTEN BY RAY BOLTZ

**RECORDED BY RAY BOLTZ
ON THANK YOU
(DIADEM, 1988)**

**PRODUCED BY STEVE
MILLIKEN**

**1990 GMA
SONG OF THE YEAR**

**1990 DOVE AWARD—
SONG OF THE YEAR**

**1997 "THANK YOU"
PERFORMED AT MOTHER
TERESA'S FUNERAL**

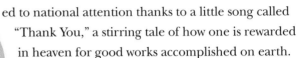

ay Boltz has captured the attention of Christian music, winning multiple Dove Awards, achieving several #1 singles and selling millions of records. But he was a virtual unknown in 1988 when he rocketed to national attention thanks to a little song called "Thank You," a stirring tale of how one is rewarded in heaven for good works accomplished on earth.

36

Boltz had been making Christian music for years by that point. In 1972, at the age of 19, he came to Christ at a Christian concert and soon started sharing his faith in prisons, nursing homes, coffeehouses and churches. In the mid-'80s, he attracted the interest of Heartland Records. He left his day job to go into music full-time when his first album, *Watch the Lamb*, was released in February 1986. Six months later, Heartland was history. As a parting gesture, the company mailed copies of the album out to Christian radio stations. Over the next year and a half, the

Karen Karki

112

seven-minute title track picked up airplay, breaking ground for the unknown artist. Consequently, when "Thank You" was released, it was an immediate hit.

Boltz says the classic song came about when someone in his church asked him to write a song for Pastor Appreciation Day. "I said I would try, and thought I had plenty of time—eight weeks. Well, the time flew by and I just was not having any success. Finally, the night before Pastor Appreciation Day, I was sitting at my piano trying to write something. As I sat there, I began to think about the people who have had the greatest impact on my life and realized that none of them were famous. They were people like Sunday school teachers, youth leaders, neighbors, and in that list I included my pastor, Eldon Morehouse. I decided to write a song that honored all of them, and I performed 'Thank You' the next morning in church."

When Boltz and producer Steve Milliken first took the song into the studio, one early arrangement sounded a bit too much like the Beatles' "Strawberry Fields." Says the artist, "It kind of went 'Thank you for giving forever . . . !' So we kept working until we created an arrangement that fit the song."

"It's a great song; it really is," says Michael English as he relates this anecdote from his days in the Gaither Vocal Band: "We were looking for songs, and this song was pitched to us. [Fellow GVB member] Gary McSpadden was so excited about it. And we're getting ready to cut it and next thing we know, somebody comes over to us and says, 'Ray Boltz is gonna try and do an artist thing; I think he wants to keep that one.' And I'm sure he's glad he did!"

> "The real heroes of the gospel are celebrated in 'Thank You,' and they are not the famous people or the ones on TV. I think we're all in for some surprises when we get to heaven!"
>
> GLORIA GAITHER

15 INCREDIBLE SONGS YOU MAY NEVER HAVE HEARD OF

"Walk to the Well"—Ashley Cleveland

"Light at the End of the Tunnel"—Ashley Cleveland

"Mourning into Dancing" or "So His Honor"—James Ward

"Double Cure"—Vigilantes of Love

"Blessed Are You"—Clear

"The Question"—Mustard Seed Faith

"The Wonders of His Love"—Phillip Bailey with Teri DeSario

"As I Am"—The Violet Burning

"You Know"—Steve Wiggins

"Love Is Not the Only Thing"—Mark Heard

"The Loving Kind"—Cindy Morgan

"Pray Where You Are"—Lost Dogs

"We Are the Beggars at the Foot of God's Door"—The Normals

"We Are a Beginning"—Sarah Masen

"You Gave Us Wings"—Billy Crockett

STEVEN CURTIS CHAPMAN

FOR THE SAKE OF THE CALL

WRITTEN BY STEVEN CURTIS CHAPMAN

RECORDED BY STEVEN CURTIS CHAPMAN ON FOR THE SAKE OF THE CALL (SPARROW, 1990)

PRODUCED BY PHIL NAISH

1992 DOVE AWARD—POP/ CONTEMPORARY ALBUM: FOR THE SAKE OF THE CALL; SONGWRITER OF THE YEAR

1992 GRAMMY AWARD— BEST POP/GOSPEL PERFORMANCE

37

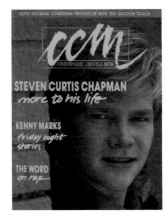

Steven Curtis Chapman's discography is really his biography as well. "I love to look back over my album titles and songs," he says, "because they usually represent seasons of life and seasons of spiritual growth, or sometimes seasons of spiritual wrestling, grappling with what was going on at the time." *For the Sake of the Call*, his fourth record for Sparrow Records, is no exception and represents an especially important time in his life. Before he went into the recording studio, he had spent almost a year immersing himself in classic Christian writings.

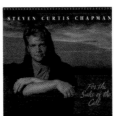

As Steven recalls, "I was asking myself a lot of questions about what I do. Like, what does it really mean to call myself a Christian, a follower and disciple of Jesus Christ?" As he delved more and more into the "whys" of his faith, he came across a book called *The Cost of Discipleship* by Dietrich Bonhoeffer. "I think it took me a year to read it, because I'm a slow reader and it's a very deep book," Steven smiles. "But it really challenged me; it was one of those times in life where God just took me by the hand and said, 'Alright, come on; I'm taking you somewhere you've never been before.' And He really did that with that book. As I was reading it, I found a passage that talked about the fact that the disciples didn't follow Christ for the sake of a great cause or a dream. It was simply because Jesus said, 'Come, follow Me.' They recognized that He was more than just a man. And though it didn't make sense to anyone, maybe even to themselves, they responded for no other reason than that He had called. I finally began to understand that to me, that's what it really means to follow Jesus Christ."

115

HE TOUCHED ME

WRITTEN BY BILL GAITHER

RECORDED BY THE BILL GAITHER TRIO ON HE TOUCHED ME (HEARTWARMING RECORDS, 1964)

PRODUCED BY BOB MACKENZIE

ALSO RECORDED BY:
BARBRA STREISAND ON THE ESSENTIAL BARBRA STREISAND

ELVIS PRESLEY ON ELVIS: ULTIMATE GOSPEL

If Bill Gaither had never picked up his pen again after writing "He Touched Me," he would have already earned his place in the songwriting history books. "That was my fifty-fourth song," Bill laughingly remembers. "I started writing in 1960 and had written a few that were strong songs, but nothing had made an impact on a national level yet. That all changed with 'He Touched Me.'"

38

Bill had been accompanying an old preacher friend of his, Dr. Dale Oldham, on several crusades. "He was a very eloquent speaker," Bill says. "One night after one of those meetings, Dr. Oldham said to me, 'Bill, the word "touch" is a very powerful word. It comes up so often in the New Testament stories about Jesus touching people's eyes and healing them, or touching people's lives and changing them. It's a special, spiritual word and you ought to write a song that praises His touch.' So I did."

Dr. Dale Oldham's son, singer Doug Oldham, was the first to record the song in 1964 on an album called *Songs That Touch the Heart.* "Doug sang it around in church circles," says Bill, "but I think it really started to get popular as people would take it back to their own congregations and sing it as a chorus. It's funny, you write 53 songs and then you write this

> "One of the first albums I ever did in Nashville was something entitled *Nothing But Praise,* which was a collection of all the Gaither tunes. My favorite song on it was 'He Touched Me.' We took a real different direction with it and it turned out so well. In fact, just the other day I was putting together a new concert list for my tour, and I sat down at the piano and started playing it. It's one of the songs I want to keep performing, because it's so well written and moving. It just still needs to be heard."
>
> **DALLAS HOLM**

one little baby, and even though it comes out of the womb the same way they all did, this baby just all of a sudden goes BOOM!"

"He Touched Me" is arguably Bill Gaither's most famous song. He says, "By the time Elvis recorded it, the cat was out of the bag." The Imperials had already done it, and when Elvis heard their arrangement of it—which was done by Henry Slaughter and is still the one the Vocal Band uses today—he said, "I need to record that." I remember when I finally got a copy of his record, I just stood there saying, 'Hey, Elvis is singing my song!' But that was all a bonus. I just really love the song."

"I literally grew up on Bill Gaither's music. When I was nine years old, my parents thought my voice was going to change and I wouldn't be able to sing anymore. They were probably right. So they wanted to make a recording of me while I could still sing. They didn't have a tape machine, but they knew there was this little studio down the street, so they spent $500 to get me on tape. The title of the record was *He Touched Me*. I never realized that one day I would actually know Bill Gaither, and more importantly, he would know my name! So even way back then I was singing Bill's songs. Of course, he's been writing forever; I think he's 10 years older than God."

MARK LOWRY

MICHAEL W. SMITH

ABOVE ALL

39

WRITTEN BY PAUL BALOCHE
AND LENNY LEBLANC

RECORDED BY MICHAEL W.
SMITH ON WORSHIP
(REUNION RECORDS, 2001)

PRODUCED BY MICHAEL W.
SMITH AND TOM LAUNE

INSPIRED TWO BOOKS:
J. COUNTRYMAN'S WORSHIP
AND BRENNAN MANNING'S
ABOVE ALL

2001 PERFORMED AT
PRESIDENT BUSH'S
INAUGURAL PRAYER SERVICE

When asked why he thinks his 1995 song "Above All" has connected with so many churchgoers in worship services around the world, Lenny LeBlanc (who co-wrote the song with Paul Baloche) pauses, and then offers, "I think because it's such a beautiful picture of how a God that is above everything would become like a rose trampled on the ground, take the fall and think of us . . . above all."

Michael W. Smith stumbled upon the song when he was looking for material to sing at President Bush's inaugural prayer service at the Boston Cathedral back in 2001. "I knew the whole thing was going to be somewhat traditional. I was just trying to find something that leaned a little bit contemporary, but I couldn't find anything," Smith recalls. "So I started going through all these worship CDs I gct in thc mail. And then on the third CD I listened to, I ran across 'Above All.' I had never heard it. And I'll never forget going, 'That's what I'm singing in Washington.'" He adds, "I even had cheat sheets on the piano because I had never sung it live before. I had not memorized it, so I had to pull these things out of my pocket and lay them on the piano—very unprofessional. But I was determined to sing it." Michael's instinctive, emotional reaction to the song mirrored the writers' experience as it was being created. Baloche says simply, "It came from an honest place. I just sincerely wanted to worship Him and praise Him for His greatness."

But what did the Commander in Chief think of Smith's rendition of the song? "I think it was received very well because every time I see the President, he wants me to play it," Smith says. "So he remembers that song very well."

While watching the inaugural prayer service on *Fox News Live,* Baloche says he couldn't hold back his emotions. "I was sitting on the floor with my children watching as Michael W. Smith walked up to the piano and began to sing," he remembers. "Tears began to pour out of my eyes. My eight-year-old daughter asked, 'Are you all right, Daddy? What's wrong?' I replied, 'Honey, these are happy tears.'

"I'm humbled and blown away that a simple prayer of worship, started at my little piano, found its way to the President of the United States. The possibility that this song could be an encouragement to him is such an honor. I pray that he would draw strength and wisdom from the One who is above him . . . and above all. It blesses me to know that Jesus will be worshiped with this song for years to come."

KEITH GREEN

OH LORD, YOU'RE BEAUTIFUL

WRITTEN BY KEITH GREEN

RECORDED BY KEITH GREEN ON SO YOU WANNA GO BACK TO EGYPT (PRETTY GOOD RECORDS, 1980)

PRODUCED BY BILL MAXWELL AND KEITH GREEN

ALSO RECORDED BY:
THE INSYDERZ ON THE INSYDERZ PRESENT SKALLELUIA!

40

In the history of contemporary Christian music, Keith Green was perhaps the first shining star, the first angry prophet, the first glorious tragedy. In his brief Christian music career he only recorded four studio albums, but his impact in Christian music is nearly unmatched in the more than 20 years since his death.

A child prodigy who recorded his first single at the age of 11, he struggled for years with his two great quests: pop stardom and spiritual meaning. At 21, he turned to Christ and his songs suddenly reflected his new life. Through honest and vulnerable lyrics, as well as preaching from the stage, the young artist relentlessly prodded his audiences, calling for them to repent and exhorting Christians to live the life they claimed to believe.

Ironically, in sacrificing his dreams of stardom, his music ministry exploded.

His first album, *For Him Who Has Ears to Hear*—released on upstart Christian label Sparrow Records in 1977—was an immediate hit. Green went from playing for crowds of 20 to playing stadiums packed with crowds of 12,000. "I fell in love with his music when I was in college," says Amy Grant. "He was one of those artists that, as a believer, I was proud to say, 'Stack this guy up against anybody—pick any Motown artist, pick your favorite rocker, and this guy will match him toe-to-toe with heart, with intelligence and with something very soulful to sing about.'"

But Green's heart and passion was to build God's Kingdom. He asked Sparrow to let him out of his contract so he could record on his own and give his

> **"Keith was my first real introduction to the Word of God. When I finally read the book of Matthew, I figured out that someone had said it way before Keith. But 'Oh Lord, You're Beautiful' is a song I loved. I probably still sing that song once a week."**
>
> PETER FURLER OF NEWSBOYS

records away. He was the label's biggest-selling artist, but Sparrow was gracious enough to let him go.

In 1980 he released *So You Wanna Go Back to Egypt*, Green's third record and the first offered by his new indie label, Pretty Good Records. His asking price was "whatever you can afford." Reportedly, the checks that came in ranged from $1 to $5,000. For what was conceived as a "give-away," the album nonetheless included many now-classic songs, from the whimsical rebuke of the title track to the sweet "I Want to Be

More Like Jesus." One of the standouts is "Oh Lord, You're Beautiful," which has since become a worship standard.

Alisa Girard of ZOEgirl has a strong memory of singing "Oh Lord, You're Beautiful" in Sunday school as a girl. "I was about seven and the Sunday school teacher led that song with his guitar. It was one of those early defining moments, helping me to worship with my heart and spirit in the truth. When I started to lead worship when I was 18, 19 years old, that was one of the songs I would always sing because it meant so much to me."

MICHAEL CARD

LOVE CRUCIFIED AROSE

WRITTEN BY MICHAEL CARD

RECORDED BY MICHAEL CARD ON LEGACY (MILK AND HONEY RECORDS, 1983)

PRODUCED BY JOHN THOMPSON AND RANDY SCRUGGS

1983 #5 ON CHRISTIAN RADIO

1983 DOVE AWARD— SONGWRITER OF THE YEAR

CCM *Magazine* has described Michael Card this way: "Always a somewhat uneasy presence within the celebrity-studded Christian music industry, Card has been content to go his own way. He has always looked beyond the passing fashions of the present moment to older, more ancient traditions." An accomplished musician and songwriter with 19 #1 songs, numerous Dove Awards, and the prestigious RIAA "Top 365 Songs of the Century" honor for "El Shaddai," Card is perhaps best known and appreciated for the tedious research and biblical scholarship that support the themes running through his songs. The bearded, somewhat professorial Card readily agrees that his passion for Bible history, philosophy and other scholarly pursuits influences everything he does. He

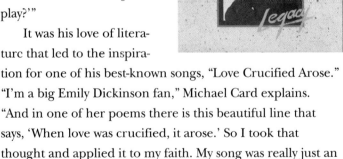

says with a laugh, "One of the reasons I started writing books was because after concerts people would sometimes say, 'Would you maybe not talk so much, and just play?'"

It was his love of literature that led to the inspiration for one of his best-known songs, "Love Crucified Arose." "I'm a big Emily Dickinson fan," Michael Card explains. "And in one of her poems there is this beautiful line that says, 'When love was crucified, it arose.' So I took that thought and applied it to my faith. My song was really just an attempt to capture that instant of resurrection—that

> "I really love Michael Card's music. 'Love Crucified Arose' is just a wonderful, epic song. It's good music and it's good theology. Michael is a deep well; there's a lot of depth to him."
>
> PHIL KEAGGY

moment when this heart that had stopped beating started beating again, this chest that had stopped breathing started to rise and fall again. We don't know exactly how it happened—the Bible doesn't give us any details—but that's what I was trying to picture. I wanted to give a poetic overview and paint the background with lines like 'Long ago He blessed the earth . . .'"

Michael Card has been "painting backgrounds" with words since his debut record, *First Light*, in 1981. *Legacy* (which contains "Love Crucified Arose") was his second album, and he's continued to turn out consistently interesting, entertaining, award-winning releases about every other year or so since then. He's also authored 14 books to date, and his skills as an author have earned him numerous industry recognitions, such as the 2002 *Publisher's Weekly* Award, the 2001 Gold Medallion Book Award, the 1998 National Religious Broadcasters Chairman's Award and a 1989 C. S. Lewis Children's Book Award Nomination for *Sleep Sound in Jesus*. And as if those weren't enough opportunities to "use his words," he also hosts a weekly one-hour national radio program called *In the Studio with Michael Card*.

Card's musical expressions are unique in that each record reflects his current passion or pursuit. He has been known to base an entire album on a single book of the Bible. He has incorporated Celtic and liturgical music into his writing and been greatly influenced in his lyrical content by the books of Brennan Manning, C. S. Lewis and various other poets, philosophers and Christian apologists. This

brings us back to Emily Dickinson and "Love Crucified Arose," which, in 1983, rose to the #5 slot and then stayed on the Christian charts for 34 weeks.

When Michael Card was told which of his many songs were judged to be among the Top 100, he smiled and said, "I was a little surprised to see 'Love Crucified Arose' there—I didn't think it was that good of a song!" Then he paused and concluded, "But I do believe in the message of it, and the real point of that song is this: Because Jesus' grave ended in the resurrection, our graves are going to end in resurrection too."

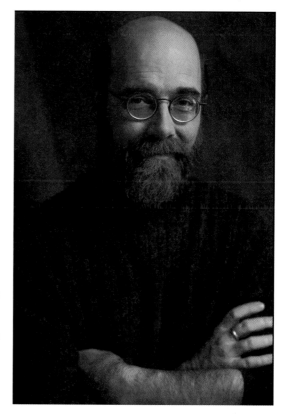

CRYSTAL LEWIS

PEOPLE GET READY, JESUS IS COMIN'

WRITTEN BY BRIAN RAY

RECORDED BY CRYSTAL LEWIS ON BEAUTY FOR ASHES (METRO ONE/MYRRH, 1996)

PRODUCED BY BRIAN RAY AND DAN POSTHUMA

1995 #1 IN CHRISTIAN RADIO FOR THREE WEEKS

1998 DOVE AWARD— FEMALE VOCALIST OF THE YEAR

42

When Crystal Lewis inked her first solo record deal, her proud father stood right beside her—because at the tender age of 17, Crystal required a co-signer. By 1996, when her hit song "People Get Ready, Jesus Is Comin'" was released, Crystal was already well into a thriving Christian music career.

Born in Corona, California in 1969 to a preaching father and a singing mother, Lewis was a natural for music ministry. At 15 she joined the kid musical *Hi Tops,* followed by a brief gig as lead singer of Wild Blue Yonder, a punkabilly band on Frontline Records. There Crystal met future husband and collaborator Brian Ray, who was the roommate of the band's drummer. When the band broke up after one album, Frontline offered her a solo contract, and Crystal Lewis (and her dad) signed on the dotted line. Throughout those first solo records, Lewis and Ray were students of the whole process, until they felt confident enough in 1992 to start their own label, Metro One. During that time, she was also stretching into other arenas, both figuratively and literally: fellow Frontline artist Benny Hester opened doors for Lewis to perform on television (Nickelodeon's *Roundhouse*) and at Greg Laurie's evangelistic Harvest Crusades.

In the early years of Metro One, Lewis and husband Ray produced several well-received projects and eventually signed a marketing and distribution deal between Metro One and larger label Myrrh. The first fruit of that new partnership was her pivotal 1996 project, *Beauty for Ashes.* The process had its difficulties: Brian and Crystal's first child, Solomon, was turning two, and Crystal was pregnant with Isabella. "I was endlessly emotional and uncomfortable during the whole process," Crystal remembers. But the finished album was a hit right out of the box, and one of the real gems from the album turned out to be "People Get Ready, Jesus Is Comin'," a triumphant anthem about preparing our hearts for the return of Christ.

Songwriter and husband Brian Ray recalls that "People Get Ready" was written in Costa Rica, where Crystal was on tour. "I remember being in the lobby lounge and there was a piano," he says. "I started to play a melody I had been humming in my head for a few days. Crystal had just finished doing some Harvest Crusades and I wanted her to have a song that

was very upfront about what it means to be a Christian. I wrote the words over the next few days, and with Crystal's help, made it into a singable tune."

Alisa Girard, of the vocal group ZOEgirl, has an especially soft spot for "People Get Ready, Jesus Is Comin'" because it was one of the songs that landed her the job in ZOEgirl. "It's an incredible song that Christians can rally around and get excited about," says Alisa.

"It's such an arresting song," agrees Benny Hester, who opened doors for Crystal all those years ago. "To this day, I just think she's one of the most powerful singers, and 'People Get Ready' couldn't be more suited to her."

125

AMY GRANT

BREATH OF HEAVEN (MARY'S SONG)

43

WRITTEN BY AMY GRANT AND CHRIS EATON

RECORDED BY AMY GRANT ON HOME FOR CHRISTMAS (MYRRH/WORD, 1992)

PRODUCED BY BROWN BANNISTER

ALSO RECORDED BY:
VINCE GILL ON BREATH OF HEAVEN: A CHRISTMAS COLLECTION

my Grant knows a good song when she hears one. Just take MercyMe's mega crossover hit, "I Can Only Imagine." Frontman Bart Millard, who wrote the song, originally offered it to Amy to record for her *Legacy of Hymns and Faith* album. After listening to it, she did decide to record the song, but she also had some advice for the band. She felt strongly that the song was a hit waiting to happen and that they needed to record "Imagine" on their own album as well. Needless to say, Ms. Grant was dead-on in her assessment, a fact that MercyMe gratefully acknowledges.

But that's certainly not the first time Amy made the right call. Step back a few years to the early '90s. Already a multi-platinum-selling artist with mainstream crossover success,

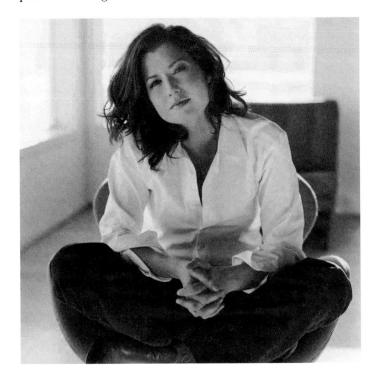

"One of the songs that makes me hold my breath is 'Breath of Heaven.' One of the reasons I love it so much is that our daughter dances to it very often. And there is just something ... that song is married to a dance. And, at best, her choreography of this song is truly 'body text.' Mary was very young, and the whole Jewish culture is so much into dance; dance is so much a part of the whole Jesus history. I cannot believe that young Mary, when she was overcome by the Holy Spirit, could not have danced her response."

GLORIA GAITHER

Amy was recording *Home for Christmas*, her second yuletide release. The first time she heard Chris Eaton's original "Breath of Heaven," it was already complete with music, verses and chorus. And while she immediately responded to the song, Amy wanted to rewrite the verses to personalize them and fit her holiday album.

Grant explains, "That song is so profound, but the chorus is so simple. It's authentic and perfectly written, because it uses an incredibly moving economy of words. And, selfishly, I just really wanted to be able to use the song on my Christmas record. So finally Chris said, 'Well, OK, just for this one version, we'll let you put a different lyric on there.' I said, 'Well, you couldn't possibly have written the lyric I'm thinking of, because I'm going to write it from a woman's perspective.' I was very pregnant at the time, and I felt like that was part of the inspiration for the song as I tried to imagine Mary's experience. We went into the recording studio with Brown Bannister producing and Shane Keister playing the piano and basically got it within one take."

It certainly seems that the newly rewritten song and the entire album were inspired, as *Home for Christmas* hit platinum status only two months after its release. The emotional,

haunting song connected with listeners in a unique way. It is written from Mary's perspective as a young girl—frightened, lonely, and expecting a child in circumstances that raised questions and eyebrows. Her viewpoint is beautifully explored in the piano-backed lyrics. Though Mary doubts her own position in God's plan, her faith in the goodness and mercy of her Father remains steadfast. Because of the intimate nature of the song, "Breath of Heaven" has become, in Grant's own words, "a prayer." As she went on to write in the CCM Books/Word Publishing book release of the same title, "It is a prayer that fits a lot of people's circumstances because it is a cry for mercy. Some nights on stage I can hardly get through the song for knowing all of the collective,

unspoken pain of the lives in front of me. And so the words become my prayer for the listener and the reader, as well as the singer."

STEVE GREEN

PEOPLE NEED THE LORD

44

WRITTEN BY GREG NELSON AND PHIL MCHUGH

RECORDED BY STEVE GREEN
ON STEVE GREEN
(SPARROW, 1984)

PRODUCED BY GREG NELSON

ALSO RECORDED BY:
RAY BOLTZ ON CLASSICS

CRAIG DUNCAN AND THE
SMOKY MOUNTAIN BAND ON
SWEET SWEET SPIRIT

Steve Green has always looked just like the squeaky-clean missionary kid he was raised to be. Handsome as a Ken doll, clean-cut and blessed with an astounding singing voice, he was the embodiment of a picture-perfect young Christian man—on the outside—at the time of his self-titled album release in 1984. According to Steve, things were actually very different on the inside.

"I guess in a nutshell, my story is that I was raised by these great missionary parents," Steve begins. "And though I picked up the rules and the regulations of Christianity, somewhere along the way I missed the heart of it. So all of my attempts at goodness were really for the wrong reasons; it was for acceptance or trying to fit into what I knew Christians wanted me to do. So eventually it became fake and phony. I was living externally one way, but in my heart a whole other way. I was trapped and caught in many areas of sin and disobedience, and all I know is, God rescued me. God turned the lights on, and for the first time I saw the mountain of my sin and understood my desperate need for a Savior. It all became clear, and I ran to Jesus for what He alone can provide."

Steve's life-changing experience was still very new when he

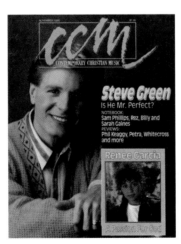

began work on his first Sparrow solo release. "I was in a very tender place spiritually, having just come through a pretty significant life turn-around," Steve recalls. "And 'People Need the Lord' was one of the first songs that was pitched to me for my record. It resonated for two reasons—first, because my parents had given their lives to evangelize,

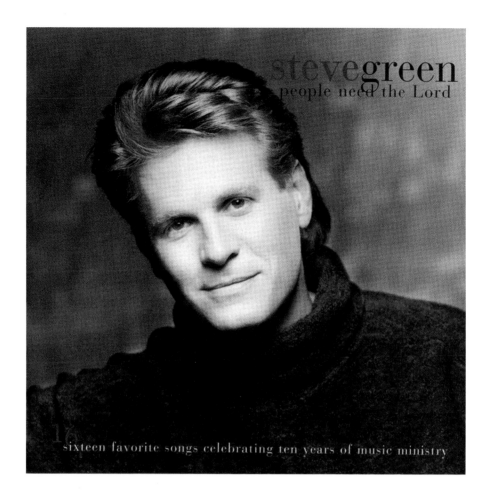

stevegreen
people need the Lord

sixteen favorite songs celebrating ten years of music ministry

and their love for the people they were serving around the world was motivated by Christ's love for them; so that was definitely one of the reasons why I gravitated to the song. The other reason was that for the first time, I suppose, I was realizing that it isn't just those who never heard about the Lord who needed Him." Steve continues slowly, "I knew that I was surrounded by people just like me who were living kind of an external, performance-based Christianity, but they had no light. I started thinking of us as the 'elder brothers'—those who never ran away from home but were just as lost as the prodigal."

"People Need the Lord" resonated with audiences as well, topping charts and paving the way for Green to win his first Dove Award for Male Vocalist of the Year. And in a perfect example of "coming full circle," the song has become the theme song for missions appeals everywhere. As pictures of a hungry, hurting world without Christ are shown, Steve's soaring voice reminds us that we all, Steve included, do so need the Lord.

BEBE & CECE WINANS

HEAVEN

WRITTEN BY BEBE WINANS AND KEITH THOMAS

RECORDED BY BEBE AND CECE WINANS ON HEAVEN (SPARROW/CAPITOL RECORDS, 1988)

PRODUCED BY KEITH THOMAS

1989 #3 IN CHRISTIAN RADIO

45

Here's a little-known fact: In 1980, BeBe Winans left his home in Detroit and traveled all the way to North Carolina to audition for the PTL Club Singers—and didn't make the cut. But his 16-year-old sister CeCe did, and a week later, Bebe was invited to join the group after all. Though the PTL Network eventually self-destructed, BeBe and CeCe emerged unscathed, with a Grammy nomination for their cover of "Up Where We Belong" to boot. In 1987, the brother and sister duo was signed to Sparrow Records and began a richly rewarding relationship with über-producer Keith Thomas, who artfully captured their unique brand of pop/R&B/gospel on their first, self-titled album. Not only were the two members of gospel music's most prominent family embraced by the Christian music industry, but

> "*Heaven*—man, I wore that record out! I remember, I went on a mission trip to Mexico and I had a jambox on my lap and played it over and over and over. I don't think anybody else in that youth group likes them anymore because of me, but I'm still a huge fan. I love every single thing about that record."
>
> **BART MILLARD OF MERCYME**

HEAVENLY REWARDS

1988 Dove Award—
New Artist: BeBe and CeCe Winans

1989 Grammy Award—
Best Male Gospel Performance: BeBe Winans;
Best Female Gospel Performance: CeCe Winans

1990 Dove Awards—
Pop/Contemporary Album: HEAVEN;
Pop/Contemporary Recorded Song: "Heaven";
Group: BeBe and CeCe Winans

by the mainstream market as well. The single "I.O.U. Me" from their first record reached #72 on Billboard's Black chart, #25 on their Adult Contemporary chart and #17 on Radio and Record's AC chart.

With Thomas again at the helm, BeBe and CeCe prepared for their second release. As CeCe remembers it, "Keith and BeBe wrote this song called 'Heaven,' and as soon as we heard it, we knew there was something magical about it. It's a song that just makes you smile, and makes you want to go to heaven too!" It became the title track of the album, which was released in 1988 and promptly propelled the duo to star status. "Heaven" featured a guest appearance by Whitney

Houston and became the first gospel recording to reach the Top 10 on Billboard's Hot R&B chart since Aretha Franklin's "Amazing Grace" did it in 1972. It was certified gold and won, among many other awards, matching Best Gospel Vocal Performance Grammy Awards in the Male and Female categories for BeBe and CeCe.

Summing up the unprecedented success of "Heaven" in an interview with *CCM Magazine*, CeCe stated simply, "I wish I could tell you that this was some great plan that we strategized, but we didn't. We just prayed, and BeBe, Keith and myself just made the album the best we could. The rest is God, as far as we're concerned."

MICHAEL W. SMITH

SECRET AMBITION

46

WRITTEN BY MICHAEL W. SMITH, AMY GRANT AND WAYNE KIRKPATRICK

RECORDED BY MICHAEL W. SMITH ON i 2 (EYE) (REUNION RECORDS, 1988)

PRODUCED BY MICHAEL W. SMITH AND WAYNE KIRKPATRICK

1988 GRAMMY NOMINATION—BEST MALE GOSPEL PERFORMANCE

1991 I 2 (EYE) IS CERTIFIED GOLD

Michael W. Smith's music video for his song "Secret Ambition" told the story of the Resurrection in a very powerful way, years before Mel Gibson's movie, *The Passion of The Christ*, became an unexpected global phenomenon.

"The cool story about the 'Secret Ambition' video is that this company that was going to shoot the video for the song offered to do it for free," Smith recalls. "They wanted it to follow the story of Jesus, and they wanted to shoot it on videotape. I just thought, *How tacky is that going to be?* I refused to do it for a year, until I finally succumbed to the pressure and said, 'OK, but we'll pay the extra—whatever it is—to shoot it on film, and we did it. In the end, it really was pretty remarkable and many, many people have come to the Lord through that video," Smith says.

As for the song that inspired the legendary video clip, the rockin' anthem complete with that killer guitar solo and unparalleled vocal delivery from Smith was yet another memorable songwriting experience alongside friends Amy Grant and Wayne Kirkpatrick.

"I'll never forget getting together with Wayne out at Amy's farm," Smith recalls. "First of all, just the music was written, and I felt like for 1988, it was a bit of a twist—especially the choruses, which were really different for me. I remember just

where I was when I said, 'This song's going on the record no matter what!' And then we still had the lyrics to write, so Wayne came up with the 'Secret Ambition' idea. I do think the song became very popular because of the video."

Michael W. Smith has made a career out of always keeping people guessing on what he will deliver next. Even after the experimental sound of *The Big Picture*, "Secret Ambition" was just one of the many musical surprises on the *i 2 (EYE)* record. That is something that's apparent from the opening sounds of the album's first track, "Hand of Providence," the unexpected but sonically effective Stryper contribution (namely Oz Fox and Michael Sweet) on the background vocals of the

relationship-themed "All You're Missing Is a Heartache," the precursor to his future instrumental work of "Ashton" and the Revelation-based inspiration on the beautiful, keyboard-driven worship ditty "The Throne."

Whether working with Smith or hanging out at his place for dinner, Sweet sings nothing but this artist's praises on any project he works on. "He's a real good friend of ours, and I actually did sing some backup vocals on a couple of his tracks," Sweet says. "He's been to our shows; we've been to his shows. What a great artist; what an incredible writer. He's really made his mark on the Christian industry in such a powerful way. I respect Michael a lot."

POINT OF GRACE

JESUS WILL STILL BE THERE

WRITTEN BY ROBERT STERLING AND JOHN MANDEVILLE

RECORDED ON POINT OF GRACE (WORD, 1993)

PRODUCED BY ROBERT STERLING AND JOHN MAYS

1994 #4 INSPIRATIONAL SONG OF THE YEAR

PEAKED AT #1 ON INSPIRATIONAL CHARTS, MAY 16

47

The debut album from Point of Grace was an undeniable industry phenomenon. Yet during the production process, the four women felt a sense of uneasiness as they acknowledged a profound absence from the project.

Shelley Breen of Point of Grace recalls: "We were doing our very first album for Word Records, and I remember us sitting around a table and telling our producer, Robert Sterling, 'We have a lot of great songs here, but feel like none of them actually say the word "Jesus,"' and that really bothered us." That night, Sterling married the words about the man Jesus to the beautiful music created by John Mandeville to create the endearing hit, "Jesus Will Still Be There." The next day, the girls cried as they heard what Shelley describes as "a universal song."

The song quickly became one of the six #1 hits off of the women's debut CD. Achieving success on the Inspirational, AC and CCM charts, there is little denying the commercial success and appeal of the song. Featuring the group's signature compelling harmonies and soaring melodies, "Jesus Will Still Be There" caught the attention of fellow musicians as well. Avalon vocalist Melissa Greene says, "They've had many great songs, but 'Jesus Will Still Be There,' I wanted to sing."

The quartet's sound seemed to have struck a chord with a generation of young women. Melissa also says that she thinks "everyone wanted to be in Point of Grace. All the girls at least."

It was all these girls

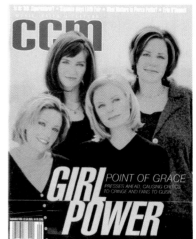

that were truly the focus of much of Point of Grace's ministry. Deeply committed and involved with Mercy Ministries and young women struggling with problems from addiction to pregnancy and eating disorders, the four women of Point of Grace modeled the same compassion that they sing about in this anthem about their Savior.

Their character has shone through, not only in the lyrics to their music, but in the holistic package and presentation of their group and music. Bonnie Keen of First Call recalls the girls' first tour. "I could see in their faces that they would try and do the right thing no matter what. And they have taken the platform where they could have just sailed through . . . they've gone out to speak hope to those girls, and I really, really respect that."

"Jesus Will Still Be There" echoes the message of endearing compassion. As Shelley says, "Whatever your situation is, you can fit yourself into that song and it's such a great

reminder that no matter what happens, one thing will always be there and that is Jesus and His love and His protection over us. . . . I always tell Rob, 'You'll never really know what you did when you went and wrote that song, and it also says the word "Jesus," and that's a good thing!'"

A good thing, indeed! An anthem of reassurance for everyone, the song says it best:

When it looks like you've lost it all,
And you haven't got a prayer,
Jesus will still be there.

Russ Harrington

135

TWILA PARIS

THE WARRIOR IS A CHILD

WRITTEN BY TWILA PARIS

RECORDED BY TWILA PARIS ON THE WARRIOR IS A CHILD (MILK AND HONEY, 1984)

PRODUCED BY JONATHAN DAVID BROWN

A 1998 CCM POLL CHOSE "THE WARRIOR IS A CHILD" AS "ONE OF THE 10 BEST CONTEMPORARY CHRISTIAN SONGS OF ALL TIME"

48

The paradox of Twila Paris's song about the frailty of the inner spirit is that it proved to be one of the strongest songs to ever grace the Christian music charts. Spending 18 weeks at #1 in 1984, the song catapulted Twila's career and reputation as a singer and inspired songwriter. As Dallas Holm puts it, "That was her defining song."

Twila looks back at the circumstances surrounding the writing of "Warrior" with a bit of wryness. "I was probably 22 when that was written, which is hilarious on some level because I had very little understanding of what the song was actually about at that age." If artistry is about reaching beyond your means, however, "Warrior Is a Child" does just that with a spiritual profundity beyond her years and life experiences. Twila says, "That's just another one of those things, another aspect of the mystery of songwriting that I've noticed over the years; I had, from time to time, written way beyond, way out of my depth in terms of concept and spiritual maturity."

The compelling and revealing lyrics—"People say that I'm amazing, strong beyond my years, but they don't see inside of me, I'm hiding all the tears"—offered audiences a peek at the vulnerability of the rising talent. Written after her second album, while still a fresh new face in the industry, Twila was beginning to feel the pressure of her developing fame. "It was really just in those first months when people were starting to hear my music and respond to it. I started realizing that people get this idea of who they think you are and they have certain expectations." The mounting stresses of her music and ministry often left Twila feeling isolated and overwhelmed. She remembers thinking, *I just write these little songs and sing them. Yes, I do try to live out and work out what I write and be faithful in it. But that doesn't mean that I'm like an elder in the church, you know!*

Luckily, however, she was seeking the counsel of the spiritual leaders in her home church. One particular Sunday night, an elder talked about this notion of vulnerability. "He used the metaphor of the army, God's army. No matter if we're a general in the army and have been serving God for years, and have all this experience and He's given us lots of responsibility—before Him, we're still a child." She continues, "So boy, I took that to heart and I went home, and with just the beginning experiences and the little bit of understanding I had, I wrote that song."

Initially Twila thought that "Warrior Is a Child" was going to be just for her. She told her producer, "We probably shouldn't record this song; it's too depressing. Everyone is going to misunderstand it, and they're not going to like it. And he was like, 'Are you nuts?' He really got it. So, thank the Lord that sometimes other people help us choose what to put on our albums!"

137

RANDY
STONEHILL

SHUT DE DO

WRITTEN BY RANDY
STONEHILL

RECORDED BY RANDY
STONEHILL ON EQUATOR
(MYRRH RECORDS, 1983)

PRODUCED BY TERRY TAYLOR

1990 LIVE VERSION APPEARED
ON STONEHILL'S UNTIL WE
HAVE WINGS

1996 STUDIO VERSION
REAPPEARED ON STONEHILL'S
OUR RECOLLECTIONS

49

With the release of his eighteenth album, *Edge of the World* (Fair Oaks Records) two years ago, Randy Stonehill is one of the few high-profile "Jesus music" pioneers who continues to record and tour more than three decades after co-founding what would become the contemporary Christian music industry. The southern California-based artist/songwriter/producer hit the music scene in 1970 under the guidance of his then-mentor Larry Norman, who is generally regarded as the patron father of modern Christian music. Stonehill got off to a fast start as he wrote and performed the early classic "I Love You," which was prominently featured on the soundtrack to the 1972 film *Time to Run*, a movie nationally distributed by the Billy Graham Evangelistic Association. Stonehill would go on to compose and record numerous Christian music staples, including renowned titles such as "King of Hearts," "Keep Me Runnin'," "Turning 30," "Christmas at Denny's" and "Who Will Save the Children?" Another potent landmark was his songwriting collaboration with Keith Green and Todd Fishkind on "Your Love Broke Thru," which became Phil Keaggy's signature song (see song #62).

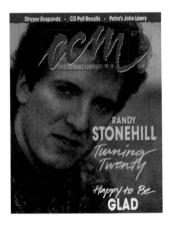

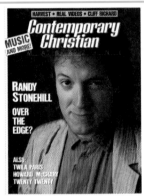

But it was Stonehill's eccentrically delightful 1983 composition "Shut De Do" which would go on to make curious inroads into Christian pop, rock, urban gospel, country gospel and choral circles. In fact, 18 years later, the song even appeared on an album recorded by the Brigham Young University Choir. (Who knew it would someday connect with the Mormon demographic?)

"Shut De Do" made its debut on Stonehill's sixth album, *Equator*, which eventually reached #3 on *CCM's* Top 50 Album Sales chart. A playful romp which employed a decidedly Jamaican flavor, "Shut De Do" featured Stonehill supported musically by only a small studio choir, a guest soloist (Regina Peoples) and a dose of creative percussion. The song became such a concert favorite that at one point Stonehill began performing a version more than 11 minutes long.

Today, after more than 20 years since its release, "Shut De Do" continues to be a popular highlight of Stonehill's live show.

SWITCHFOOT

DARE YOU

50

TO MOVE

WRITTEN BY JON FOREMAN

RECORDED BY SWITCHFOOT ON LEARNING TO BREATHE (SPARROW, 2000)

PRODUCED BY CHARLIE PEACOCK

2003 "WE'RE CHRISTIAN BY FAITH, NOT GENRE."— SWITCHFOOT BASSIST TIM FOREMAN TELLS *ROLLING STONE*

ACTIVE IN THE FIGHT AGAINST HIV/AIDS AND POVERTY IN AFRICA, SWITCHFOOT CONSISTENTLY DIRECTS FANS TO VISIT DATA.ORG AND TAKE ACTION

When artist/producer Charlie Peacock discovered the young San Diego rock band Chin Up in 1996, he knew he'd found something special. Special, yes, but one of the world's future big-time rock acts? Signing the alternative trio to his own re:think label, Peacock convinced the musically inclined surfers to change their band's name. Lifting a term from their favorite recreational activity, the lads dubbed themselves "Switchfoot" and set sail with their 1997 debut, *The Legend of Chin*. Averaging 150 shows each year, the band enjoyed a growing and increasingly devoted fanbase as it released its first three albums. The third, 2000's impressive *Learning to Breathe*, featuring the standout track, "I Dare You to Move," would go on to be nominated for a Grammy Award.

The following year, as Warner Brothers entered pre-production on the 2002 motion picture *A Walk to Remember*, the film's star, singer Mandy Moore, lobbied to have Switchfoot represented prominently on the movie's soundtrack. Apparently, when Mandy Moore speaks, Warner Brothers listens. When all was said and done, the film (and accompanying CD soundtrack) featured no less than four previously released Switchfoot songs and a duet by the band's lead singer, Jon Foreman, and Moore. "I Dare You to Move," already a favorite among Switchfoot fans, was emphasized as the opening song on the motion picture soundtrack.

Asked about the emerging track, Switchfoot's Foreman responds, "I love to write songs. I've been at it since I could reach the piano. It's one of my favorite ways to pass the time. Music helps me sort out who I am, so my songs usually end up being somewhat autobiographical. I've always felt the deepest connection with honest songs, so I try to write with sincerity. ['I Dare You to Move'] is an attempt to honestly face the gap between who I am and who I want to be; between the way the world spins and the way it should be. I've heard that we only use a small part of our brain. Maybe our soul is the same way. And maybe we're half asleep most of our lives, simply reacting to the stimulus our brain receives. Action, true action, is rare indeed."

With *A Walk to Remember*'s popularity at the box office, the film's soundtrack served as a mass introduction of Switchfoot to the general market. Then came 2003 and the release of *The Beautiful Letdown*, Switchfoot's first effort to be backed by a major mainstream label (Columbia). The powers that be were so impressed with "I Dare You to Move," they took the original version, retooled it and included it on Switchfoot's Columbia debut, making this the third album it appeared on in a three-year span. (Curiously, the song was given the slightly revised title: "Dare You to Move.")

"We always make it a point to talk to people outside after the shows," says Foreman as he contemplates the song's connection with fans, "and I recently had a kid come up to me and give me a big hug because he was so affected by 'Dare You to Move.' Apparently, he was going through some really rough times and wasn't sure if he wanted to live anymore, but heard the song and was inspired. That's incredible. On days when you're wondering what you're doing playing a show in

some small town in the middle of nowhere, you think about moments like that and realize that you're part of a bigger story than your own."

Switchfoot and its label elected to launch *The Beautiful Letdown* with a different song, "Meant to Live," as the lead single. By year's end, the song camped out in the top five of America's alternative rock radio charts, pushing sales of their new album to more than half a million copies. As 2004 unfolded, Switchfoot became video darlings for both MTV and VH1 as "Meant to Live" became a multi-format hit, also entering the top echelon of the pop radio charts.

The table had been set. Even as "Meant to Live" continued to gain airplay at Top 40 stations, Switchfoot unloaded its brilliant "Dare You to Move" single on alternative radio. As the second faith-charged track from *The Beautiful Letdown*, "Dare You to Move" immediately wiped out any naïve notions of Switchfoot being a one-hit wonder. By mid-2004 "Dare You to Move" entrenched itself in the top 10 of the alternative charts and further fueled *The Beautiful Letdown*'s momentum—at one point, the CD had become one of the 20 best-selling albums of any kind in America, while logging total sales of more than one million copies.

EVIE

MIRROR

WRITTEN BY RON HARRIS

51

RECORDED BY EVIE ON
MIRROR (WORD
RECORDS, 1977)

PRODUCED BY PHIL NAISH

1977 AND 1978 DOVE
AWARD—FEMALE VOCALIST
OF THE YEAR

Before Amy Grant, before Rebecca St. James, there was Evie. Contemporary Christian music's first sweetheart, this dimpled blonde pioneered the style we now call "inspirational." She was born Evie Tornquist to Norwegian immigrant parents and began her Christian music career in 1971. Signed to Word Records, she was soon paired with songwriter Ron Harris and began a successful partnership that resulted in many of her signature songs, including the way-too-cute classic, "I'm Only 4 Foot 11 But I'm Going to Heaven (And That Makes Me Feel 10 Feet Tall)." She was a huge hit at the very first Estes Park Christian Artist's Seminar in 1975 and became a regular guest performer at Billy Graham crusades.

But behind the adorably marketable face was a deeply spiritual young woman who eventually grew tired and a little disenchanted with the emerging corporate side of the Christian music industry. In 1981, after marrying a minister named Pelle Karlsson, Evie quietly bowed out of her flourishing career. She became the mother of two children and spent the next couple of decades more or less out of the public eye, with an occasional appearance on a Gaither Homecoming video or as a spokesperson for the Sky Angel Network.

Speaking recently from her home in Florida, the ever gracious Evie Tornquist Karlsson cheerfully offered these thoughts about "Mirror."

> "Evie is a lady that definitely impacted my life. I listened to 'Mirror' and all her albums. I'd go buy her songbooks and sit at the piano and sing her stuff all day! What always impressed me was her genuineness, her realness."
>
> SANDI PATTY

"Ron Harris is a masterful, skilled songwriter, and I love the fact that this one is always such fun to sing. When I first heard the song, I was very, very taken by the thought that even my simple little face—and all of our faces as believers in Jesus Christ—can be a direct manifestation of God's love to somebody. As someone looks upon our countenance, our eyes—being the windows of the soul—can exude a powerful presence that comes from the living Holy Spirit within us. And even as we laugh or weep or speak seriously, from our countenance comes a living testimony, if you will; a living story of what Jesus means to us."

DALLAS HOLM

RISE AGAIN

52

WRITTEN BY DALLAS HOLM

RECORDED BY DALLAS HOLM ON DALLAS HOLM AND PRAISE LIVE (BENSON RECORDS, 1977)

PRODUCED BY PHIL JOHNSON

ALSO RECORDED BY:
RAY BOLTZ ON THE CLASSICS

CRISTY LANE ON ONE DAY AT A TIME

BILL GAITHER ON REVIVAL

GREG LONG ON BORN AGAIN

In 1976, a young singer named Dallas Holm, traveling with the evangelist David Wilkerson, decided to branch out and begin a youth ministry. Wanting to take the message to college campuses and the beaches at spring break, Dallas figured that a singer with a band would relate much better than a solo artist. His friend Phil Johnson suggested he audition Phil's brother Tim and his wife, LaDonna. There also happened to be a pretty good bass player working at their warehouse named Randy Adams. So "Dallas Holm and Praise" was born, and now all they needed were some songs to sing.

Dallas began writing new material, but it wasn't coming easy. "Normally I can sit down and come up with some kind of idea either musically or lyrically," Dallas says. "But this time I was totally dry. Finally out of frustration I began to pray, 'Well, Lord, if You were transported to this time and this place, what would You say?' And as hokey as it may sound, I got this mental image of Jesus with the beard and the robe and the whole thing just standing onstage with a guitar. I didn't hear any voices from heaven, no thunderclaps or lightning flashes, but I began to write, and it was literally like taking dictation. In 10 minutes tops, the music and words came out and it was done."

Six weeks after the band was formed, they decided to cut a record. "We didn't know anything; we did everything wrong you could possibly do," Dallas laughingly recalls. "First of all, we decided to record it live, and nobody was buying live albums! We spent a whopping $4,500 producing the whole thing, using semi-professional equipment with these cheesy eight-track channel boards set up in a camping trailer. We recorded it at Lindale High School in a 300-seat auditorium. It was truly live with no fixes. We just blew through it and sang our songs; the whole thing took 45 minutes."

Dallas knew immediately from

the audience's reaction to "Rise Again" that something special was happening. But the powers that be at the record company chose another single to be the first release. That song didn't exactly burn up the charts, and Benson Records, which had optimistically shipped an unprecedented 100,000 copies to bookstores, began to receive an alarming amount of returns. But in those heady days of pre-playlist Christian radio, station managers pretty much spun whatever they liked. "Everybody started discovering 'Rise Again,'" Dallas says. "Every time they played it on the radio, the phones would all light up. People started rushing to the bookstores saying, 'Where can we get that song?' And the bookstore owners were all going, 'Well, uh, we just shipped it back!'"

"Rise Again" went on to win the 1977 Dove Award for Song of the Year. In press releases and interviews, it is repeatedly referred to by countless Christian music artists as one of the songs that most influenced their lives, music and ministry. Looking back on the comedy of errors that produced the song, Dallas shakes his head. "Our hearts were in the right place, but we truly didn't know what we were doing," he says. "And it was like God just said, 'Oh yeah? Well, watch this!'"

"Rise Again" has also been covered by more artists than Dallas Holm can count. His personal favorite? "No question—the best cut anybody ever did of that song was Bob Dylan," Dallas says. "Somebody gave me a bootleg copy of a 1980 Dylan concert in Seattle when he was doing his *Slow Train Coming* material. He even called it the 'Rise Again Tour.' It was just killer; I mean, can't you just hear that voice singing, 'Go ahead . . . drive the nails'? Dylan really got it."

SONGS OF RESURRECTION

"O DEATH, WHERE IS YOUR VICTORY? O DEATH, WHERE IS YOUR STING?"
(1 Cor. 15:55, NASB)

"Easter Song"—2nd Chapter of Acts
"He's Alive"—Don Francisco
"RISE AGAIN"—DALLAS HOLM
"Still Rolls the Stone"—Bob Bennett
"The Rock (That Was Rolled Away)"—Clay Crosse
"Was It a Morning Like This?"—Sandi Patti
"Driving Nails"—Bruce Carroll
"Sunday's on the Way"—Carman
"He Rolled away the Stone"—Michelle Pillar
"Here He Comes Back"—Michelle Pillar
"Didn't He"—Randy Matthews
"How Could You Say No"—Billy Sprague
"The Great Exchange"—Bruce Carroll
"The Cross That Bears His Name"—Cheri Keaggy
"The Warrior"—Chuck Girard
"The Victor"—Jamie Owens-Collins/Keith Green
"Wood Between the Worlds"—Bob Ayala
"He's Risen"—John Michael Talbot and Terry Talbot
"Alive and Well"—Cindy Morgan
"It Is Finished"—Scott Wesley Brown
"Why?"—Michael Card
"Up from the Dead"—Dana Key

DON FRANCISCO

HE'S ALIVE

53

WRITTEN BY DON FRANCISCO

RECORDED BY DON FRANCISCO ON FORGIVEN (NEWPAX, 1977)

PRODUCED BY JOHN W. THOMPSON AND SHANE KEISTER

1998 FRANCISCO RECORDED A NEW VERSION OF "HE'S ALIVE," WHICH APPEARS ON HE'S ALIVE AND HE'S STILL ALIVE

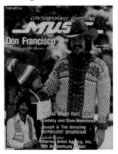

Don Francisco is best known for his unique, narrative style of songwriting. He developed this craft during his first years as an artist on Benson's New Pax label. Born in Louisville, Kentucky in 1946, Francisco was the son of an Old Testament teacher at Southern Baptist Theological Seminary.

In his teen years, he rebelled against his parents' faith and pursued a secular music career. But a supernatural experience in his twenties turned him around, and he decided to use his music to express his relationship with God. His first album, 1976's *Brother of the Son*, included his first story-song, "Come and Follow." After that, it became a conscious choice to write songs in that style; he had learned that painting a picture, rather than pointing a finger, was a more effective way of getting the gospel into listeners' hearts. As he told *CCM* in 1982, "The songs that tend to have the most power are stories."

"For years—it still happens—people come up and say, 'I love your song "He's Alive." ' And I'll go, 'I didn't write that,' and they go, 'Yes you did!' 'No, I didn't write "He's Alive." ' 'Yes, I have it on record.' 'No, I wrote "Rise Again." ' 'Oh.' And I asked Don one time some years ago, 'Don, do people ever come up to you and thank you for writing "Rise Again?" ' And he just cracked up and said, 'All the time! Every concert, somebody always comes up and says, "You're gonna sing 'Rise Again,' right?" ' And Don goes, 'I didn't write "Rise Again.'" 'Yes, you did! . . .' "

DALLAS HOLM

His second album, *Forgiven,* included a few more character-driven songs, including "Jehoshophat" and "Adam, Where Are You?" But the one that forever labeled Don a storyteller was "He's Alive," which went on to earn a 1980 Dove Award as Song of the Year, with Don also taking home the award for Songwriter of the Year. The song holds the record for the longest-running chart single in the history of Christian radio (in fact, it was the #1 song when *CCM*'s first chart was published).

The inspiration came from a different song Francisco had been playing in concert at the time. That song, about the Crucifixion, focused on suffering and death. "I sat down with the intention of trying to write a song about the Resurrection," Francisco says in the liner notes for *Don Francisco: The Early Works* (Benson), "because, let's face it, the Crucifixion is just half the story, and the worst half by far."

Gloria Gaither remembers the first time she heard the song, when a friend had brought Francisco to come in and play for her and Bill. "He came in and basically did the very same rendition that we've heard him do a thousand times since, just by himself. And I'm telling you, I was just shaking, and the tears were streaming down my face the first time I heard it. This is such truth and so like it must have been—and it was said so well."

In writing the song, Francisco originally tried to tell the story from the perspective of Thomas, envisioning the room where the disciples were when Jesus appeared to them and spoke to Thomas. But he couldn't make it work. "So, I tried it from Peter's perspective," he said. "I was able to put a lot of my deep-set feelings in Peter's experience."

KEITH GREEN

THERE IS A REDEEMER

54

WRITTEN BY MELODY GREEN

RECORDED BY KEITH GREEN ON SONGS FOR THE SHEPHERD (PRETTY GOOD RECORDS, 1982)

PRODUCED BY BILL MAXWELL AND KEITH GREEN

1992 BROWN BANNISTER AND KELLY WILLARD PERFORMED "THERE IS A REDEEMER" ON NO COMPROMISE: REMEMBERING THE MUSIC OF KEITH GREEN

2002 YOUR LOVE BROKE THROUGH: THE WORSHIP SONGS OF KEITH GREEN INCLUDES A NEW VERSION OF "THERE IS A REDEEMER," PERFORMED BY MICHELLE TUMES

Songs for the Shepherd was released just a few months before the horrific plane crash that would take the life of Keith Green, two of his young children and another entire family. It was only Green's fourth album, and it was as full of his trademark passion and conviction as ever.

"We're calling it an album of praise and worship," Keith told *CCM* in May 1982, "because every single song is written as a worship song to the Lord or as a message from God to us, His beloved Christians." He explained that the album would certainly have its upbeat moments, with electric guitars and such, but mentioned that he had also been quite moved during the recording process. "There's one or two songs on there where I almost could not record the vocal because I was crying so hard," he said. "And the anointing of the Spirit falling was so strong I almost had to stop recording."

One of the standout cuts from that album is "There Is a Redeemer," written by Keith's wife, Melody. It is a song that has long stuck in the hearts of listeners, serving as a bridge between conservative-leaning worshipers and the growing presence of modern praise music.

"As a young lad growing up in England, 'There Is a Redeemer' was a big song," remembers Martin Smith, vocalist for the praise/rock band Delirious?. "Even in the church that I grew up in, which was quite conservative, where the ladies wore hats and the men wore suits, they would all be singing 'There Is a Redeemer.' The days of drum kits and electric guitars in church were still far away at that stage."

As *Songs for the Shepherd* was still only beginning to circulate, on July 28, 1982, there was a small plane crash, which took the lives of Keith, 3-year-old Josiah and 2-year-old Bethany Green. Wife and mother, Melody, was home with 1-year-old Rebekah and was six weeks pregnant with their fourth child, Rachel. Keith was only 28.

music . . . There's a station here that plays him once in a while and they'll wedge it between whatever's on the radio now, and it actually sounds better than most of the stuff they're playing," he laughs. "It's like you want to call them up and go, 'This is song-writing! This is what we're supposed to be doing here!'"

Keith Green once said, "The only music minister to whom the Lord will say, 'Well done, thou good and faithful servant,' is the one whose life proves what their lyrics are saying, and to whom music is the least important part of their life. Glorifying the only worthy One has to be a minister's most impor-tant goal."

And although Keith is now with Jesus, his songs, performances and words continue to impact lives. Last Days Ministries, started by Keith and Melody, is still going strong, more than 20 years later.

Dallas Holm has come to appreciate the songs and performances of Green even more today than he did 20 years ago. "Oh man, his

"I actually took Keith and his two oldest kids fishing about two weeks before his plane went down. Keith had never fished and he always used to make fun of me for doing it. So finally I said, 'Keith, have you ever fished?' 'Well, no . . .' And I said, 'Then you've got nothing to say until you come fishing with me!' So he came fishing and they actually caught some! The last memory I have of Keith was when we got back to the house and we had brought some little sunfish with us. There was an inflatable pool there, just about five feet around, and we filled it up with water and put the fish in the pool and his little boy in the pool with them. And he was just in heaven playing with all those fish in that water! And that was the last I ever saw Keith."

DALLAS HOLM

GOD'S PROPERTY

STOMP

55

WRITTEN BY KIRK FRANKLIN, GEORGE CLINTON JR., GARRY M. SHIDER, WALTER MORRISON

RECORDED BY KIRK FRANKLIN AND GOD'S PROPERTY ON GOD'S PROPERTY FROM KIRK FRANKLIN'S NU NATION (B-RITE, 1997)

PRODUCED BY BIG YAM AND VICTOR M.

#1 ON BILLBOARD'S R&B ALBUMS CHART FOR FIVE WEEKS

1998 BILLBOARD'S YEAR-END CHART: TOP GOSPEL ARTIST

1998 GRAMMY AWARD— BEST GOSPEL ALBUM BY A CHOIR OR CHORUS

1998 DOVE AWARD—URBAN ALBUM OF THE YEAR

Long before it was commonplace to see a few of your favorite Christian artists on MTV and VH1, Kirk Franklin did what seemed like a cataclysmic feat back in 1997: He introduced gospel to pop radio and MTV viewers without sacrificing the integrity of the message in the process, with a little ditty called "Stomp."

When describing her friend and fellow artist, CeCe Winans found herself at a loss for words. "Well what can I say? He put another face to gospel music, and he opened the door, I think, for a lot of young people to come to the Lord," she says. "'Stomp' was a song that made you ready to get up, dance and move; then when you heard the lyrics, it was like, 'OK, it's fine to move to this!' And so I thank God for him and his ministry and all his songs. But

'Stomp' was definitely a great one that I think we'll dance to forever."

Charismatic, outspoken and a proponent of diversity inside and outside of the church walls, Franklin used his real-life struggles to relate to the masses along with a soundtrack that was simply irresistible to listeners. And apparently his strategy worked, as he became one of the biggest sellers in the history of gospel music. Later on, he would collaborate with a myriad of artists—in and outside of Christian music—including U2's Bono, Mary J. Blige, R. Kelly, Crystal Lewis, TobyMac and more.

Kirk's testimony is akin to that of the prodigal son. He grew up with music and faith as an integral part of his life and began learning to play the piano at the age of four. He was offered a record contract when he was only seven; however, his aunt and uncle turned down the offer. Instead, Franklin was one of the key players in his church choir at the Mt. Rose Baptist Church in Dallas, Texas.

As a teenager, though, Kirk fought against his roots and rebelled against his beliefs and music. In his biography, he says, "Trust me, there were times when I could've been killed, I could've been shot, I could've been addicted to drugs or alcohol . . . until a friend was killed."

After that reality check, he returned to the path he knew was right all along and began creating his own brand of gospel music. Franklin achieved crossover stardom when he hooked up with God's Property—a gospel group from Texas consisting of more than 50 members and a five-piece backup band. Of this unique partnership, Franklin comments, "Our music transcends race . . . our music is about sending the only message that can save the lives of our youth . . . white, black and otherwise . . . the message that God loves them and has a plan for them."

7 TAKES ON THE PRODIGAL SON

"While he was still a long way off, his father saw him, and felt compassion for him. . ." (Luke 15:20). Songs for all of us who come to our senses and come home.

"Love Waits for You"—Brown Bannister

"The Prodigal (I'll Be Waiting)"—Amy Grant

"When God Ran"—Benny Hester

"The Prodigal Son Suite"—Keith Green

"Prodigal Son"—Steve Grace

"The Prodigal"—Russ Lee

"Please Come Back"—Michelle Tumes

SANDI PATTI

VIA DOLOROSA

WRITTEN BY BILLY SPRAGUE AND NILES BOROP

RECORDED BY SANDI PATTI ON SONGS FROM THE HEART (WORD, 1984)

PRODUCED BY GREG NELSON

ALSO APPEARED ON SANDI'S THE FINEST MOMENTS (1989) AND LIBERTAD ME DAS (1998)

SANDI GRACED THE COVER OF CCM MAGAZINE IN JANUARY 1983, DECEMBER 1984 AND APRIL 1988

56

S andi Patti's voice and music have long been associated with church music—and for good reason. Growing up in Oklahoma and later California with a music minister father and a mother who taught piano, Sandi traveled and sang with her parents as the Ron Patty Family. In college, she moved on to recording jingles in order to earn money, and in 1978 recorded a custom record. While performing concerts in California, Sandi came to the attention of the legendary Bill Gaither, who hired her as a background vocalist and soon gave her a featured spot in his concerts. Word Records promptly signed her and released her first album, which officially began the astounding 20-plus year career that would ultimately bring Sandi 39 Dove Awards (including 11 consecutive Female Vocalist of the Year honors), five Grammy Awards, three platinum records and five gold albums.

One of Sandi's all-time favorite songs is her 1984 vocal masterpiece, "Via Dolorosa." When asked to comment on it, she immediately pays homage to the writers of the song. "I think the challenge for a songwriter is always to find a new way to say the same story. When 'Via Dolorosa' came along my path, I just was so blown away because it did just that. It told the story but in a new and fresh and incredibly artistic way." Sandi adds, "Because of the words *via dolorosa* being Latin and Spanish, we chose to do part of the song in Spanish. And that was always one of those little spur-of-the-moment decisions that proved to be a really powerful one as well." The result was a beautiful, bilingual epic that features Sandi's soaring vocal set to a backdrop of lush orchestral music. As *CCM Magazine*'s cover story on Sandi in December of 1984 noted, the centerpiece of *Songs from the Heart* "is an electrifying retelling of

Christ's climb to Calvary titled 'Via Dolorosa.' It fully reveals Sandi Patti's unquestioned vocal artistry, as she makes the song her own with a virtuoso performance."

The years surrounding this song and album proved to be golden ones for Sandi, with multiple radio hits, gold- and platinum-selling records, and mainstream media appearances such as her much-heralded National Anthem performance at the ABC-televised rededication ceremony of the Statue of Liberty. And while later years brought a divorce scandal that threatened to end her award-winning career, Sandi ultimately weathered the storm with humility and grace. But her amazing voice—the voice for church and inspirational music—has never wavered, and her loyal fans have remained intact and supportive.

In 2004, the Gospel Music Association inducted Sandi into the Gospel Music Hall of Fame. During that ceremony, the humble "girl from Oklahoma" gave an acceptance speech that expressed her heart's desire. She said simply, "I want to be remembered as a woman who loved the Lord with her whole heart, who loved her family and loved life. And, when she got a chance, she sang about it."

Michael Gomez

153

ANDRÁE CROUCH

JESUS IS THE ANSWER

WRITTEN BY ANDRÁE CROUCH

RECORDED BY ANDRÁE
CROUCH & THE DISCIPLES
ON LIVE AT CARNEGIE HALL
(LIGHT, 1973)

PRODUCED BY ANDRÁE
CROUCH

BEFORE IT BECAME
COMMONPLACE TO SEE
CHRISTIAN ARTISTS ON
TELEVISION, ANDRÁE
CROUCH & THE DISCIPLES
WERE MUSICAL GUESTS ON
SUCH SHOWS AS *THE
TONIGHT SHOW WITH
JOHNNY CARSON* (1971) &
SATURDAY NIGHT LIVE (1980
& 1984)

57

One of the most influential figures in modern Christian music, it would be difficult to overestimate the contributions of songwriter, conductor, performer and pastor Andráe Crouch. Long before Kirk Franklin melded church music with funk, before Fred Hammond bridged the gap between traditional black gospel and praise and worship, before Amy Grant, before Michael W. Smith, there was Andráe Crouch—opening doors, building bridges and innovating contemporary Christian music in ways the casual observer could not imagine.

"Oh my goodness, Andráe Crouch, all these songs," gushes Amy Grant. "I mean, how many times have we all sung and re-sung these songs? 'To God Be the Glory,' 'Soon and Very Soon,' 'The Blood Will Never Lose Its Power.' His songs are powerful because they are highly emotional and have a lot of theology. That's a dynamic combination."

Born in 1950 in San Francisco, California, Crouch got his musical start at his father's church and began playing piano and writing music at the age of nine with no formal musical training. By the mid-'60s, he had formed Andráe Crouch and the Disciples, establishing a reputation for electrifying live performances all over the globe. Over the next 20 years, Andráe Crouch and the Disciples appeared on television, performed at the Hollywood Bowl and Carnegie Hall, and toured around the world.

The early albums gave glimpses of his genius, but the first one to really connect with record buyers was the 1973 classic *Live at Carnegie Hall*, possibly because it was the first to capture the fervor of the live performances. "This album is not a slick or watered-down album," it boldly stated on the back cover. "It is rough and honest."

"*Live at Carnegie Hall* was life-changing for me," notes Michael W. Smith. "I grew up on Andráe

Crouch. All of his songs are great, but 'Jesus Is the Answer,' that's the one I would truly recommend." Evie Tornquist agrees. "I love that song. In fact, I was talking to someone recently who was going through tremendous doubts, and that individual asked me, 'If it's true that Jesus is the answer and He is the only way, why are the Christians with this message not taking it more seriously?' And that challenged the snot out of me; I felt humbled and convicted."

The song's simple, singable chorus has been embraced by the church as an anthem, but is also a vital clue to Crouch's work in the secular arena. After all, the entire line says, "Jesus is the Answer for the world today." Working as salt and light in the culture at large, Crouch has collaborated over the years with the likes of Elvis Presley, Michael Jackson and Quincy Jones, and has composed and conducted for such films as

The Color Purple and *Free Willy.* (He even provided the voice of Yertle the Turtle for the 1994 television special *In Search of Dr. Seuss.*)

Andráe Crouch now serves as Senior Pastor at New Christ Memorial Church of God in Christ in San Fernando, California, the church founded by his parents.

Steve Green

CHRIS RICE

WELCOME TO OUR WORLD

WRITTEN BY CHRIS RICE

RECORDED BY CHRIS RICE
ON DEEP ENOUGH TO DREAM
(ROCKETOWN RECORDS, 1997)

PRODUCED BY MONROE JONES

ALSO RECORDED BY:
AMY GRANT ON A CHRISTMAS
TO REMEMBER

MICHAEL W. SMITH ON
CHRISTMASTIME

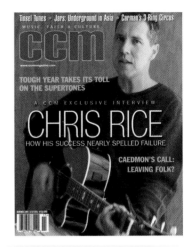

58

C hris Rice is a money-where-your-mouth-is kind of guy. Christian artists are expected to have a desire to touch the lives of young people, but they usually expect to do so while standing on a stage, singing. Chris, on the other hand, juggles a successful recording, songwriting and performing career with what he considers his real job: working as an itinerant youth pastor, a guitar-strapped camp counselor who leads college retreats and youth weekends across the country.

Outreach, mentoring and building relationships are quite simply, he says, why he's alive.

Chris Rice was the first artist signed to Michael W. Smith's fledgling Rocketown Records in 1997, primarily based on the strength of his songwriting ability. His lyrics often take a familiar concept and gently turn it on its ear. "That's what's exciting to me about writing," Chris says. "You can make people think differently about something they thought they've known forever."

Jimmy Abegg

"Welcome to Our World" is a perfect example. *CCM Magazine* called it "a treasure, an exquisite anthem to the Christ child that speaks volumes in its simplicity." Chris calls it a song that wasn't intended to be a Christmas song but became one. "It deals with the reality that God invaded our planet and became one of us, which is just astounding to me," Chris explains. "I wrote about God coming to our world in a naïve way, knowing that it's not ours anyway, it's His. The thoughts that went through my head were about how tiny He was and how He came into the world just like the rest of us do. How much did He know at that point? When He was human flesh, was He aware at all that He was really God, or did He just accept all the limitations and start from scratch? I thought of that progression, and about the fact that He took on what He did so that we would be able to find God and be found by God."

An accidental Christmas song or just a new way to look at an old story, Chris Rice's "Welcome to Our World" touched listeners and helped launch Chris's career. Fittingly, the debut album *Deep Enough to Dream* helped launch Rocketown Records, doubling its projected sales and sending several singles to the top of the charts.

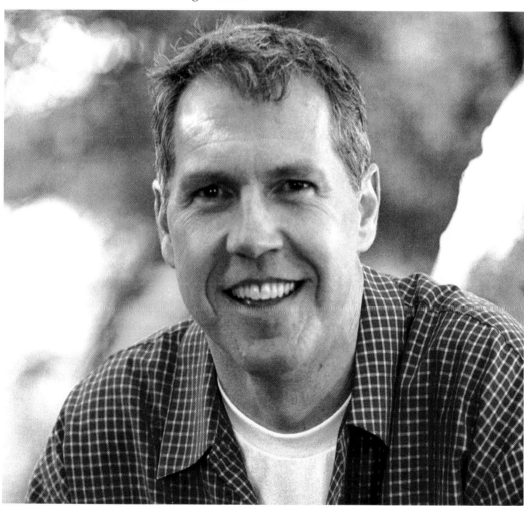

157

ANDRÁE CROUCH

MY TRIBUTE (TO GOD BE THE GLORY)

WRITTEN BY ANDRÁE CROUCH

RECORDED BY ANDRÁE
CROUCH ON KEEP ON
SINGIN' (LIGHT, 1971)

PRODUCED BY BILL COLE

1998 CROUCH INDUCTED
INTO THE GOSPEL MUSIC
HALL OF FAME

59

All of Andráe Crouch's songs testify to the enduring power of faith, but few of them express that message as beautifully as "My Tribute." The lyric is elegantly simple and eminently personal; a private moment between a humble, grateful heart and its Creator.

Andráe Crouch's catalogue of songs is so thick with classics, there was quite a debate in the course of assembling this book —not about whether to include Andráe, of course, but which songs and how many. It was nearly impossible to choose.

"My Tribute" is particularly a favorite among many contemporary Christian household names. "What a great song," says Sandi Patty. "I mean, like Bill Gaither says, that one sticks to the wall." "'My Tribute' became a benchmark," Steven Curtis Chapman adds, "because this is what a great song is—a song that moves you and proclaims the glory of God. Andráe was writing true worship songs before there was

In 2004, Pastor Crouch received his own star on the Hollywood Walk of Fame. He is only the third gospel artist to receive this honor, following the great Mahalia Jackson and the Rev. James Cleveland. Photo by Michal Pasco

such a thing as the worship music we know now. They shaped my heart and understanding of what it really means to make music to the glory of God. In fact, the very first concert I ever attended as a kid was Andraé Crouch. I never experienced anything like it in my life, this guy who was just so passionate, and making all this incredible music." "His songs are all fantastic," agrees Phil Keaggy. "There was such a life and an honesty and a humility in so many of the old ones. There's pure gospel in the songs of Andraé Crouch."

Andraé's gospel music career started at an early age in his parents' church in southern California. He was only 14 when he wrote "The Blood Will Never Lose Its Power." His first band had a decidedly un catchy name — The COGICS (Church of God in Christ Singers)—but in 1965, Crouch founded Andraé Crouch & The Disciples. The 1971 classic *Keep on Singin'* was the group's sophomore release and was chock-full of greats, including "I'm Gonna Keep On Singin'" and "I've Got Confidence," later recorded by Elvis Presley. The slow-building bal-

lad simply titled "My Tribute" garnered little notice at first, but it has since become one of the most recognized and recorded songs in gospel music history.

Throughout his career, Crouch has remained multi-faceted. While he has been active in general market circles for years, the passionate, emotional celebration of God's greatness found in "My Tribute" makes it easy to understand why he is also now a full-time pastor, taking up where his father left off at the family church in Los Angeles.

In 1996, some of the biggest names in contemporary Christian music paid honor with *Tribute: The Songs of Andraé Crouch* (Warner Alliance), including CeCe Winans, The Brooklyn Tabernacle Choir and Michael W. Smith. The finale, "My Tribute (To God Be the Glory)," featured Crouch himself leading a 70-member all-star choir that included Patti Austin, Susan Ashton, Vestal Goodman and many others. The album was awarded Best Contemporary Gospel Album at the 1997 Grammy Awards.

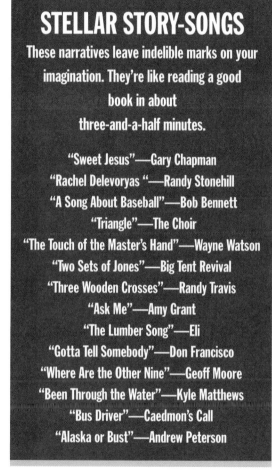

STELLAR STORY-SONGS

These narratives leave indelible marks on your imagination. They're like reading a good book in about three-and-a-half minutes.

"Sweet Jesus"—Gary Chapman
"Rachel Delevoryas "—Randy Stonehill
"A Song About Baseball"—Bob Bennett
"Triangle"—The Choir
"The Touch of the Master's Hand"—Wayne Watson
"Two Sets of Jones"—Big Tent Revival
"Three Wooden Crosses"—Randy Travis
"Ask Me"—Amy Grant
"The Lumber Song"—Eli
"Gotta Tell Somebody"—Don Francisco
"Where Are the Other Nine"—Geoff Moore
"Been Through the Water"—Kyle Matthews
"Bus Driver"—Caedmon's Call
"Alaska or Bust"—Andrew Peterson

AMY GRANT

LEAD ME ON

(60)

**WRITTEN BY AMY GRANT,
MICHAEL W. SMITH, WAYNE
KIRKPATRICK**

RECORDED BY AMY GRANT
ON LEAD ME ON (MYRRH/
A&M, 1982)

PRODUCED BY
BROWN BANNISTER

ALSO RECORDED BY:
BETHANY DILLON ON
BETHANY DILLON

It would be difficult to overstate the importance of Amy Grant's *Lead Me On* project. Released in the summer of 1988, the album's stark, soul-baring honesty and stripped-down acoustic-based sound was a radical departure from the slick mass-market pop of her previous effort, 1985's crossover hit *Unguarded.* That album had positioned her as the undisputed Queen of Christian Pop. Several national publications even went so far as to refer to Grant as a "cheerleader for Jesus."

So to say that *Lead Me On* caught people by surprise is to minimize the shock. But what a pleasant shock it was. Grant's vocals sounded earthy, filled with a gritty maturity scarcely hinted at in her previous recordings. Having endured a miscarriage, a battle to save her marriage and intense spiritual growth and upheaval, Grant chose songs for *Lead Me On* that were by turn joyful and bleak,

full yet sparse, contemplative yet celebratory. *Lead Me On* was drenched with honesty, blunt honesty that to this day remains relatively rare in Christian music. "Who knew that Amy Grant had it in her?" everyone seemed to ask when listening to it. It was, quite simply, startlingly good. The public responded in droves, keeping *Lead Me On* at #1 for five months on the sales charts. The project resulted in Grant's fifth Grammy Award, as well as three Dove Awards and five *CCM* Readers' Choice Awards.

Though the 12 songs on *Lead Me On* (only 10 were included on the vinyl and cassette versions) were all solid, the anthemic title track remains the most well known, and it is the only song from the album that Grant still regularly performs live. Though never a major pop

hit, it did manage to crack *Billboard* Magazine's Hot 100 chart, and Christian radio received it with open arms.

Amy recalls, "Wayne and I wrote the lyrics, and Michael wrote the music. He wanted the song to be 'Rain Down, Rain Down,' or something like that, and he was singing all these goofy things." But inspired by memories of a seventh-grade English project called "Man's Inhumanity to Man," Grant took the song in a different direction, touching on American slavery and the Nazi concentration camps and the hope that God offered in the midst of such pain. "History repeats itself, and we keep relearning the same lessons. So we felt as song-

writers it was a great thing to try to recapture some hard-learned lessons in a song that really was a cry to God to continue leading the way through the love He created," she reflects. "It's always made me want to say to teachers, 'Never underestimate the impact you can have upon your students.'"

In 2001, 13 years after its release, *CCM Presents the 100 Greatest Albums in Christian Music* named *Lead Me On* the #1 Christian album of all time. In 2003, Grant was honored both by ASCAP for 25 years of membership and by the Gospel Music Association, which inducted her into its Hall of Fame.

4HIM

FOR FUTURE GENERATIONS

WRITTEN BY DAVE CLARK, MARK HARRIS AND DON KOCH

RECORDED BY 4HIM ON THE RIDE (BENSON, 1994)

PRODUCED BY DON KOCH

1994 AND 1995 DOVE AWARD—GROUP OF THE YEAR

1994 4HIM PRODUCED THE DOCUMENTARY FILM THE RIDE COMES ALIVE

61

"There's really no way to tell what generation it was written for because it's a timeless message," says Mark Harris of 4Him.

The enduring lyrics and trademark musical quality of the group certainly struck a chord with a generation of contemporary Christian music listeners. "For Future Generations" scored the 1994 *CCM* Readers' Choice for Song of the Year.

Quite a feat for a song sprung from tiny inspiration—Mark's son, who was only four weeks old when the song was written. Like many new fathers, Mark was looking for a way to share the gospel and the message of the cross to his newborn, who hadn't quite caught on to this thing we call language.

Suddenly, it hit him that his message was bigger than words.

"I thought it's really how I live and if I live what I say. The simple message in this song is that we cannot compromise because kids are looking at us, and what they see in us basically gives them a foundation for the way that they live their lives."

Mark's personal revelation was certainly in accord with the mission driving this group from the start. Mark comments, "We as 4Him know what we've been called to do; our songs were written to challenge the church and also to encourage the believer."

The clear vision has certainly paid off. Garnering nine Dove Awards and a Grammy nomination since the group's conception in 1990, 4Him has indelibly left its mark on the world of Christian music. From commercial success to inspirational anthems, it seems fitting that one of 4Him's trademark songs reflects just the kind of men they feel called to be.

As Mark puts it, "We all need to continue to be . . . a light for the kids that come behind us—for future generations."

"**G**enius" is one of those terms that publicists like to throw around with abandon. In the case of Phil Keaggy, however, it is not hype, though his small stature and unassuming demeanor can fool you. He is in fact a guitar virtuoso, a musician's musician who has inspired artists and fans for over 30 years.

In 1976, a newly married Phil Keaggy was living in a Christian "commune" in upstate New York. He had taken a break from his own solo recording career and had been touring with 2nd Chapter of Acts and Honeytree. Ready to go back into the studio, he began work on a new project with 2nd Chapter's Buck Herring at the helm. Phil describes finding his signature song, "Love Broke Thru," and his historic encounter with the late, great Keith Green like this:

"I was working on my second solo album with Buck as the producer and engineer, and we were sitting around sorting through songs and discussing our time frame. So in bounces this guy, Keith Green, and it was great. He was so full of life, full of Jesus, full of song. Buck says, 'Brother, I'd like to introduce you to Keith.' And Keith says with this big grin, 'Hi, how are you doing, praise the Lord! I've got a new song I want to play for you!' We went into one of the extra bedrooms and he sat down at the piano and played 'Love Broke Thru,' smiling the whole time and looking directly into my eyes. Buck told me that he really thought I should do it on my new album, and I said, 'I'd love to— what a beautiful song!' So I did. We went in and cut the track and then did the vocals. Keith personally taught me the song; he wrote it all out for me and we actually used his handwritten lyric sheet taped up by the microphone when I sang it. It's a really good memory. I had such a great deal of respect for him as an artist, and I still do today."

PHIL KEAGGY

62

YOUR LOVE BROKE THRU

WRITTEN BY KEITH GREEN, RANDY STONEHILL AND TODD FISHKIND

RECORDED BY PHIL KEAGGY ON LOVE BROKE THRU (NEWSONG, 1976)

PRODUCED BY BUCK HERRING

ALSO RECORDED BY:
RANDY STONEHILL ON LOVE BEYOND REASON

DAVID MEECE

WE ARE THE REASON

63

WRITTEN BY DAVID MEECE

RECORDED BY DAVID MEECE ON ARE YOU READY (MYRRH, 1980)

PRODUCED BY BROWN BANNISTER

ALSO RECORDED BY: AVALON ON JOY: A CHRISTMAS COLLECTION

DAVID MEECE ON THERE I GO AGAIN

Hailing from Houston, classically trained singer/songwriter/musician David Meece was only 14 when he first conducted Andre Previn's Houston Symphony. At age 16, he regularly appeared as the symphony's pianist. Upon graduation from the Peabody Conservatory of Music in Baltimore, he began recording in 1976.

Although he had a few Christian hits before, and has had several since, the song that has forever put Meece on the map is "We Are the Reason," a touching ode that encapsulates both Christmas and Easter in explaining why Jesus came to earth in the first place.

"The most important thing in the song 'We Are the Reason' is how important it is to realize that He died for each and every one of us," Meece explains. "The individual nature of Christ's sacrifice is something we need to really focus on."

However, he also admits that in writing the song, he really didn't know what he was doing. "It's not my intellect that did it; it wasn't my profound theological thought. I was a piano teacher; I never went to Bible college or seminary or anything. I was probably the last person in the world anybody would expect to write a song as profound as that one—not to sound pompous at all; I mean, it just kind of wrote itself. When I took it in and played it for Brown Bannister, my producer, he was the one who recognized it for what it was. I really didn't know; it was just one of those things that God plopped in my lap."

Meece adds that every time he performs that song, he feels humbled by how easily it came to him. "You know, I've published hundreds of songs, thousands of songs, and I'll tell you, most of the time I had a concept and I constructed it or I worked it and I used my intellect and my songwriting craft. But the biggest songs in my career were just always the ones that—there they were. And it's probably because I didn't mess it up and for that, I'm most grateful."

n the mid-'70s, despite astounding earlier successes like "Jesus Is the Answer," "My Tribute (To God Be the Glory)" and a host of others, Andráe Crouch was really just getting warmed up. Though by that time his songs had already been adopted by the likes of young white hippies in mainstream churches, his fellow black Pentecostals and Elvis Presley—some of his best music was yet to come.

In 1976, the latest creative endeavor from Andráe Crouch & The Disciples was *This Is Another Day*, which turned out to be the last studio album by the group before Andráe went solo. It is rich with Crouch-penned gems, but the most famous song on the record is the soul-stirring proclamation "Soon and Very Soon." With its infectious melody and African rhythms, the joyous anticipation of Christ's return is celebrated with the call-and-response promise that "Soon and very soon, we are going to see the King!" It is instantly recognizable and immediately singable, the kind of song that has audiences on their feet and swaying before the first line is even sung.

CeCe Winans agrees. "His music, I think, more so than anybody in history, has torn down walls between races and ages—it just has no barriers to it."

Crouch (along with his former group, The Disciples) was inducted into GMA's Gospel Music Hall of Fame in 1988. Crouch was also the first inductee into *CCM Magazine*'s Hall of Fame in 2003.

> "When people ask me who I grew up listening to, I have to admit I didn't listen to Aretha, or all that music—I grew up on Andráe. 'Soon and Very Soon' was one of the first songs I remember singing. And you know, every Sunday in all the black churches from here to there, we all sing it like it's still brand new."
>
> NICOLE C. MULLEN

ANDRÁE CROUCH

64

SOON AND VERY SOON

WRITTEN BY ANDRÁE CROUCH

RECORDED BY ANDRÁE CROUCH & THE DISCIPLES ON THIS IS ANOTHER DAY (LIGHT, 1976)

PRODUCED BY ANDRÁE CROUCH AND BILL MAXWELL

1997 DOVE AWARD—SOUL/BLACK GOSPEL ALBUM: THIS IS ANOTHER DAY

2003 CROUCH INDUCTED INTO THE *CCM MAGAZINE* HALL OF FAME

SANDI PATTI

WE SHALL BEHOLD HIM

WRITTEN BY DOTTIE RAMBO

RECORDED BY SANDI PATTI
ON LOVE OVERFLOWING
(WORD RECORDS, 1981)

PRODUCED BY NEAL JOSEPH

ALSO RECORDED BY:
VICKIE WINANS ON THE BEST
OF ALL

THE RAMBOS ON THE VERY
BEST OF THE RAMBOS

ANTHONY BURGER ON
ATLANTA HOMECOMING

65

"I was mesmerized by that song." Sandi Patty's first impression of "We Shall Behold Him" mirrors the response of the millions of people who have heard it since then. But Sandi is referring to a demo tape by an unnamed artist. The rest of us are, of course, remembering the first time we heard Sandi sing it.

In 1981, Sandi was meeting with her arranger, David Clydesdale. "We were sitting at my little spinet piano, talking about that song," Sandi says. "And while we were sitting there, he started arranging the orchestration, and two hours later, it was done. Wrote it right there on the spot, and the next day the musicians were playing it!"

Right after the *Love Overflowing* album was released, Sandi was invited to travel and sing back-up vocals for Bill and Gloria Gaither. She says, "They graciously let me do a song during their program, so I decided to sing 'We Shall Behold Him.' I had just seen Dottie Rambo, who wrote the song, on television and her daughter Reba did sign language to one of their songs. I was just spellbound. I'm always trying to find a way to make a song more interesting, and I thought, *'We Shall Behold Him' would be really beautiful in sign language."* Sandi learned to sign the lyric, and it became a moving, eloquent addition to an already breathtaking vocal performance. It was also the source of one of her favorite memories.

"Our concerts always had a section for the deaf," Sandi recalls, "and one night while I was singing the song, right at the chorus the entire deaf section stood up and began to sign back to me. The spotlight guys were paying attention, thankfully, and so they quickly put the spot over on them. That was just one of those moments that is imprinted forever on my heart. You know, 'Every eye will see, every ear will hear.' They were saying, 'We are going to behold Him too, in all of His glory, with our new bodies and our new ears.' It still gives me chills when I think about that."

Some songs are born out of intense meditation, emotion or circumstance. According to Twila Paris, though, the praise anthem "He Is Exalted" just kind of happened. "Well, it doesn't really have a story behind it. You know, it's a worship song and I was up on this mountain . . ."

It must have been some mountain that prompted this transcendent song that has crossed so many musical and cultural borders. Bob Hartman, from the Christian rock band Petra, commented that it is "one of the greatest praise songs I've ever heard." Even Twila acknowledges that "He Is Exalted" has seemed to capture the essence of worship for people around the world; people from every ethnic background and from every musical sphere.

Reflecting on her role as a worship songwriter, she says, "It's so incredible to hear how the songs have gone to places you've never been and maybe you'll never go, and are being sung by people who don't know your name." She goes on, "It feels so appropriate, you know, because God gives the ability to write a song. He gave the gift of this song. You share it with the body of Christ and then it just makes its way out there. And soon it's being lifted up by somebody on the other side of the world, in a language you don't understand, to worship the One who gave it in the first place."

"He Is Exalted" has certainly "made its way out there." In 1991, Twila re-recorded the song in Portuguese at the request of a missionary friend serving in Brazil. Of that experience, Twila says, "It illustrates that whole concept of how the worship songs just go so far beyond us and accomplish the purpose that they're meant to accomplish. They're used for what they should have been meant for."

Meant for worship, meant for everyone—from rock to gospel, from America to Brazil, "He Is Exalted" highlights Twila's consistency as an inspired and undeniably gifted songwriter.

TWILA PARIS

66

HE IS EXALTED

WRITTEN BY TWILA PARIS

RECORDED BY TWILA PARIS ON KINGDOM SEEKERS (STAR SONG, 1985)

PRODUCED BY JONATHAN DAVID BROWN

1992 DOVE AWARD— PRAISE AND WORSHIP ALBUM. KINGDOM SEEKERS

1991 RE-RECORDED BY TWILA PARIS ON SANCTUARY FEATURING BRAZILIAN RHYTHMS AND LYRICS SUNG IN PORTUGUESE

IMPERIALS

PRAISE THE LORD

WRITTEN BY BROWN BANNISTER AND MIKE HUDSON

67

RECORDED BY IMPERIALS ON HEED THE CALL (DAYSPRING, 1979)

PRODUCED BY CHRIS CHRISTIAN

1979 GRAMMY AWARD— BEST GOSPEL PERFORMANCE: HEED THE CALL

1980 DOVE AWARD—MALE GROUP OF THE YEAR

A 1998 *CCM* POLL NAMED "PRAISE THE LORD" ONE OF THE "10 BEST CONTEMPORARY CHRISTIAN SONGS OF ALL TIME"

Don't let the retro, matching-suit-look of their '70s-era album covers fool you. The Imperials were cutting-edge Christian artists, arguably the industry's first real mavericks.

In 1964, Jake Hess of the Statesman Quartet decided to handpick the best singers he could find to form a "super group" that he called Imperials. The southern gospel world was more than a little skeptical as the quartet began incorporating more contemporary musical styles and changing their appearance and performance to suit the times. But their talent was unquestionable, and in the late '60s The King of Rock and Roll himself hired them to tour, record and perform in his Vegas act. Following their stint with Elvis, the Imperials became regulars on Jimmy Dean's weekly television show, once again taking gospel music into unfamiliar territory.

Their most groundbreaking move came in the early 1970s when the Imperials literally changed the face of the industry by hiring Sherman Andrus as their lead singer, becoming the first southern gospel group in history to break the racial barrier. Andrus left in 1976, replaced by a young vocal powerhouse named Russ Taff. For the next four years, Taff's signature sound completed the Imperials' transition from southern gospel quartet to award-winning contemporary Christian group. "Praise the Lord" is the perfect example of the Imperials at their very best, with Russ Taff's tour-de-force lead vocal surrounded by soaring, seamless harmony.

Over the decades the group has undergone many personnel and stylistic changes. The Imperials released over 40

albums, won 12 Grammy Awards, 13 Dove Awards and had 14 #1 songs. These were all fitting milestones for a group that took traditional gospel music farther than some thought it should go, and then helped define the emerging sounds of contemporary Christian music.

With a career spanning more than 20 years (and counting), Wayne Watson has regularly written about his family and his faith in a rich and vulnerable manner. The title track of his 1987 Dove Award-winning album *Watercolour Ponies* (one of the few songs on this list to later become a children's book) is a bittersweet reminder to parents to cherish their children while they're still young, and before it's too late.

"For every parent who's had kids' artwork on the refrigerator and who just blinks an eye and the kids are gone," notes fellow artist Steve Green, "I think that song just embodied every parent's yearning and the tenderness in our hearts toward our kids growing up and riding off."

"Watercolour Ponies" was born in the kitchen, Watson admits. ("The lyrics give the whole thing away.") He was sitting at the kitchen counter and noticed a school painting by one of his sons, Adam, sticking to the door. "It sort of looked like a pony," Watson says, "but there were elements and other things I couldn't identify. The house was cluttered with kid stuff; I thought of how soon the clutter would change to other stuff and then be gone altogether. It helped me take a deep breath and appreciate the gift in front of me—children in my care."

Watson co-produced the track with Paul Mills, who Watson credits as being "way ahead of the curve" with the keyboard and string arrangements. As for the distinctive opening chords, Watson says prior to making the record, he had recently taken a few jazz guitar lessons. "The chords in the song are a direct result of those lessons," he says. "I've never really used them in any other songs. Even now, in concerts, audiences recognize 'Ponies' from the first chord."

WAYNE WATSON

WATERCOLOUR PONIES

WRITTEN BY WAYNE WATSON AND PAUL MILLS

RECORDED BY WAYNE WATSON ON WATERCOLOUR PONIES (DAYSPRING, 1987)

PRODUCED BY WAYNE WATSON AND PAUL MILLS

APPROPRIATELY ENOUGH, WHEN WATSON RE-RECORDED THE SONG FOR THE ACOUSTIC RETROSPECTIVE SIGNATURES (SPRING HILL), THE NEW VERSION WAS PRODUCED BY HIS OLDEST SON, NEAL

68

2ND CHAPTER OF ACTS

69

EASTER SONG

WRITTEN BY ANNIE HERRING

RECORDED BY 2ND CHAPTER OF ACTS ON WITH FOOTNOTES (MYRRH RECORDS, 1974)

PRODUCED BY BUCK HERRING

ALSO RECORDED BY: KEITH GREEN ON FOR HIM WHO HAS EARS TO HEAR

1998 *CCM* POLL SELECTED "EASTER SONG" ONE OF THE "10 BEST CONTEMPORARY CHRISTIAN SONGS OF ALL TIME"

The opening notes to "Easter Song" just may be the single most recognizable intro in contemporary Christian music. Lilting and melodic, it eases the listener into the song, then quickly soars into the stratosphere on the wings of the crystalline, impossibly close sibling harmonies of Annie, Nelly and Matthew Ward. And by the time the two-minute-and-twenty-second song triumphantly modulates into the only-dogs-can-hear-it high notes of the chorus, "Joy to the world! He is risen! Hallelujah!" —well, by that time the listener may well have imploded.

2nd Chapter of Acts was formed when newlyweds Buck and Annie Herring opened their home to Annie's younger brother and sister after both parents died tragically within a two-year period. Nelly, 15, and Matthew, 13, made the heartbreaking cross-country move from their native North Dakota to the Herrings' home in California. Numb and grieving, the two siblings found themselves harmonizing around the old, beat-up piano in the living room as older sister Annie began trying to express her newfound Christian faith by tentatively writing praise choruses. This led to a few small public performances in the early '70s, which caught the ears of Pat Boone and Barry McGuire. Mightily impressed, Boone helped land the newly christened 2nd Chapter of Acts a deal with MGM, which released two singles but no album. Billy Ray Hearn remedied that by signing the group to his new label, Myrrh, and their first album hit the airwaves, such as they were, in 1974.

"Easter Song" was enthusiastically embraced by the Christian audience, and despite its blatant biblical lyrics, even managed to find moderate success on mainstream radio. Annie, Matthew and Nelly spent the next 17 years as 2nd Chapter of Acts, writing, touring and releasing another 15 albums before officially disbanding in 1988. The purity of their blended voices and the poetry of their songs have assured that 2nd Chapter of Acts and their beloved "Easter Song" hold a well-deserved place of honor in the history of contemporary Christian music.

Nobody in Christian music saw Stryper coming. Oh sure, there were some contemporary Christian groups that rocked, like Petra and Rez Band. But a full-out hard glam metal band, complete with spandex, make-up and cascading, Aqua-Netted hair? Uh, no.

To the horror of parents and pastors and the utter delight of young Christian metalheads everywhere, Stryper exploded onto the music scene in 1984. The band's in-your-face stage persona sparked endless debate, scrutiny, criticism and even hatred in Christian circles. They were denounced from pulpits and picketed at their concerts. And lead singer Michael Sweet says he can't really blame them. "If you go back and look at the Christian music scene at that time, we were certainly from another planet," he says. But their commitment to Christ was as blatant as their look. They ended concerts by hurling Bibles into the outstretched arms of their head-banging audience. The band's moniker, Stryper, is an acronym that means Salvation Through Redemption Yielding Peace, Encouragement, and Righteousness. The Isaiah 53:5 reference, always boldly displayed under the Stryper logo, is a Bible verse that states, ". . . by His stripes we are healed."

Signed to Enigma records, Stryper's first two releases rocketed up the metal charts and set the stage for their third album, *To Hell with the Devil*. "That album just turned out exceptionally well," says Michael Sweet, looking back. "With the title song, we were really striving to write something that would not only be musically unique and different, but to lyrically hit people in a fresh way." The song became a signature Stryper rocker, with its blistering twin guitars and Sweet's trademark higher-than-high notes. *To Hell with the Devil* spent over 40 weeks on Billboard's Top 200 album chart, was certified platinum-plus and produced the #1 most-requested video on MTV. Stryper broke all the rules and won over both Christian and mainstream fans with their hard-edged music, solid musicianship and killer live shows.

STRYPER

TO HELL WITH THE DEVIL

70

WRITTEN BY MICHAEL SWEET AND ROBERT SWEET

RECORDED BY STRYPER ON TO HELL WITH THE DEVIL (ENIGMA RECORDS, 1986)

PRODUCED BY STEPHAN GALFAS, MICHAEL SWEET, ROBERT SWEET AND OZ FOX

1987 TO HELL WITH THE DEVIL IS RIAA CERTIFIED GOLD

1987 A HIGH SCHOOL STUDENT WAS SUSPENDED FOR WEARING A "TO HELL WITH THE DEVIL" STRYPER T-SHIRT TO SCHOOL

CHARLIE PEACOCK

IN THE LIGHT

WRITTEN BY CHARLIE PEACOCK

RECORDED BY CHARLIE PEACOCK ON LOVE LIFE (SPARROW, 1991)

PRODUCED BY CHARLIE PEACOCK AND RICK WILL

ALSO RECORDED BY:
DC TALK ON JESUS FREAK

SARA GROVES, PHIL KEAGGY AND BELA FLECK ON CHARLIE PEACOCK: FULL CIRCLE A CELEBRATION OF SONGS AND FRIENDS

1997 DOVE NOMINATION— SONG OF THE YEAR FOR DC TALK'S VERSION

C harlie Peacock is a songwriter, teacher, producer, musician, executive, singer, visionary and author. In his spare time, he also serves as a mentor to gifted young Christian artists and a conscience to the industry they want to be a part of. And his view of what it truly means to be "salt and light" in the world challenges many of contemporary Christian music's most widely held beliefs.

From the outside, Charlie looks like an insider. His 20-year résumé includes Dove Awards, Grammy nominations, #1 singles (including "In the Light") and production credits for heavy hitters such as Avalon, Nichole Nordeman, Audio Adrenaline and Switchfoot (as well as multiple books, a pioneering

record label and the creation of the Art House ministry). But his intent is always to reach beyond the safe confines of Christian music. He believes an artist's job is not to avoid popular culture but to transform it. Charlie says, "The power to imagine and create is given by God and can be lived out in every sphere of influence and activity, not just the church."

In 1991's *Love Life* album, Charlie made his point and raised a few eyebrows with his candid look at relationships, primarily the ones between husbands and wives. He tastefully but openly extolled the pleasures of married love, particularly in "Lovin' You" and the PG-rated "Kiss Me Like a Woman." But the song

that stood out on the record and ultimately received the most attention was "In the Light," a testament to the struggle between who we are and who we want to be.

"Musically, I started out with a groove inspired by Johnny Clegg and Savuka, a South African Zulu pop group," Charlie explains. "I wanted it to be very singable and simple." dc talk covered "In the Light" on their *Jesus Freak* album and took it to the top of the charts. Michael Tait says, "It's probably one of our top three songs of all time. Charlie did an incredible job writing that one."

Never say dinosaur when you talk about Petra. True, they have been rocking for 30 years, have released 20 albums, sold over seven million records, won four Grammy Awards, 10 Dove Awards and been inducted into the Gospel Music Hall of Fame. But the talent, the passion and the calling are as strong as ever.

Petra, perhaps more than any other Christian rock act that followed, helped define the genre for a whole generation of music lovers. Petra was formed in 1972 by guitarist Bob Hartman, who was attending the Christian Training Center in Fort Wayne, Indiana at the time. He recruited several fellow students and they began performing in a Christian coffee shop. The wet-behind-the-ears rock band had the backing of the school, but quickly encountered resistance from several local churches who felt that the rock and roll beat itself was inherently evil. Petra stubbornly

countered that notion by pioneering the concept of developing ministry tools for kids and youth leaders to enhance their message, with innovative Bible studies, video events, a praise album, devotional books and retreat materials.

1982's "More Power to Ya" could go in a time capsule as a classic slice of pure, unadulterated Petra. There were many personnel changes to come, but at that time Bob Hartman and Greg X. Volz were at the height of their creative collaboration. One review noted, "The guys are note-perfect and watertight from beginning to end, drenching the whole project with their signature, multi-part vocal harmonies."

"I really have a lot of fond memories about 'More Power to Ya,'" Bob Hartman says. "We actually recorded it in the desert. There was an old studio that had been abandoned, but there was some kid running it that had rebuilt this thing literally in the middle of nowhere. So we just went out there among all the herds of jackrabbits and scorpions and made a record!"

PETRA
MORE POWER TO YA

72

WRITTEN BY BOB HARTMAN

RECORDED BY PETRA ON MORE POWER TO YA (STAR SONG RECORDS, 1982)

PRODUCED BY JONATHAN DAVID BROWN

ON THE MORE POWER TO YA TOUR, PETRA SET A PRECEDENT BY GIVING AWAY FREE TICKETS TO THEIR EVANGELISTIC SHOW

SANDI PATTI

LOVE IN ANY LANGUAGE

73

WRITTEN BY JOHN MOHR
AND JOHN MAYS

RECORDED BY SANDI PATTI
ON MORNING LIKE THIS
(WORD RECORDS, 1986)

PRODUCED BY GREG NELSON

1987 DOVE AWARD—
FEMALE VOCALIST AND
INSPIRATIONAL ALBUM:
MORNING LIKE THIS

Morning Like This was a huge record for Sandi Patti, netting her a Grammy Award, two Dove Awards and certified platinum status. This was due in no small part to the single "Love in Any Language," a lilting, audience-friendly anthem which caused countless young women in countless churches across the country to buy the soundtrack and attempt their best Sandi Patti impressions, complete with sign language.

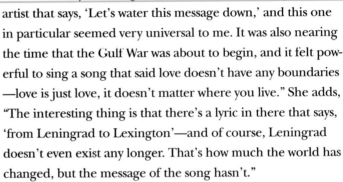

Sandi had a strong reaction to the song as soon as she heard it. "It was already completed when it was played for me," she says, "and I just loved it. I've never really been an artist that says, 'Let's water this message down,' and this one in particular seemed very universal to me. It was also nearing the time that the Gulf War was about to begin, and it felt powerful to sing a song that said love doesn't have any boundaries —love is just love, it doesn't matter where you live." She adds, "The interesting thing is that there's a lyric in there that says, 'from Leningrad to Lexington'—and of course, Leningrad doesn't even exist any longer. That's how much the world has changed, but the message of the song hasn't."

The timeliness of "Love in Any Language" combined with the one-time-through-and-you've-got-it chorus turned the song into an instant favorite in live concerts. "I know it's been performed a lot by children's choirs too," Sandi says, "and of course, I love hearing that!"

In February of 2004, Sandi Patty was inducted into the Gospel Music Association Hall of Fame. Word Records recording artist Kristy Starling surprised her by singing "Love in Any Language" as part of the ceremony honoring her contribution to the industry. "I'll never forget it," smiles Sandi.

> "Our youth group sang every Sandi Patti song there was, and especially 'Love in Any Language' because of course, we had the whole hand motion thing down!"
>
> JODY MCBRAYER OF AVALON

t's been nearly two decades since NewSong founding members Eddie Carswell and Billy Goodwin first hit the road together, and although the group has gone through almost as many member changes as the Imperials, they show no sign of slowing down. The band has scored 17 #1 singles, six Gospel Music Association Dove Award nominations, numerous songwriting awards and five of the Top 100 Christian radio singles of the past decade.

NewSong started out as a nine-man band singing in the Morningside Baptist Church in Valdosta, Georgia. In 1981, four of the nine—Eddie Carswell, Billy Goodwin, Eddie Middleton and the late Bobby Apon—decided to pursue music and ministry full-time. "I don't think we ever thought we'd be doing this for 20 years," Goodwin comments on the group's longevity. "The commitment that we made was, 'God, we'll do this as long as Your hand is on it, as long as we see You working.'"

One of the group's signature songs is "Arise My Love," a majestic, emotionally charged anthem of resurrection that inevitably brings the audience to their feet. It first appeared on their 1994 Benson album, *People Get Ready*, and quickly became an Easter service classic. In 1999 NewSong released *Arise My Love: The Very Best of NewSong*, which again featured the hit single.

NewSong's energetic live performances with all the band members getting involved have become a mainstay on the Christian music touring circuit. That spirit of friendship and collaboration spilled over into a concept the group started several years ago when they began to put together a series of small multi-artist concerts they labeled "Jam" events. The "January Jam" and "Summer Jam" events have now grown to an audience count of over 150,000 and include artists like Rebecca St. James, Newsboys, Audio Adrenaline, Reliant K and others. The concerts evoke a true community feeling among the artists on stage, as their music is intertwined throughout the evening and multi-artist collaborations on stage are frequent.

NEWSONG

ARISE
MY LOVE

74

WRITTEN BY EDDIE CARSWELL

RECORDED BY NEWSONG ON PEOPLE GET READY (BENSON RECORDS, 1994)

PRODUCED BY CHRISTOPHER HARRIS AND PAUL MILLS

1996 DOVE NOMINATION— POP/ CONTEMPORARY ALBUM: PEOPLE GET READY

LARRY NORMAN

WHY SHOULD THE DEVIL HAVE ALL THE GOOD MUSIC?

WRITTEN BY LARRY NORMAN

75

RECORDED BY LARRY NORMAN ON ONLY VISITING THIS PLANET (VERVE, 1972)

PRODUCED BY LARRY NORMAN

"WHY SHOULD THE DEVIL HAVE ALL THE GOOD MUSIC?" HAS BEEN COVERED BY GEOFF MOORE & THE DISTANCE AND BRITISH POP SUPERSTAR CLIFF RICHARD

It's a question that has been asked by many a Christian youth starving for a culturally relevant expression of a timeless faith, but Christian rock pioneer Larry Norman was first to put it to a beat: "Why Should the Devil Have All the Good Music?" The song, which became an anthem for a generation of young believers, was just one of the classics on Norman's 1972 Christian rock manifesto *Only Visiting This Planet*, one of the most significant statements in contemporary Christian music. With big guitars, a rock gospel chorus and raw, vulnerable lyrics that spoke to all facets of life (religious, political and personal), *Only Visiting* also included "Why Don't You Look into Jesus," "The Outlaw," "The Great American Novel" and a remake of "I Wish We'd All Been Ready."

Petra founder and songwriter Bob Hartman points to Norman as a real influence. In fact, Hartman was in a rock band when he became a Christian and struggling at the time with whether rock music could be used to glorify God. When he first saw Larry Norman perform, it was like a light bulb had been turned on. "I'll never forget that first time I heard him," Hartman says. "The freedom Larry had onstage, that freedom to just be himself, really set me free in my songwriting; it really set me free in the establishment of Petra."

Norman went on to form Solid Rock Records, working with such pioneers as Randy Stonehill, Daniel Amos, Mark Heard, Tom Howard and Pantano-Salsbury. Tired of the business and struggling with health issues, in the early 1980s he started his underground label, Phydeaux, and has been releasing studio compilations and bootleg-style recordings in the years since.

Larry Norman

In 2001, Larry Norman was inducted into the GMA Hall of Fame. Though recent bypass surgery prevented him from attending the ceremony, his name was added to the ranks of gospel music's finest, including fellow inductees Elvis Presley and Norman's old friend, fellow pioneer Keith Green.

S

eptember 11, 2001 was the day the unthinkable happened and America lost its innocence. It was also the release date for P.O.D.'s second album, *Satellite*, which at the time seemed irrelevant, as well as unfortunate. But as *CCM*'s Brian Quincy Newcomb noted, the hard rocking band's album was filled with a "positive energy-laden statement of hope and thanksgiving," and apparently the message was timely. During a time when most heavy metal bands were wallowing in their own misery singing about pain and sadness, P.O.D. was offering a more optimistic alternative.

Satellite, the band's sophomore album, entered the Billboard Top 200 album chart at #6, selling over 133,000 units in its first week, making it the highest-selling Christian music debut ever. Following suit, the video for "Alive," the disc's first single, rose to the #1 most- requested slot on MTV's *Total Request Live*, and the song spent three weeks at #1 on Christian rock radio. "Alive" was also nominated for the 2002 Grammy Award for Best Hard Rock Performance.

In a press statement released by Atlantic Records' Vice President/General Manager Barry Landis, he called this "an incredible accomplishment for P.O.D. They are pioneers, redefining the perception of Christians who are creating music for the world."

The critics' response to *Satellite* was just as unprecedented, particularly in the mainstream media. *Rolling Stone* rated it 4 out of 5 stars and offered the opinion that "If P.O.D.'s religious devotion inspired them to turn out the most soulful hard-rock record so far this year, then maybe more new-metalheads should get down with God." But perhaps the most significant observation came from *Billboard* Magazine, which noted that "*Satellite* not only has the juice to elevate P.O.D. to much-deserved superstar status, it could very well blow some desperately needed hope into the air."

P.O.D. earned its reputation as one of the hardest touring bands in America. Their live shows built a loyal following and their albums delivered the goods with songs that inspired the listener to celebrate life, not despise it.

P.O.D.

ALIVE

76

WRITTEN BY P.O.D.

RECORDED BY P.O.D. ON SATELLITE (ATLANTIC, 2001)

PRODUCED BY HOWARD BENSON

2002 MTV VIDEO MUSIC AWARDS NOMINATION— BEST VIDEO OF THE YEAR: "ALIVE"

2002 SATELLITE REACHES RIAA TRIPLE PLATINUM

SATELLITE HAS GONE GOLD IN IRELAND, SINGAPORE, MALAYSIA AND THE PHILIPPINES

WAYNE WATSON

FRIEND OF A WOUNDED HEART

WRITTEN BY WAYNE WATSON AND CLAIRE CLONINGER

RECORDED BY WAYNE WATSON ON WATERCOLOUR PONIES (DAYSPRING, 1987)

PRODUCED AND ARRANGED BY WAYNE WATSON AND PAUL MILLS

ALSO RECORDED BY: THE BROOKLYN TABERNACLE CHOIR ON LIVE ... AGAIN

77

Veteran songwriter Wayne Watson started a string of Christian radio hits throughout the 1980s, including such time-honored perennials as "New Lives for Old" and "Touch of the Master's Hand." But the 1987 album *Watercolour Ponies* was a benchmark for Watson, showcasing his growth and maturity as an artist and songwriter.

One of the big singles from that album, "Friend of a Wounded Heart," garnered him the 1989 Dove Award for Song of the Year (following a 1988 win for Album of the Year for *Watercolour Ponies*). "It put words to the feelings I was having about Jesus," Watson says. "Knowing him most of my life as Savior, I was getting to know Him as my friend."

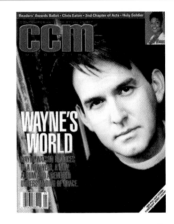

When he hit a rough patch while writing the lyrics, he called on Claire Cloninger to help with the finishing touches. "She made it happen," Watson says. "I had an idea for the music of the chorus but nothing else."

The musical side of the equation came to Watson in Houston, when he was in a recording studio singing background on a Kim Boyce record with some friends. "At the dinner break, I stayed behind for some solitude," he recalls. "[Producer] Paul Mills' keyboard was hooked up through these huge wall speakers in the control room, so I turned them up and started playing. Something about the sound in that room was inspiring and I pretty much finished it on the spot."

During recording, executive producer Neal Joseph asked if Watson was sure he wanted to record in such a high key—after all, he reasoned, Watson could be singing this song for a while. "I wish I had listened," Watson admits. "But the truth is, unless you're going for it vocally and knocking the sides of the box out a bit, it just doesn't sound as good."

There is a case to be made that if Steven Curtis Chapman did not have Scotty Smith as his pastor, Christian music fans would have missed out on a lot of good music. Steven freely admits that Smith's sermons have inspired, provoked or served as the foundation for many of his best songs over the years. "Dive," from his twelfth album, is a prime example.

One Sunday morning at Christ Community Church in Franklin, Tennessee, Steven listened as Scotty Smith told a tale of trout fishing with his friend. They had found an

idyllic bend in the stream and waded out chest deep with their fly fishing rods. The afternoon turned into every angler's dream as the two men found themselves in the middle of a trout-feeding frenzy culminating in a total of over 200 fish. Happily exhausted, they finally looked up and noticed a group of envious fishermen watching them from the shore. They were apparently unwilling or ill equipped to come out into the deep water where the fish were. Pastor Smith drew an analogy to the Christian life, encouraging his congregation to not sit on the sidelines, but to brave the deep waters and fully experience the scary, sometimes dangerous places God has called His people to walk.

"I knew I wanted to write that, somehow," Steven says. "I wanted to capture the emotions of finding the courage to dive in deep and lose yourself in the flow of the living water." He masterfully turned his pastor's challenge into "Dive," an exhilarating, techno-tinged rock song with a hook-filled chorus that won him the 1999 Grammy Award for the album *Speechless*.

78

STEVEN CURTIS CHAPMAN

DIVE

WRITTEN BY STEVEN CURTIS CHAPMAN

RECORDED BY STEVEN CURTIS CHAPMAN ON SPEECHLESS (SPARROW, 1999)

PRODUCED BY BROWN BANNISTER AND STEVEN CURTIS CHAPMAN

2000 DOVE AWARDS—
ARTIST OF THE YEAR,
MALE VOCALIST,
POP/CONTEMPORARY
ALBUM: SPEECHLESS AND
POP/CONTEMPORARY
SONG: "DIVE"

WES KING

THE ROBE

79

WRITTEN BY WES KING AND PHIL NAISH

RECORDED BY WES KING ON THE ROBE (REUNION RECORDS, 1993)

PRODUCED BY PHIL NAISH

IN ADDITION TO MUSIC, WES IS KNOWN FOR HIS COMIC IMPRESSIONS; "TIM CONWAY"AND "ELVIS" APPEAR REGULARLY AT HIS CONCERTS

Wes King sort of backed into the music business. He was a Bible student at Covenant College in Stone Mountain, Georgia when he met singer Kim Hill through his work with local youth groups. "I was doing some playing and singing around town," Wes remembers. "But I wasn't really pursuing music as a career." Hill was putting together a tour to support her debut album and asked Wes to play guitar and sing back-up for her. With no performing aspirations of his own, Wes agreed and was a standout addition to the tour. Kim cut two of Wes' songs, "Snake in the Grass" and "Charm Is Deceitful," for her second album and Wes suddenly found that his budding songwriting talent was bringing him even more industry attention.

Finally realizing that he was in the middle of the music career he hadn't pursued, Wes signed with Reunion Records. He released two albums with moderate success, but it was 1993's *The Robe* that brought him a much wider audience and commercial success.

While searching for material for *The Robe*, producer Phil Naish played some music he had been working on for Wes, who immediately loved it and promptly forgot about it. As they prepared to start recording, Wes suddenly remembered Naish's music and hurried to finish it. He had an idea of where he wanted to go with the song, but wasn't quite coming up with the words. He had been looking for a new way to close out his live performances, a new way to present an invitation to accept Christ that didn't include a thousand verses of "Just As I Am" and threats of a fiery hell. So, for inspiration, he dug out a collection of sermons by Charles Spurgeon called *Sovereign Grace* that he had read the year before. In an interview with *CCM*, Wes told what happened next:

"I went back and re-read the parts I'd highlighted, and I found this: 'Sinner, you say you have no faith. You're right. You have no faith. Faith is of God. Come as you are, and He will give you the faith that you need. You say you're guilty. You're right. You are guilty. Come as you are and God will pardon you. Sinner, you say you're naked and ashamed. Come as you are, and the robe that He will clothe you in is made of a garment of the grace of His Son. Come as you are.'

"And I said, 'That's it. That's the song.'"

onsider this: a new group hits #1 on radio with the first single it ever releases, garners successful sales on a debut album and is voted Best New Artist by the Gospel Music Association the following year. Talk about making a good first impression! It sounds improbable, but that's exactly what happened when four friends—Kirk Sullivan, Marty Magehee, Andy Chrisman and Mark Harris—formed 4Him and released their self-titled debut album. And, as if the story couldn't get any better, the group wasn't even a "real" touring group at the time the song hit #1. As Chrisman explains it, they were still touring members of Truth when the song released.

While just having the opportunity to perform and record as 4Him was a miraculous blessing to the four, the discovery and recording process of "Where There Is Faith" was equally special. Chrisman says 4Him's A&R contact, Andy Ivey, had the song—after it had been passed around to several "A"-level artists—and begged the group to record it. While they agreed to record it, no one was anxious to sing it because it was completely different from anything they'd heard. But Chrisman stepped up to the plate and, only hours before having to get back on the road with Truth, he went into the studio.

As he describes it, "I literally went in and ran through that song maybe four times, and I had to leave to go to Atlanta. And the guys were behind me about 12 hours. They went in and threw some background vocals down on it. You know, crazier things have happened, and it turns out to be this great song that starts our career. We still sing it every night."

"When we got married, Jack was my manager. We traveled together; we did everything together. But Jack started to have more and more problems with his health. I was in one of the darkest, deepest times when he was feeling so bad that he had to start staying home. Suddenly I was out on the bus by myself. And I remember sometimes everyone else would have gone to bed, and it was just me and the bus driver. And I'd be sitting up front just weeping and listening to 'Where There Is Faith'. That song was just pouring into me encouragement and hope and strength."

TWILA PARIS

4HIM

WHERE THERE IS FAITH

80

WRITTEN BY BILLY SIMON

RECORDED BY 4HIM ON 4HIM (BENSON, 1990)

PRODUCED BY JONATHAN DAVID BROWN

1993, 1994 AND 1995 DOVE AWARDS—GROUP OF THE YEAR

BENNY HESTER

WHEN GOD RAN

81

WRITTEN BY BENNY HESTER

RECORDED BY BENNY HESTER ON BENNY FROM HERE (WORD RECORDS, 1985)

PRODUCED BY DAN POSTHUMA

1985 #1 FOR 13 WEEKS ON CHRISTIAN RADIO

The year was 1972, and a teenaged Benny Hester was about to release his first album, a mainstream pop/rock project entitled, appropriately enough, *Benny*. The brand-spanking-new records were being temporarily stored and awaiting shipment when the warehouse mysteriously burned to the ground, destroying all copies and preventing the project from ever being released. It took six more years, but in 1978 a Benny Hester album finally saw the light of day. By this time Benny was a music teacher in Las Vegas, Nevada, and the project was a self-titled Christian release on Sparrow Records. It proved to be a groundbreaking debut for Hester, and by the time his third album, *Benny from Here,* was released on Word Records in 1985, he was on a roll. "When God Ran" quickly rose to #1 on the CHR and AC radio charts, and when combined with another rock single from the album, a song called "Secret Thoughts," Benny had three simultaneous chart toppers, a feat which had never been achieved up to that point in Christian music.

By 1992 Benny was executive producer and president of his own music and television production company, Rebel Entertainment, which produced the MTV Networks/Nickelodeon hit show *Roundhouse.* The show ran for four years, earning Benny the 1993 Cable Ace Award for best Original Song with "I Can Dream."

"I was on the road with Benny Hester when he released 'When God Ran.' I have a lot of memories of those times, just writing songs and throwing them out there trying to figure out what was going to stick. Boy, that one did."

AMY GRANT

" 'When God Ran' was a song my best friend and I listened to all the time. We wore that record out; I never could sing that high, but I kept trying. And in my youth group, we made up a drama to that song and we did it in our church camp every year. Hopefully no one filmed it."

BART MILLARD OF MERCYME

Contemporary Christian music has had many famous prodigal sons, but it is Michael English's talent that has placed him in a class by himself. Possessing one of the most admired and recognizable voices in the business, his stunning fall from grace in May of 1994, on the heels of a scandal involving an extramarital affair, rocked the industry and saddened his fans. Michael made a public confession, returned his six recently awarded Dove Awards, lost his recording contract and, ultimately, his marriage.

The next few years were spent in virtual exile from Christian music, though Curb Records released a number of mainstream pop albums with him, even landing a Top 10 single on the Adult Contemporary charts. Michael continued to struggle and eventually faced addiction and arrest. In 2000, he doggedly began the agonizing struggle to conquer his demons and rebuild his life and ministry. Sobriety, remarriage and a new baby girl fill Michael's life today, and he gratefully reflects on a song that was as true in the dark times as it was the first time he sang it.

"That song almost slipped through my fingers," Michael says with a smile. "It kind of got lost in the shuffle of the millions of tapes we were wading through, trying to find material for my first solo record. I guess I had heard it, but it didn't register or something. And then I was in the car one day listening to the songs, and I got a call from Brown's office and somebody said, 'Have you heard "In Christ Alone"?' I said that I probably had, and they said, 'Well, maybe you should listen to it again!' So I went back home and listened to it, and I was like, 'HOW did that get by me?' Thank God I found it; it has been the perfect song for me, especially the lyric. It kind of says it all.

"In Christ alone will I glory/ For only by His grace I am redeemed/ And only His tender mercy could reach/ Beyond my weakness to my need."

Russ Harrington

MICHAEL ENGLISH

IN CHRIST ALONE

WRITTEN BY SHAWN CRAIG AND DON KOCH

RECORDED BY MICHAEL ENGLISH ON MICHAEL ENGLISH (WARNER ALLIANCE RECORDS, 1992)

PRODUCED BY BROWN BANNISTER

1993 DOVE AWARDS— INSPIRATIONAL SONG OF THE YEAR; MALE VOCALIST OF THE YEAR

82

MARK SCHULTZ

HE'S MY SON

83

WRITTEN BY MARK SCHULTZ

RECORDED BY MARK SCHULTZ
ON MARK SCHULTZ
(MYRRH, 2000)

PRODUCED BY MONROE
JONES

SCHULTZ GARNERED SEVEN
2001 DOVE AWARD NOM-
INATIONS INCLUDING SONG OF
THE YEAR FOR "HE'S MY SON"

2001 LEUKEMIA AND LYMPHOMA
SOCIETY GAVE SCHULTZ
THE BEACON AWARD FOR
HIS AWARENESS-RAISING
EFFORTS

Mark Schultz will forever be the man responsible for writing the crossover phenomenon "He's My Son." But if you ask him, "the only thing I had to do with this song is that I just happened to be there when God sat it in my lap."

For music lovers of every genre, we are all grateful that Schultz took what was in his lap to the top of both Christian and secular music charts, peaking at #22 on Billboard's Adult Contemporary Chart. However, the true success of this song cannot be captured by rankings or commercial figures; rather, it can be seen in the many lives touched by this moving story of a family dealing with their son's cancer.

Mark wrote the song when he was a youth minister at a church in Nashville, Tennessee. Upon the diagnosis of leukemia in a young man at the church, Mark says, "I learned how to walk through life with two parents who thought they were going to lose their child."

Mark observed the grieving of a mother and father. He recounts: "Louise often stayed up with [Martin] until he fell asleep. She would rub his back and try to comfort him, but she felt helpless." He goes on: "Some nights, John would wake up and walk down the hall to Martin's room and watch him sleep. As he stood there, he would try to imagine what life would be like without his son."

Mark "tried for several months to write a song for John and Louise, but nothing seemed to capture what they were going through . . . I couldn't begin to understand the depth of pain John and Louise faced every day—but God did. This is the song He chose for them."

Healthy and happy, Martin Baird and his father, John Baird.

And it is the song listeners continue to choose as the signature work from this masterful storyteller. Amidst all the success and accolades from the music industry, Mark maintains that "my favorite part of this story is that Martin is 20 years old and has been cancer-free for five years."

The typical Nashville story goes something like this: young hopeful moves to town with the dream of becoming a star, pounds the pavement looking for a record deal and, in the meantime, slaves away at some hourly job, just scraping to get by until that "big break." The path for Susan Ashton was anything but typical.

Susan Rae Hill (she changed her recording name to her mother's maiden name, Ashton, to avoid confusion with Kim Hill) was barely out of her teens when Sparrow spotted her talent as a background singer and offered her a contract. In fact, things moved so quickly that Ashton completed her first album before ever playing a concert! But, although she's quick to admit she had a lot of learning to do when it came to stage presence, fans didn't seem

to notice. Her debut record, *Wakened by the Wind*, went on to score five radio singles, including a #1 Adult Contemporary hit for "Stand." The record sold more than any new artist in Sparrow Records' history, and Ashton also claimed *CCM Magazine*'s title as Favorite New Artist in 1992.

Although Ashton rarely penned the songs she sang, she has always been praised for her song choice and interpretation. And much of that praise can be attributed to the special musical bond she and longtime collaborator and producer Wayne Kirkpatrick shared. In *CCM*'s March 1994 cover story, Ashton said, "It's like somebody gave him the key to my heart and he walked in, opened it up, looked at everything and said, 'Okay. Now I know what to write.'" While she was the first to give credit to her writers, she often defended the role of the vocalist (as opposed to the songwriter). Ashton once noted in *CCM*'s January 1997 cover story, ". . . The song belongs to the person that can truly communicate the heart of it the best. And whoever that song lives inside, that's who the song belongs to." If that's the case, then Ashton owned every song she ever sang.

SUSAN ASHTON

84 | STAND

WRITTEN BY LORRAINE FERRO, TANYA LEAH AND JOANNE SONDERLING

RECORDED BY SUSAN ASHTON ON WAKENED BY THE WIND (SPARROW, 1991)

PRODUCED BY WAYNE KIRKPATRICK

SUSAN ASHTON GRACED THE COVER OF *CCM MAGAZINE* THREE TIMES—IN APRIL 1992, MARCH 1994 AND JANUARY 1997. SHE TOURED AND SANG BACKGROUND VOCALS WITH GARTH BROOKS ON UNITED STATES AND EUROPEAN TOURS AND LATER RECORDED A COUNTRY ALBUM, CLOSER, WITH CAPITOL RECORDS

LARNELLE HARRIS

HOW EXCELLENT IS THY NAME

WRITTEN BY DICK TUNNEY, MELODIE TUNNEY AND PAUL SMITH

RECORDED BY LARNELLE HARRIS ON I'VE JUST SEEN JESUS (BENSON, 1985)

PRODUCED BY GREG NELSON

1985 GRAMMY AWARD—BEST GOSPEL PERFORMANCE

ALSO RECORDED BY:
FAMED PIANIST DINO ON MORE THAN THE MUSIC . . . LIVE

85

Now in his fourth decade of recording, Larnelle Harris has a mantle full of honors (including multiple Grammys, several Doves, a Silver Bell, a Stellar and a People's Choice Award), has made numerous network TV appearances, performed for presidents and kings all over the world and sold millions of records.

He began studying piano as a child and sang his first solo in church at age nine. A native of Danville, Kentucky, he received his first formal vocal training as a music major in college. Earning a degree in classical music by day and playing drums in local bands by night, he had an eclectic course of study that ran from German lieder and Elizabethan love songs to James Brown and Ray Charles.

With stints with both the Spurrlows and the New Gaither Vocal Band on his résumé, his solo career stretches back to 1976. It was nine years later when he released *I've Just Seen Jesus* (Dove winner for Inspirational Album of the Year), which includes the Grammy-winning performance of "How Excellent Is Thy Name."

Of the track, Harris first gives credit and thanks to songwriters Dick and Melodie Tunney and Paul Smith for writing a great song. "I remember the assurance that I had all during the recording session that 'How Excellent' was going to be one of those songs that would be a great blessing to the church," he beams. "I was right."

Sandi Patty, who has performed on more than one duet with Harris (whom she refers to as "an amazing gentleman"), remarks that "How Excellent Is Thy Name" is "just one of those amazing praise songs that's still very much alive."

It should be noted that Harris has received "letter after letter" informing him that "How Excellent Is Thy Name" is being used in exercise classes around the country.

Personal experience was the inspiration behind Twila Paris's song "Runner"—sort of. "I have never been and never will be a runner," she laughs. "I'm a walker. But 'Walker' just doesn't have the same ring!"

OK, so she's not a marathoner, and she still smiles when she hears that actual runners listen to her song during workouts; but it wasn't the idea of exercise that led to the song that ran straight up the Christian music chart in the mid-'80s. Rather, Twila says the song was written "specifically for missionaries."

A trip to Venezuela at the age of six was the beginning of a life infused with the spirit of the mission field. "My immediate and my extended family have worked for years in missions," Twila says, "and so I've just always grown up with a deep heart for evangelism." The depth of her passion for ministry has consistently revealed itself in her work. Her fervent, meaningful lyrics have resonated with people from every walk of life and have marked her as a writer of substance. The humble songwriter shrugs off the accolades and simply credits the power of music and the strength of the message. "That's how music is, really. When we go back and pull out our old music, it's timeless, and we can actually recall that time and that place in our world and what our thoughts were. Music can revive us and give us comfort."

People from around the world have written letters of gratitude to Twila, sharing how "Runner" has touched them in any number of circumstances. "I think it's a song that most believers can relate to because really, we are all missionaries in the field," Twila says. "I've found that God has used it to just encourage people, especially if they might be going through a difficult time in their lives and they're beginning to feel weary."

> "Twila opened for us the first year she ever traveled. She's such a wonderful writer, and I always have this sense of fatherly pride that we had a small part in getting her songs out there."
>
> **DALLAS HOLM**

TWILA PARIS

86 RUNNER

WRITTEN BY TWILA PARIS

RECORDED BY TWILA PARIS
ON KINGDOM SEEKERS
(STAR SONG, 1985)

PRODUCED BY JONATHAN
DAVID BROWN

1986 #7 ON CHRISTIAN
RADIO CHART (SUNG WITH
DAVID MEECE)

2001 KINGDOM SEEKERS
INCLUDED IN *CCM*'S 100
GREATEST ALBUMS IN
CHRISTIAN MUSIC

RICH MULLINS

MY DELIVERER

WRITTEN BY RICH MULLINS AND MITCH McVICKER

RECORDED BY RICH MULLINS AND A RAGAMUFFIN BAND / VARIOUS ARTISTS ON THE JESUS RECORD (MYRRH RECORDS, 1998)

PRODUCED BY RICK ELIAS

1998 DOVE AWARD— ARTIST OF THE YEAR

1999 DOVE AWARD— SONGWRITER OF THE YEAR

87

On September 10, 1997, Rich Mullins was in Chicago with a few of the Ragamuffins working on Mitch McVicker's upcoming solo record. During a break, Rich wandered over to a nearby abandoned church and sat down inside. He took out his guitar and his brand-new K-Mart tape recorder and proceeded to sing and play nine songs he had written for a new project he was affectionately calling *Ten Songs for Jesus*. Nine days later Rich was gone. A tragic car accident claimed his life and silenced the irreplaceable man who seemed to have so much music left to make.

It seemed obvious that Rich's *Jesus Record* would never see the light of day. But Myrrh Records and the Ragamuffins decided to try to creatively pick up the mantle and finish what Rich had started. Rick Elias had already been chosen to produce the record, and he began the process of "cleaning up" Rich's roughly recorded cassette demo of the nine songs. That became the first CD of the two-disc project, entitled *The Jesus Demos*. The second CD is *The Jesus Record*, with Rich's songs fully realized by guest artists such as Amy Grant, Ashley Cleveland, Michael W. Smith and Phil Keaggy. The end result is exceptional.

The first single was "My Deliverer," a classic Mullins hymn that conveyed unshakable faith and yearning for personal deliverance. Rich had hoped the song's worship chorus and confession of need could create the same sort of feeling that "Awesome God" stirred, but in the context of a mature, biblically grounded reflection. It quickly became #1 in the nation in August of 1998.

By all accounts, *The Jesus Record* fully accomplished its goal of providing a kind of musical closure for the countless friends and fans that were touched by the life and music of Rich Mullins. "My Deliverer" won the 1999 Dove Award for Song of the Year, and Rich was posthumously awarded the Dove for Songwriter of the Year—an honor that, ironically, had never been bestowed on him while he was alive.

B. J. Thomas was not the first "secular" singer to cross over into contemporary Christian music, but he may have been the first one to face such a bewildering barrage of mixed reactions. A hugely successful recording artist in several genres, B. J. Thomas had a solid career going with gold records, awards and top 40 hits on the pop, country and adult contemporary charts. But success also brought temptation, and Thomas came dangerously close to becoming another substance-abusing-burned-out pop music statistic. He had a spiritual renewal that saved his life as well as his marriage and career, and in 1976 he was eager to express his newfound Christianity in song.

Myrrh Records signed him, and *Home Where I Belong* was

rushed into record stores. It was eagerly snapped up to the tune of over a million copies by both existing B. J. Thomas fans who were thrilled to have a new release from their favorite singer, and curious Christian music fans who wondered what the "Raindrops Keep Falling on My Head" guy had to say about God and faith.

B. J. Thomas, a new Christian in the first flush of his spiritual walk, quickly found himself in the awkward position of having to justify his artistic choices to both sides of the music industry. Longtime fans found the new direction worrisome and wondered if their good-looking, sexy pop star might be crossing too far into Pat Boone territory. And the Christian media alternately embraced and vilified him as they publicly debated the validity of his conversion. It all came to a head in Thomas's live performances, when Christian concert crowds bristled, booed and even walked out when he innocently performed his pop hits such as "Hooked on a Feeling" side by side with "Amazing Grace."

B. J. Thomas eventually moved away from performing in the Christian arena, but never walked away from the music. As he explained in a 2002 interview, " I won five Grammys for my gospel records, but trying to get along in the Christian music business was just almost impossible. So I had to leave it, although I'll always love to sing gospel and I still do sing it today."

B.J. THOMAS

88

HOME WHERE I BELONG

WRITTEN BY PAT TERRY

RECORDED BY B. J. THOMAS, ON HOME WHERE I BELONG (MYRRH RECORDS, 1976)

PRODUCED BY CHRIS CHRISTIAN

ALSO RECORDED BY:
MARK LOWRY ON GOING HOME

PAT TERRY ON THE BEST OF THE PAT TERRY GROUP

1976 DOVE AWARD—BEST ALBUM BY A SECULAR ARTIST: HOME WHERE I BELONG

CINDY MORGAN

I WILL BE FREE

WRITTEN BY CINDY MORGAN

RECORDED BY CINDY MORGAN
ON A REASON TO LIVE
(WORD, 1993)

PRODUCED BY MARK
HAMMOND

ALSO APPEARS ON THE BEST
SO FAR (WORD, 2000)

1994 DOVE AWARD
NOMINATIONS:
NEW ARTIST OF THE YEAR,
FEMALE VOCALIST OF THE
YEAR, CONTEMPORARY ALBUM
OF THE YEAR, CONTEMPORARY
RECORDED SONG OF THE
YEAR AND RECORDED MUSIC
PACKAGING

89

Cindy Morgan burst onto the Christian music scene in the early '90s and quickly and firmly established herself as a major new talent. In fact, her debut album, *Real Life*, earned her the Dove Award for New Artist of the Year. She wrote or co-wrote the bulk of her outstanding material from the beginning, proving to have a knack for articulating the pains, fears and joys of life in a rare way, especially in her ballads.

"I Will Be Free" is one of the best of the best. A stunning, poetic tale of hope in the midst of pain, the song was intensely personal to Morgan. She says, "I was struggling through a lot of different issues in my life. I had been reading the book *Hinds Feet on High Places* by Hannah Hurnard in an effort to get some insight with my own issues with fear. And I prayed, 'Lord, when will I be free of this sense of dread, of fear?' I started humming the tune and the words followed . . . The mountains are steep and the valleys low . . ."

"I Will Be Free" is one of Morgan's most vulnerable and memorable performances ever, and that was felt by fans far and wide. She recalls a young girl of about 12 sharing with her that she had sung it to her mother on her deathbed. She also recounts how Karla Faye Tucker, a convicted murderer who became a born-again Christian while on death row, asked for it to be played before she became the first woman executed in Texas.

Over the years, Morgan has heard many other stories from listeners who were profoundly affected by the song, and although she has released four fine albums since, "I Will Be Free" is a memorable highlight in a career full of many.

Though the song won a Dove Award for "Short Form Music Video of the Year," its personal impact remains more important to Morgan.

"This song still gives me chills. The first time I heard it, I wept against my will. I was stunned. It is one of these rare songs that bypasses all the defenses and gets straight to the center of the heart."

MARGARET BECKER

Kathy Troccoli recently celebrated 20 years as a recording artist. This husky-voiced alto could never have foreseen the success she would later have when she was working on her debut release, *Stubborn Love*, in the early '80s. Having moved from her native Long Island to Nashville, Troccoli lived for a time with the family of Dan Harrell, who co-managed the career of his sister-in-law, Amy Grant. Troccoli found a job in a local Christian bookstore as she worked on her debut album under the direction of Blanton & Harrell Management. In 1982, *Stubborn Love* released and had the distinction of being the fastest-selling debut album by a female Christian artist. The title track, "Stubborn Love," launched a career that would include co-headlining a tour with Michael W. Smith, a major crossover pop hit ("Everything Changes"), a stint opening for comedian Jay Leno, speaking at women's conferences and authoring several books.

Oddly enough, "Stubborn Love" never even hit #1 on the Christian radio charts, though to this day it remains one of Troccoli's best-loved songs. The well-crafted song centers on God's faithfulness in spite of our faithlessness, and its big chorus will run through your head for days after listening. Though in hindsight Troccoli admits that her debut album wasn't really reflective of her own musical tastes and identity, she is grateful for the introduction it provided her to Christian music fans the world over. The feeling is mutual.

A few years after the album released, Troccoli visited the Christian bookstore where she had worked when she first moved to town, and was humbled to hear them playing her album in the store. "In only three years," she reflects, "the Lord had been so faithful. I was once the girl behind the cash register, and now my music was playing in the store!"

KATHY TROCCOLI

90

STUBBORN LOVE

WRITTEN BY AMY GRANT, GARY CHAPMAN, SLOAN TOWNER, BROWN BANNISTER AND MICHAEL W. SMITH

RECORDED BY KATHY TROCCOLI ON STUBBORN LOVE (REUNION RECORDS, 1982; RE-RELEASED, 1994)

PRODUCED BY BROWN BANNISTER

1983 #2 ON CHRISTIAN RADIO CHARTS

CARMAN

THE CHAMPION

91

WRITTEN BY CARMAN

RECORDED BY CARMAN
ON THE CHAMPION (MYRRH
RECORDS, 1986)

PRODUCED BY KEITH
THOMAS

BILLBOARD MAGAZINE HAS
TWICE NAMED CARMAN
CONTEMPORARY CHRISTIAN
ARTIST OF THE YEAR

"THE CHAMPION" INSPIRED
CARMAN TO WRITE AND
PRODUCE THE FILM
THE CHAMPION

Love him or loathe him, the guy's got staying power. For the last 26 years Carman has baffled critics and delighted audiences with his patented brand of ever-changing musical styles and over-the-top showmanship. To his credit, Carman has never pretended to be anything other than what he is: a minister first, who uses his albums and concerts primarily to evangelize. He doesn't indulge in artistic posturing —he simply wants to get his message across in the most entertaining and effective way possible.

Having said that, Carman is not for the faint of heart. His biggest songs are traditionally a version of the same story; the power of good, which is Christ, locked in a fierce battle showdown with the power of evil, Satan. Carman has said that he writes primarily with live concerts in mind, so his songs are often a mixed bag of dramatic lyrics and music, with theatrical sound effects and extensive spoken-word sections. "The Champion" is a prime example of Carman's signature style. The showpiece and first single from the same-titled 1986 album is almost eight minutes long. This time the epic showdown is staged in a boxing ring, with Jesus and Satan duking it out for the eternal heavyweight championship title and God the Father as referee. The outcome is never in question as Jesus is knocked down but never out, and ultimately gives the Prince of Darkness the good thrashing he deserves. The song was a huge hit with the flocks of faithful Carman fans and spent four weeks in the #1 spot in April of 1986.

In 2001, Carman teamed with the folks at Gener8Xion Films and co-wrote and starred in a dramatic film called *Carman: The Champion*. The PG-13 rated film was released in theaters with predictable results—Carman-lovers loved it, the critics . . . not so much.

Carman continues to successfully sell tickets to his huge, dazzlingly produced live shows, continues to turn out increasingly well-received album projects and continues to unabashedly evangelize in his incomparable style.

Contemporary Christian

CARMAN
EVANGELICAL
ENTERTAINER

One of the most influential bands in Christian music history is White Heart, both for its own output, as well as for the many alumni who have gone on to work as songwriters, producers and session players with some of the biggest names in Christian and general market music. Their 1984 sophomore release, *Vital Signs*, yielded one of the band's biggest hits, the perennial anthem "We Are His Hands."

Songwriter Mark Gersmehl recalls the years when he first migrated to Nashville from Fort Wayne, Indiana (some guys he played with in the back-up group for the Bill Gaither Trio were starting a rock band). "Bill and Gloria (Gaither) had graciously allowed us to blow up their house system after sound check for years," he says, "but it was time for us to tell our own stories."

He arrived in Nashville with a bagful of songs but clueless about the Christian music business. Fellow White Heart co-founder Billy Smiley told Gersh he needed to find a publisher and set up some meetings for him, instructing him to take three or four of his best songs on tape with lyric sheets.

Gersh approached the meetings with "a barely concealed terror," he says. "However, there was one song that I felt pretty confident about playing for people. It was the tune that I played first at every one of those soirées."

On hearing the song, Publisher No. 1 loved the chorus but said the verses needed to change. In the next meeting, Publisher No. 2 loved the verses, but said the chorus had to change.

"My songs have been greatly aided by constructive criticism throughout my entire career," Gersh says. "But this was one time when I didn't change a single word or note. The name of that song was 'We Are His Hands.'"

WHITE HEART

WE ARE HIS HANDS

92

WRITTEN BY MARK GERSMEHL

RECORDED BY WHITE HEART ON VITAL SIGNS (MYRRH, 1984)

PRODUCED BY WHITE HEART

THE SONG'S ALL-STAR CHOIR INCLUDES SCOTT WESLEY BROWN, DAVID MEECE, AMY GRANT, STEVE GREEN, RUSS TAFF AND KATHY TROCCOLI, AMONG OTHERS

FIRST CALL

UNDIVIDED

93

WRITTEN BY MELODIE TUNNEY

RECORDED BY FIRST CALL
ON UNDIVIDED (DAYSPRING
RECORDS, 1986)

PRODUCED BY KEITH THOMAS

1987 AND 1988 DOVE
AWARDS—GROUP OF THE
YEAR

F irst Call, with their soaring, flawless, intricate harmonies, was who producers always called first to come
sing back-up vocals on their albums. But the trio, with
original members Bonnie Keen, Melodie Tunney and
Marty McCall, accidentally ended up with an award-winning
career of their own.

Bonnie Keen says, "First Call was doing a lot of studio
work in town, but we decided that we had no interest
in pursuing a deal of our own. So
we made a pact that we would
do all of the studio work that
came our way but we would
never record or tour as a group."

In 1983, during Gospel Music week in
Nashville, budding writer Melodie Tunney was preparing to
perform a new song for a publisher's showcase. Bonnie continues, "During a break, Mel grabbed Marty and me and said,
'You've got to come sing it with me! It will make a much better
impression if we do it together.' So Marty and I ran down with
her to the luncheon showcase. We started singing 'Undivided,'
and the room got very quiet. The people were obviously
moved by our performance. Long story short—that ended up
being our first single."

First Call's debut album and single grabbed the attention of
the industry, and they became featured performers on Sandi
Patti's tour. The group recorded five increasingly successful
albums until Mel Tunney left in 1989. Mel was replaced by
Marabeth Jordan, who stayed until 1994. Marabeth was
involved in the Michael English scandal and resigned from
the group after admitting to an extramarital affair.

First Call barely survived the scorched earth aftermath of
Marabeth's departure. Devastated and hurting for their friend,
Marty and Bonnie fully expected to retire the group forever.
But God had other plans and slowly, first with interim members
and finally as a duo, First Call rose from the ashes with a strong
testimony to God's overwhelming grace and faithfulness.

S truggling, searching, focused, passionate, intentional—those words have been used to describe Jennifer Knapp's songwriting and, we can assume, offer some insight into her character as well. In a March 2000 interview with *CCM,* Jennifer said, "Music is a really great example of how we can take something, pour ourselves into it, do it with excellence and make an emotional connection. I'm building a career out of being able to communicate a few basic things that God has taught me in life. That's the way you evangelize."

Jennifer Knapp came to the attention of Toby McKeehan of dc talk fame through an indie project she recorded after quitting college in her senior year to pursue music full time. Intrigued by her well-crafted lyrics and soulful acoustic sound, he immediately signed her to his new label, Gotee Records, and in December 1997 released her debut album, *Kansas.* The gold-certified album produced both critical acclaim and commercial success, landing the young artist five Top 10 radio singles and two Dove Awards in 1999 for New Artist of the Year and Rock Song of the Year, for "Undo Me."

Looking back to that time in her life, Jennifer said, "I'm willing to admit that first record is a process of recovery and just going, 'Man I've just got to spill this out.' Honestly that's all I ever thought it was; I didn't think that it was going to be splattered in front of everybody, and I didn't really think about the consequences of it either."

But it is her willingness to be transparent that causes audiences to connect with Jennifer, and that is the backbone of her songwriting success. "Undo Me," a painfully honest confession of how her human failings have hurt the ones she loves and the One who loves her most, is a perfect, powerful example.

"Jennifer definitely brought the whole chick-rocker thing back into Christian music! I think 'Undo Me' is one of the best songs she has ever written. It's about just stripping everything away and being honest before the Lord."

JOEY ELWOOD, PRESIDENT, GOTEE RECORDS

JENNIFER KNAPP

94

UNDO ME

WRITTEN BY JENNIFER KNAPP

RECORDED BY JENNIFER KNAPP ON KANSAS (GOTEE RECORDS, 1998)

PRODUCED BY MARK STUART

JENNIFER HAS PLAYED MANY BENEFIT CONCERTS INCLUDING SHOWS FOR RONALD MCDONALD HOUSE, MERCY MINISTRIES, CHILDREN'S HOSPITALS AND WOMEN'S SHELTERS

"UNDO ME" ALSO APPEARS ON JENNIFER KNAPP'S THE COLLECTION: A DIAMOND IN THE ROUGH

SCOTT WESLEY BROWN

HE WILL CARRY YOU

WRITTEN BY SCOTT WESLEY BROWN

RECORDED BY SCOTT WESLEY BROWN ON SIGNATURE (SPARROW RECORDS, 1982)

PRODUCED BY DAN COLLINS

SIGNATURE FEATURES ORCHESTRAL BACKING FROM THE NATIONAL PHILHARMONIC OF LONDON

IN 1984 SCOTT COMPILED A PROJECT CALLED ALL THE CHURCH IS SINGING SUPPORTING RUSSIAN CHURCHES BEHIND THE IRON CURTAIN

95

Scott Wesley Brown may be the only contemporary Christian music artist whose résumé includes covert missions behind the Iron Curtain. But Scott's music and career has always been about more than just building a following and maintaining a lifestyle. His eyes are firmly on the bigger picture, which to him means global mission work.

Scott's original intent when he moved to Nashville from Washington, D.C. in 1981 was to break into the Christian music biz as a writer and performer. He achieved a measure of success relatively quickly and was signed to Sparrow Records as a solo recording artist. His 1982 album, *Signature*, produced the single "He Will Carry You," which entered the charts in November and remained there for the next 13 weeks. Scott also began writing songs for such artists as Sandi Patti, Amy Grant, Bruce Carroll, the Imperials, Petra and even opera superstar Placido Domingo.

But in the mid-'80s, Scott Wesley Brown found himself drawn more and more towards the mission field, particularly the Soviet Union in the Cold War era. His calling was crystallized in August of 1989, when he conducted the U.S.S.R.'s first publicly promoted Christian music event for an audience of over 15,000 people. Scott also stood side by side with East German brothers and sisters as the Berlin Wall came down. He has taken over 100 musicians on trips to the mission field and provided countless musical instruments to musicians and missionaries in Third World and restricted access countries.

"I saw a transformation take place in Scott when he got involved with missions. He was a musician who had successful songs like 'He Will Carry You,' and had gained this level of recognition that he kind of struggled with. But then he started going to Russia when it was still a closed country, and I don't think I've ever seen a person so impacted by an experience. He came back and basically said, 'I'm not working for myself and my own fame anymore.' And it wasn't just short-term missionary zeal, you know; that's what he's still doing, that's where his heart is."

MICHAEL CARD

The name Chuck Girard instantly evokes warm memories for music lovers "of a certain age." The Jesus movement, Love Song, Calvary Chapel, Maranatha—all of these words will forever be associated with the '70s contemporary Christian pioneer.

In 1970 in Costa Mesa, California, Chuck Girard helped found Love Song, a group many people credit with defining what came to be called Jesus Music. They were together for four years and released several recordings. Chuck's self-titled solo project came out in 1975 and included "Sometimes Alleluia," a simple worship song that has become a standard. Here's how Chuck tells it:

"In the early days when Love Song first started out, we didn't know how to say no. We thought if the phone rang, it was God. Sometimes we played two or three times a day for weeks on end. Well, one weekend a bunch of us went up to a cabin for some R&R. We sat around the fireplace the first night to just worship. I had a guitar and I'd been thinking about the different ways in which we express our heart to God. I just started singing, 'Sometimes alleluia, sometimes praise the Lord . . .' and the chorus was born. Then I basically forgot about it until a few years later when I was preparing to record the *Chuck Girard* album. I told my wife that I wanted to put a worship song on the album. She reminded me about the little chorus we sang up at the cabin. I said 'Naw, that's too simple; I need a real song.' Karen said, 'No, I have a feeling about that one. You need to finish it.' I went to the piano and the verses were written in about 20 minutes. It came out as the final song on the album, and in this case, the rest truly is history."

"I remember even as a very young girl watching the reaction of the crowd when my dad sang this song. They all remembered it and I could see them, in a sense, being ushered back into the spirit of that time in their lives. I think that's how God uses music, as a vehicle to connect people with Him and to memories that are significant to them."

ALISA GIRARD OF ZOEGIRL

CHUCK GIRARD

96

SOMETIMES ALLELUIA

WRITTEN BY
CHUCK GIRARD

RECORDED BY CHUCK GIRARD ON CHUCK GIRARD (WORD RECORDS, 1975)

PRODUCED BY CHUCK GIRARD

ALSO RECORDED BY:
THE IMPERIALS ON HALL OF FAME SERIES

"SOMETIMES ALLELUIA" IS A POPULAR CHORUS NOW FOUND IN MANY HYMN BOOKS

LESLIE PHILLIPS

STRENGTH OF MY LIFE

97

WRITTEN BY LESLIE PHILLIPS

RECORDED BY LESLIE PHILLIPS ON DANCING WITH DANGER (MYRRH RECORDS, 1984)

PRODUCED BY DAN POSTHUMA

"STRENGTH OF MY LIFE" HAS BEEN INCORPORATED INTO MANY CHURCH HYMN BOOKS

Leslie Phillips had a four-year career in Christian music before she changed her name to Sam, married producer T-Bone Burnett (Counting Crows, Jakob Dylan) and became a critically acclaimed, if not wildly popular, general market rock/pop singer.

Those are the facts if not the heart of the talented, troubled, enigmatic artist's brief sojourn in the contemporary Christian music world. Though it sometimes appears that she has spent the last 20 years doggedly trying to put that part of her life behind her, a look back at the *CCM* interview she did in 1984 reveals an earnest, literate, deeply introspective young woman with a wary eye towards organized religion but a deep faith in God.

Dancing with Danger was her second Myrrh release, following 1983's *Beyond Saturday Night*, and while her self-penned songs accurately reflected her age and inexperience, they also hinted at the gifted writer she was on her way to becoming. "Strength of My Life," her well-matched duet with Russ Taff, is a melodic ballad with an indelible hook that became a Top 10 single. The lyric expresses the comfort and relief of depending on God's strength instead of our own, and the prayerful chorus became a standard praise and worship sing-a-long.

Phillips recorded two more albums for the Christian marketplace, but she chafed against the restrictions and unrealistic expectations she felt were imposed on her. Her frustration with corporate Christianity and what she saw as the pre-packaging and homogenizing of her artistic vision ultimately left her feeling as if she had no choice but to get out of the business.

Her final Christian market project, *The Turning*, was an intensely personal recording focusing on spiritual struggle and shattered love as well as restored faith. As her swan song to the Christian music world, the bittersweet goodbye left the industry and her fans with something to think about.

Leslie ultimately married her producer, T-Bone Burnett—another gifted expatriate from mainstream Christianity—signed with Virgin Records and released seven albums with varying success under the name Sam Phillips.

V ocalist/guitarist Dana Key and keyboardist Eddie DeGarmo formed DeGarmo & Key in 1977. The pioneering Memphis-bred duo initially crafted blues-oriented rock & roll and helped fuel contemporary Christian music's first wave during the mid- to late '70s. Christian radio responded tentatively to DeGarmo & Key's evolving guitar-driven rock sound, while moody classics such as "Addey" and "Livin' on the Edge of Dyin'" left Key dubbed as the "Prophet of Pain," a moniker he would shy away from.

The band's fifth album, *Mission of Mercy*, marked a jarring change in artistic direction—a change that alienated many longtime fans while winning over throngs of new devotees, including Christian radio. In the October 1983 issue of *CCM*, music critic Devlin Donaldson anchored his review around the project's defining opening track. "With all the bands that have hyped themselves as the 'band of the '80s' or have claimed they have the 'music for the '80s,' DeGarmo & Key actually make the shift into '80s pop rock," he wrote. "*Mission of Mercy* opens with a wonderfully danceable tune, 'Ready or Not.' … Indicative of almost the entire album, the song is built around a very strong hook. It has layers of keyboard parts swirling underneath the basic melody, which rings clear and rides above its adventuresome underpinnings. Dana Key's vocals are the best ones I have ever heard from him, supplemented with thick vocal harmonies which add yet another tasty layer to this musical feast."

"Ready or Not," which lyrically anticipated the Second Coming of Christ, established itself as a multi-format Christian radio hit and joined three other songs from *Mission of Mercy* on the charts (including "Let the Whole World Sing," which reached #1 on both Christian pop and rock radio). The addictive connection of "Ready or Not" with listeners wasn't lost on the band. Down the road—even with music from their next album in hand—DeGarmo & Key would open their concerts by walking onstage as John Williams's *Superman* theme played over the sound system. The theme concluded on the same note as the "Ready or Not'" synthesizer intro, forming a flawless overlap with which to launch their shows.

DEGARMO & KEY

98

READY OR NOT

WRITTEN BY EDDIE DEGARMO AND DANA KEY

RECORDED BY DEGARMO & KEY ON MISSION OF MERCY (POWERDISCS, 1983)

PRODUCED BY EDDIE DEGARMO AND DANA KEY

MISSION OF MERCY, LISTED AMONG THE 10 BEST ALBUMS OF 1983 BY *CCM*, BECAME ONE OF THE TOP 5 BEST-SELLING CHRISTIAN ALBUMS IN AMERICA

"READY OR NOT"—TOP 40 HIT AT CHRISTIAN POP RADIO AND A TOP 5 HIT ON THE CHRISTIAN ROCK CHARTS

199

MARGARET BECKER

SAY THE NAME

WRITTEN BY MARGARET BECKER AND CHARLIE PEACOCK

RECORDED BY MARGARET BECKER ON SOUL (SPARROW RECORDS, 1993)

PRODUCED BY CHARLIE PEACOCK

2003 MARGARET BECKER HONORED WITH THE PRESTIGIOUS LEMIERE DU MONDE AWARD FOR HER HUMANITARIAN EFFORTS

1994 *AMERICAN SONGWRITER MAGAZINE*'S CONTEMPORARY CHRISTIAN SONGWRITER OF THE YEAR

99

Margaret Becker is on the short list of the finest female singer/songwriters Christian music has known. From her early rock 'n' roll days of the late '80s to her R&B/pop leanings of the '90s, Becker has articulated faith, spiritual passion and struggle in a way that few before or since have managed. Her fans were uncommonly devoted and, despite her rock roots, they identified perhaps most strongly with her ballads.

"Say The Name" is one of Becker's crown jewels. *CCM Magazine* wrote upon its release that it ". . . may just be one of the most beautiful songs to ever come from Becker, and she's had plenty."

Becker says, "I wanted to write a song about protecting the sanctity of the name of Jesus in our culture. I wrote for weeks on this song, but no matter how I tried, it seemed too dense. Charlie Peacock had just bought the Art House, where he now lives, and it was still a church setting. One evening, I sat by the sanctuary window in an old wooden chair and prayed, 'Lord, fill me with the ability to communicate the magnificence of Your Name, as it has been spoken in this structure—this simple house of worship—for years.' It wasn't immediate, but shortly after that, I found my entrance into the final song. I realized that instead of trying to explain my concept, I should just do it. 'Say The Name' became a demonstration of how to illustrate the beauty and the power of the name of Jesus by describing all its wonderful benefits. I did that by remembering all the things I could attribute to it in my own

life. I purposefully held back the actual utterance of it until the bridge — late in the song, as an example of my respect."

Before they became renowned songwriters and producers, Derri Daugherty and Steve Hindalong were best known as the founding members of the pioneering alternative rock band The Choir. With Daugherty on lead vocals and guitar, and Hindalong, the primary lyricist, on drums, the Los Angeles-born group launched 20 years ago and went on to establish a devoted following among Christian music enthusiasts. Just prior to moving their band to Nashville in the early '90s, Hindalong and Daugherty composed and produced the various artists' contributions for the stirring 1992 concept album *At the Foot of the Cross, Volume One: Clouds, Rain, Fire* (Glasshouse). Though it released several years prior to the modern worship explosion, the album featured the reverent "Beautiful Scandalous Night," which is now a classic.

Explains Hindalong, "Derri gave me this handheld tape player with all these songs that he'd demo'd up, and you could hear a football game [on TV] in the background. He's watching the game and strumming his guitar. . . . For "Beautiful Scandalous Night" and the album it was on, we were just focusing on the death of Christ and His sacrifice. That was just a real powerful offering for us and a very special song. It was our dream, our fantasy, that Russ Taff would sing it . . . We didn't get that to happen, but Bob Bennett did a great job. Recently Sixpence None the Richer (and Bebo Norman) covered it [on 2003's *City on a Hill: The Gathering* (Essential), which Hindalong himself produced along with Daugherty and Marc Byrd], and I think that's the definitive version. Leigh Nash is just fabulous."

Ironically, it wasn't until 1997 that The Choir officially recorded the song themselves when their live album, *Let It Fly* (Tattoo), featured an acoustic rendition. Three years later the band released a studio-recorded version of "Beautiful Scandalous Night" on the Grammy-nominated album *Flap Your Wings*. That same year, veteran artist Sheila Walsh included the song on her album, *Blue Waters* (Integrity).

THE CHOIR

BEAUTIFUL SCANDALOUS NIGHT

100

WRITTEN BY STEVE HINDALONG AND DERRI DAUGHERTY

RECORDED BY THE CHOIR ON FLAP YOUR WINGS (GALAXY21 MUSIC, 2000)

PRODUCED BY DERRI DAUGHERTY, STEVE HINDALONG AND TIM CHANDLER

FIRST RECORDED ON AT THE FOOT OF THE CROSS, VOLUME ONE (GLASSHOUSE, 1992)

ALSO RECORDED BY: SMALLTOWN POETS ON THIRD VERSE

LOST DOGS ON MUTT

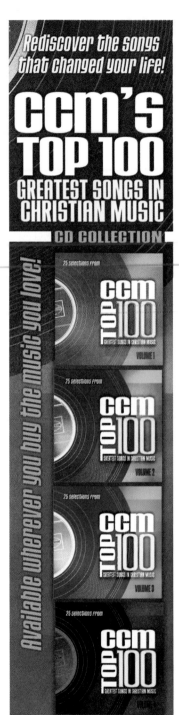

Rediscover the songs that changed your life!

CCM'S TOP 100 GREATEST SONGS IN CHRISTIAN MUSIC

CD COLLECTION

Available wherever you buy the music you love!

25 selections from
CCM TOP 100 GREATEST SONGS IN CHRISTIAN MUSIC
VOLUME 1

25 selections from
CCM TOP 100 GREATEST SONGS IN CHRISTIAN MUSIC
VOLUME 2

25 selections from
CCM TOP 100 GREATEST SONGS IN CHRISTIAN MUSIC
VOLUME 3

25 selections from
CCM TOP 100 GREATEST SONGS IN CHRISTIAN MUSIC
VOLUME 4

creativeTRUST   PROVIDENT DISTRIBUTION

ACKNOWLEDGMENTS

A special thank you to the photographers who gave us permission to use their photos in this book. Every effort was made to contact copyright holders. In case of omission, please notify the publisher and acknowledgment will be made in future printings.

Thank you also to the many industry veterans, executives, and music-makers who served on our list-making committees—for your input, passion and invaluable insights.

Music Fans: We'd love to hear from you! You can write to us at 100greatest@ccmmagazine.com. Tell us your stories. Tell us what songs we missed! Your stories and opinions could be part of a special feature in *CCM Magazine!*

Tori Taff would like to offer props:

To all of the artists and writers who make the music we love. Thank you for graciously telling the "story behind the song" for the ten millionth time.

To Roberta, who artfully conceals a CEO's brain beneath those pre-Raphaelite curls.

To "JuiceBox Jay" Smith—a gentleman—whose hard work and creativity made this book look better than anyone had a right to expect.

To Kelly—I thought I was getting an indentured servant, but instead I ended up with a friend and colleague whose inexhaustible efforts made this whole thing happen.

To Mike Nolan, whose generosity of spirit is matched only by his talent and humor. We love us some Nolan around here.

To all of the additional *CCM* writers who worked so hard— thank you Chris, Jay, Christa, Michael, Caroline and Stephanie.

To our many Talking Head Focus Groups, especially the *CCM* staff, which has a passion for music and a Rain Man-like grasp of trivia.

Especially to my beautiful, book-orphaned Maddie Rose and Charlotte, who gave me grace, tolerance, glasses of water and much-needed laughs—and my treasured parents, who think I can do anything.

And lastly, to the lovely and talented Russ Taff, who I love with all my heart. Thank you for bringing me to the party and for being the kind of husband, father, artist, friend and human being that I am grateful to get to live with. And doggonnit, people like you!